"EVEN THE OLD DUDE IS COOL!"

"EVEN THE OLD DUDE IS COOL!"

William Burroughs on the Wheels of Steel and the Silver Screen

by
Simon Strong

This book has been produced by The LedaTape Organisation on behalf of the author who retains all copyrights in the material.

October 2013

This work is licensed under the Creative Commons Attribution-NonCommercial-ShareAlike 3.0 Unported License. To view a copy of this license, visit http://creativecommons.org/licenses/by-nc-sa/3.0/deed.en_GB.

This book has been produced in complete conformity with the authorised economy standards

Contents

Preface 7
Introduction 9
Bibliography 12

It is a Long Trip

Legend 14
Chronology 15
Posthumous releases 22

Show All Your Cards

How to read the cards 24
The cards 25

Any Number Can Play

Index by type 108
Index of creators 111
Index of titles 113

About the author 116

Preface

Why didn't you?

This is a book, kind of, about the film and recording career of a writer who never wrote a produced film and whose sole composition is amongst the least-known work in his oeuvre.

How did that happen? and why? and why not? I don't know. And I'm not sure I care. Am I the right man for the job? See above. I've been waiting two decades or more for some other cunt to do this so I'm sorry if you don't dig my stab but I reckon it's better than nowt. Plus it'll be easier now for someone else to step up and do it proper.

It might help if you keep in mind that I'm an experimental novelist by convincement. That means I'd rather fail on a mission than enlist for a certain victory. If you're interested to know more about why this project turned out the way it did then you can read the introduction that comes next, but be warned that it's all about me though, not much WSB slop there but there's Bill-ions of words about him already so that's only equitable.

So here at last is my own meagre tribute to the last important thinker of age before the internet and the first one of the one after. It's not a puzzle book or a quiz book but you can use it for that if you like. Or perhaps as an operator's manual if that's your special kick. You can cut out the cards and sort them into any order you like but you might need to buy two copies for that. Better still, you could play a very unsatisfying game of snap or try your hand at telling fortunes in a Tarot stylee, or even use them to con suckers with 324-card Monte. Either way, I reckon WSB would approve. The fuck I know?

Tubes of fury

Choke. Sob. This book was put together very quickly with limited resources. Most info came from my own collection of WSB artefacts and the notes I'd compiled in a previous millennium for the first version of this work.

Following the praxis of high-school students all over the world, I used common internet resources to generate leads and get access to media that I couldn't otherwise locate. the main sites included: allmusic.com, discogs.com, imdb.com, wikipedia.org and youtube.com. I also found much useful info on lawrence.com, the local portal for WSB and JWG's home town.

The leading WSB site is without question realitystudio.org but I consulted that one only sparingly to resolve puzzles and verify completeness. It's a truly spectacular resource but I avoided a comprehensive assessment of it for a few reasons. First, the sheer volume of data simply made it impossible to review adequately within the projected time-frame for this project. Secondly, the information is of such high quality that it would overwhelm more idiosyncratic readings. Thirdly, the site has a sense of canonical authority that I feel compelled to challenge on principle.

I found many useful artefacts on the archive at ubu.com, which is truly one of the wonders of the internet; a huge repository of otherwise unavailable avant-garde film, music and books. You can find some of my shit on there too if you want to. That's how hep it is.

Big up massive

The aforementioned time and budget restrictions entailed that I couldn't make any purchases for the purposes of this project, so I was fortunate to have access to some excellent libraries: City of Yarra Libraries (Collingwood), City of Darebin (Northcote) and the University of Melbourne Libraries. And of course, I also frequented my fave video libraries: Video Dogs (Fitzroy) and Movie Reel (Northcote).

None of this would have been possible, or anywhere as funty, without the help of these folks, some of whom I haven't seen in twenty years or more: Paul Cecil, David Cox, Graham Duff, Paul Elliott, Aaron Goldberg, Ken Goldsmith, Michael Helms, Stewart Home, Andy Kirk, Iain McIntyre, Will Prentice, Richard Rees Jones, Jack Sargeant. Thanks lads. My shout. If there's anything fucked up here, it's their fault... right?

Melbourne,
Australia
1 October 2013

Introduction

Thanks for sticking with it. If you're reading this, you'll probably know that it's mandatory for Burroughs fanboys not only to dream about the old dead writer, but also to relate those dreams at every inappropriate opportunity, and furthermore for the dreams to be unrelentingly tedious. This convention makes it easy to distinguish serious Burroughs scholars from their anoraknid competitors. All you have to do is avoid any book that makes mention of unconscious encounters.

I never got to meet Burroughs on the mortal plane but I did run into him twice on the astral plane. The first time I was in a boozer and spied him across the room. All my mates said I should go and have a word since I was always banging on about the old bastard but I was too chickenshit and by the time I got my gander up he was exiting the pub and I couldn't get through the thirsty throng in time. I woke up spewing. That probably wasn't down to the dream though. It happened quite a bit in those days.

The second dream was probably a couple of years later. There was the recurring angle of the boozer and everything but this time I didn't dawdle and barged straight over immediately on clocking him. I managed to introduce myself pretty cool and asked him something clever. As he opened his mouth to reply I realised I was dreaming. There was no room in the crowded pub to spin myself round like a dervish (which is a good trick to help you stay in the lucid state) so I shoved a beermat and a biro at him and asked for his number to follow up later. The pub was noisy and this seemed the quickest safest way. Burroughs wrote on the coaster and rolled it back to me. I knew I had to memorise the number fast before I surfaced into consciousness but I only managed to get the first three digits. What a shittener! Oddly, those first digits of the number had been 021, the STD code for Birmingham. What the fuck was he doing in the Midlands? I dunno. The Move and ELO were from there so maybe it's good. I've never been so I wouldn't know. Maybe he was visiting the BSA factory, the one for guns rather than motorbikes.

You cannot call the Old Doctor a twat

So from c.1987–1992 I was carrying an oil-burner WSB habit like the worst kind of Burroughs bore. Got the old junky crawling up my back for the fans of recursive puns. For a few years I even dressed like him in a gaberdine and fedora, and I question whether WSB was called "El Hombre Invisible" by the Mexican street kids for occult reasons. I reckon it's more likely they just thought he looked like Claude Rains out of the 1933 Universal Picture like when I got the exact same thing dressed like that. Also, I was into spouting Burroughsisms anywhere they were least wanted. I memorised the first five minutes of *The Last Words of Hassan I Sabbah* and would declaim them stumbling through spooky forests or pissing in alleyways. People were way too indulgent. This was Brighton after all but I should've known better. I was in my twenties and had a girlfriend and everything. I didn't take it quite so far as hitting up smack like some did. Not smug though. I had limited will-power and much less good sense but I never had the wedge for scag after blowing it all on piss.

Around this time I belatedly heard Talking Head's 1980 LP *Remain in Light* and wondered if their tune *Seen and Not Seen* (about a bloke choosing what his own face will look like) would actually work in practise. I didn't expect it would so for a laugh, I decided to look like William Burroughs. After a decade or so, I realised I'd got half-way there without realising and chickened out like one of the losers in the tune.

Just checking your summer recordings

For a long time I'd figured that a book on Burroughs' recording career would be a good earner. For one, I'd buy it since I'd been collecting WSB discs and compiling data since the mid-eighties. You couldn't viably collect films back in those days as there were only VHS tapes and only mainstream slop had surfaced meaningfully. Things was very different then. There was no internet and any kind of research was fucking hard. Mind you, it was handy I was working in underground music distribution so it was easy to build my collection and to get in touch with fellow Burroughsians. Plus I had connections who I knew could get the book out if I finished it. Nice.

Originally I was going to call the book *Just Checking Your Summer Recordings* but when I heard about WSB's *Beavis and Butthead* cameo, I changed it to what it is

Introduction

now and it stayed that way ever since. The subtitle came much later, courtesy of an Edwin Pouncey review of *Elvis of Letters*. So I slogged away sporadically over the data for a few years. It would all come to the top of the pile and then vanish again beneath more urgent or immediately innaresting shit.

Then, in the mid-nineties, I suddenly left the UK for reasons we don't need to go into here. I took most of my archives with me but all my mates and contacts were left behind in Blighty. By now I was running on fumes anyway. I'd been immersed for years and Cronenberg's *Naked Lunch* film had very effectively manifested everything I didn't like about Burroughs right there. Later there were rumours Burroughs had done a US tv ad for the fucking Nike Corp. Well, that was his business but I was (still am) out as a lippy lefty wanker so it gave me the shits. Longer and longer intervals (of time) elapsed between the periods when ETODIC came to the top of the to-do pile.

Disappointingly, word of my book had leaked out to well-informed Burroughsians, and they continued to ask, albeit with dwindling frequency, when (or whether) it was finally coming out. At first I'd tell them it was on hold, then I'd say it was never going to happen, and eventually it wasn't even a book anymore, just a box of yellowed clippings and floppy disks in obsolete file formats that wouldn't even fit in the slot on my new PC. I knew coz I tried.

Sipple out deh

Suddenly two more decades had passed and I was in a different place altogether. A new hemisphere, a family man, reasonably comfortable, and a successful writer myself me, albeit in the Burroughsian tradition of indiscriminate media, making records, films and artwork as well as books.

Something was bugging me though. Besides the NSA. When I'd started writing all those years before I'd been told there was a hierarchy of authority for books. It started with poetry, progressed through fiction (pulp through to literature) and thence to general nonfiction, ending up with academic books, PhD theses, and technical manuals. I lacked much of a formal education, beyond a seventies comprehensive that made the school in *Kes* look like fucking Hogwarts, so it took me a while to get my head together to be able to digest the heaviest academic shit. Even the technical manuals seemed much easier and I wondered why that was. Winds of time eventually tossed me through the world of academic publishing just as it was imploding post-internet. Of course, the answer was that academics treat their subjects as fixed dead entities, animated only in decomposition, twitching reflexes and noxious death-farts. Whereas enthusiasts know their subjects are alive, and act more like physicians than morticians.

I realised that I had just bought the authority scam lock, stock and barrel. It was just a damage limitation exercise to try and mitigate any cultural material that had been produced with the tiniest degree of autonomy. At this point, Reactionary Forces had infiltrated fully everywhere and the whole fucking shithouse was completely burned down. From the codification by consensus of extra-galactic quasars to the most private recesses of your brains' responses conditioned with cascading contingencies. All stitched up tighter than a nun's cunt. The fucking bastards!

It put me in mind of the dystopias of Huxley, Orwell and Bradbury. You couldn't get WSB slop in Yorkshire in those days ya dig. So we used to argue at the Sheffield SF Club about which of them would be closest to the future and none of us figured that the triple-whammy was even an option. Fucking greasebag brainrapists! Seems like every SF nightmare had been gobbled up by reactionary agents for inspiration and/or hints on deployment. By 2013, it was a cliché to say "1984 is not an instruction book" but back then you'd sound dumber than a cunt using a laptop in a cafe. I guess the RF stooges weren't as cocky back in the olden days.

Poor old Burroughs fared even worse than the canonical dystopians did do. His books started out as sci-fi gay porn and wound up as social realism. Inevitable as J.G. Ballard had said "Sex times technology equals the future" back in the sixties.

Deliberately or not, Burroughs had put a lot of effort into defending his work against recuperation. There was transgression there, obscurism, underground dissemination, unseriousness and lots lots lots lots more. But even he couldn't withstand assimilation by the Beast of Babylon, or any other aliases of the RF, forever.

For instance, look at Cronenberg's children, whatever this season's *Human Centipede* is, make *Naked Lunch* look like a teddy bears' picnic. Such the calculated idiocy of the arms race of grotesqueries that Burroughs might have the good grace to take some credit for.

"Are you taking the piss? An R rating will cut penetration in the primary demographic by up to 15%! Make the castration a disembowelling and we'll call it even."

"Fuck you! The knob-choppery stays. Nothing makes any sense without it. How about the eye-gouging sequences? If we make it a teen instead of a toddler?"

"MA 15+ Strong Themes?"

So now that disgust is safely commodified, canonical transgression is about as threatening as satanism ever was to the christian church. From Sunday arvo detective shows, with statutory gorefest PSAs to cancer-porn full-colour illustrated fag packs, we're as surrounded by pro-necrophile propaganda as Pooh ever was by water. Put the circles in a wagon Mary.

The Exterminator speaks with his voice

By now one of my kicks was to do a sporadic radio show with my pal Dr Gonzo (no relation to HST) and I was halfway through a 23 hour survey of the limits of protest tunes called *Because Fuck You! That's Why*. I was doing episodes on my entire stable of hobby-horses: Sheffield electro music, skinhead reggae, French ye-ye tunes of 1968, tunes about bananas, etc. I figured I should do a show about WSB even though I didn't really want to anymore. I still had the shit in my archives so it would be easy and I knew that the kids would dig it more than ever. Plus I could spin some Hawkwind.

I prepared for the show by getting more hammered than was customary and getting round to watching the WSB-inclusive episode of *Beavis and Butthead* thanks to the "miracle" of YouTube. Then I dug through my old files and Gonzo and me did the show. Feedback was positive. But then we turned the speakers down and it was okay.

Having looked at my WSB notes for the first time in decades, I figured I could easily use this new-fangled internet thing to quickly fill in the holes in the abandoned book and knock it off in about a week or so. That was the easy bit. The challenge would be to minimise the book's utility to the RF.

Show all your cards to all players

A couple of days afterwards, I was having a game of *Horrible Histories* Top Trumps and it occurred to me that autonomous children's culture still displayed some resistance to heavy assault from the RF, despite the dismantling of their traditional barricades against extreme media and commerce. Humour was fighting a losing battle too, but might provide some last meagre cover. So maybe a William Burroughs Top Trumps deck would be more defensively effective than a more conventional form of book. It would certainly be less work. But most importantly of all, it was a piss-funny idea. For the benefit of those who may confuse seriousness with intelligence, I will admit a distinct familiarity with the "but that's not funny" contention, and I have a universal response which in itself becomes funnier with each deployment. You'll note that my deliberately shallow comments help accommodate a much broader vision. Alternatively, keep in mind that a clown on a unicycle will get to most places faster than a funeral cortege.

If you can't be just, be arbitrary

As in any book with pretensions to veracity, I have excluded some information on spurious or arbitrary grounds. The difference is that I'll fess up to and iterate the instances of which I'm aware. This is done to self-consciously undermine any potential accusations of authority. Beyond this section, and entirely beyond this book, are some other items that are comprehensively excluded where the Burroughs influence has not been detected or the item as yet unrealised, or unconceived.

Obviously I omitted WSB references by Transvision Vamp and 10,000 Maniacs on the grounds of their overwhelming shitness, but where's Patti Smith for example? or even more mysteriously, why didn't I make room for Hawkwind? They're the most influential English group since the Beatles. Or I could have filled you in on my hypothesis about the old blues tune from c.1927 called "Cocaine Blues" but that's absent here for no good reason. And I just found out that Thurston Moore's new outfit Chelsea Light Moving have a tune called "Burroughs" which is pretty cool but that's not here either.

In terms of films, I completely forgot to include the recent version of *On the Road*, which is not surprising since I forgot to watch it too. *Kill Your Darlings* isn't out yet, and neither is Steve Buscemi's film of *Queer* but at least they get a mention in the relevant places. I also know about a 2011 film called *Lives and Deaths of the Poets* which has Josh Anderson as WSB but I couldn't be bothered chasing it up. Also, the German film *Tanger - Legende einer Stadt* (2000), has Ulrich Günther as WSB in a portrait of Old Tangiers ya dig. And I saw Storm Thorgersen's film *Drug-Taking and the Arts* (with John Sessions as WSB) when it came out round 1994 but it has vanished off the face of the internet. Most troublingly, I completely overlooked Nik Sheehan's excellent recent Gysin doco *FLicKeR*, but I don't feel bad about it since I also overlooked my own WSB movie *The The Naked Lunch and the Naked The Naked Lunch*. Now, on the topic of WSB references in *Doctor Who*, I can... no I can't. Thanks. Stay cool now won't you?

Melbourne, Australia.
14 August 2013

Bibliography

Bockris, Victor. *With William Burroughs: A Report from the Bunker*. New York: St Martin's Press, 1996. Print.

Burroughs, William S. *The Adding Machine: Collected Essays*. London: John Calder, 1985. Print.

Burroughs, William S., and Brion Gysin. *The Third Mind*. New York: John Calder, 1979. Print.

Burroughs, William S., and Daniel Odier. *The Job: Interviews with William S. Burroughs*. London: John Calder, 1984. Print.

Burroughs, William S., James Grauerholz, Ira Silverberg, and Ann Douglas. *Word Virus*. London: Flamingo, 1999. Print.

Ely, Roger. *The Final Academy: Statements of a Kind*. London: The Final Academy, 1982. Print.

Goodman, Michael B., and Lemuel B. Coley. *William S. Burroughs: A Reference Guide*. New York: Garland, 1990. Print.

Grauerholz, James. *The Death of Joan Vollmer Burroughs: What Really Happened?*. American Studies Department, University of Kansas, 2002. Web. 15 June 2013.

Maynard, Joe, and Barry Miles. *William S. Burroughs: A Bibliography, 1953-73: Unlocking Inspector Lee's Word Hoard*. Charlottesville: University of Virginia, 1978. Print.

Miles, Barry. *The Beat Hotel: Ginsberg, Burroughs, and Corso in Paris, 1958-1963*. New York: Grove, 2000. Print.

Miles, Barry. *In the Sixties*. London: Jonathan Cape, 2002. Print.

Morgan, Ted. *Literary Outlaw*. London: Bodley Head, 1991. Print.

Murphy, Timothy S. *Wising up the Marks: The Amodern William Burroughs*. Berkeley: University of California, 1997. Print.

Sargeant, Jack. *Naked Lens: Beat Cinema*. London, Eng.: Creation, 1997. Print.

Schottlaender, Brian E.C. *Anything But Routine: A Selectively Annotated Bibliography of William S. Burroughs, v. 3.0*. UC San Diego Libraries, UC San Diego, n.d. Web. 15 July 2013.

Shoaf, Eric C. *Collecting William S. Burroughs in Print: A Checklist*. Rumford, RI: Rock N' Roll Research, 2000. Print.

Sobieszek, Robert A. *Ports of Entry: William S. Burroughs and the Arts*. Los Angeles: Los Angeles County Museum of Art, 1996. Print.

Stevenson, Jack. *Witchcraft through the Ages: The Story of Häxan, the World's Strangest Film, and the Man Who Made It*. Guildford: FAB, 2007. Print.

Vale, V., and Andrea Juno. *Re/Search #4/5: A Special Book Issue*. San Francisco, CA: Re/Search, 1982. Print.

IT IS A LONG TRIP

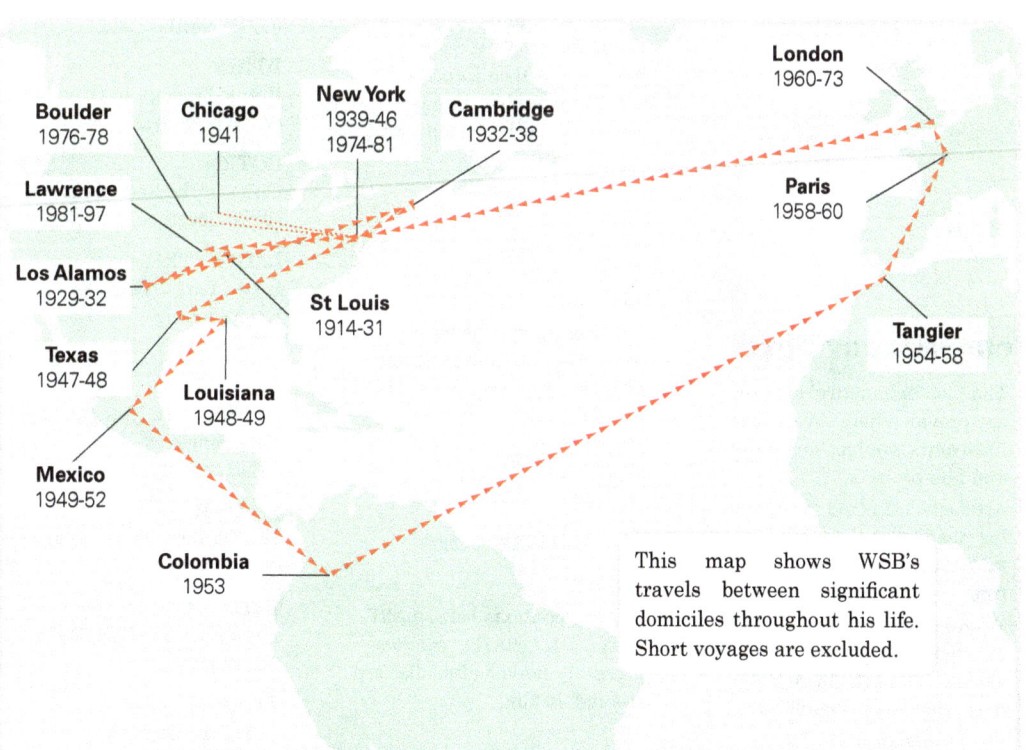

This map shows WSB's travels between significant domiciles throughout his life. Short voyages are excluded.

Legend

KEY TO SYMBOLS

▪ Only physical artefacts have been included in this book. Ebooks and download only items are excluded.

BOOK

▪ 46 items.
▪ Books by or relating to WSB have only been included if they relate to his work in media other than print.

RECORDING

▪ 172 items.
▪ Some musical groups (e.g. Soft Machine) have overt but non-specific WSB influences. In these cases, they are listed under their most WSB-centric artefact.
▪ Where several musical groups are named for a WSB reference (e.g. Naked Lunch), the earliest manifestation is included and others mentioned.

FILM

▪ 102 items.
▪ TV programmes using brief extracts of previously noted WSB footage have been excluded.

MULTIMEDIA

▪ 4 items.
▪ In some contexts here, multimedia artefacts (i.e. random access audio-visual media) are treated as film.

ABBREVIATIONS

▪ **WSB**
William S. Burroughs

▪ **JWG**
James W. Grauerholz

▪ **GPS**
Giorno Poetry Systems

▪ **TMMOJ**
The Master Musicians of Jajouka

▪ **ADHITMOAC**
A Diamond Hidden in the Mouth of a Corpse
(GPS comp) 117

▪ **ATHWBITT**
And the Hippos Were Boiled in Their Tanks
(WSB novel) 295

▪ **BAODTANG**
Better an Old Demon Than a New God
(GPS comp) 109

▪ **BOTTOAC**
Biting Off the Tongue of a Corpse
(GPS comp) 51

▪ **BTIGR**
Break Through in Grey Room
(WSB record) 124

▪ **COTRN**
Cities of the Red Night
(WSB novel) 79

▪ **LAGIWYTKC**
Like a Girl, I Want You to Keep Coming
(GPS comp) 156

▪ **NHNBTR**
Nothing Here Now But the Recordings
(WSB record) 81

▪ **TDIOTM**
The Doctor is on the Market
(WSB record) 128

▪ **TTTE**
The Ticket That Exploded
(WSB novel) 6

▪ **YTGIWTSMMW**
You're the Guy I Want to Share My Money With
(GPS comp) 88

CHRONOLOGY NOTES

The (non-exhaustive) chronology provided here covers major life events emphasising music and film projects.

▪ Artefacts are noted in the item listings rather than in body text, unless unrealised at the time.
▪ Where space permits, names of artists (other than WSB) are given in brackets for recordings other than compilations.
▪ The most significant WSB artefacts are given in the item listings bold type.

Chronology

1914
- **5 Feb.** WSB born at 4664 Pershing Ave., St. Louis, MO, USA, son of Mortimer and Laura Lee Burroughs.

1920-32
- Attends Community School and John Burroughs (no relation) School in St. Louis, then Los Alamos Ranch School, NM, and Taylor School, St Louis.

1932-36
- Harvard University, studies English literature and graduates with BA.

1937
- Medical studies at University of Vienna.
- **Aug.** WSB marries Ilse Herzfeld Klapper, a Jewish German, so she could emigrate to the US to avoid Nazi persecution.

1937-38
- WSB at Columbia University, NY, studying psychology.

1938
- Graduate studies in Anthropology at Harvard.
- Meets Kells Elvins and collaborates on "Twilight's Last Gleamings".

1940
- **Apr.** Following self-amputation of a finger, WSB is admitted to Payne Whitney Psychiatric Clinic through late May. Then heads to St. Louis.

1942
- In Chicago, working as an exterminator, shipping clerk and employee-fraud detective.
- After four unsuccessful attempts (1939-1941) volunteers for US Army at Jefferson Barracks, St. Louis and is accepted as private first class
- **Sep.** Honourable discharge following mental breakdown.

1943-44
- Settles in New York working as a bartender and process server.
- Meets **Jack Kerouac & Allen Ginsberg**.

1944
- In the Columbia University area. Meets Joan Vollmer.
- **Aug.** Lucien Carr kills David Kammerer on the banks of the Hudson River. WSB and Kerouac arrested as material witnesses / accessories.
- With Kerouac, WSB starts writing *And the Hippos Were Boiled in Their Tanks* based on the murder case.
- WSB is introduced to morphine by Herbert Hunke.

1945
- First narcotics addiction.

1946
- WSB divorces Ilse Klapper and she returns to Europe.
- **Jan.** Moves with Joan Vollmer and her daughter to Texas where they live on a farm in The Rio Grande Valley.

1947
- **21 Jul.** Son William, Jr. born in Conroe, TX.

1948
- **Jun.** Moves to New Orleans but soon becomes re-addicted to junk.
- Admitted to Hospital in Lexington, KY, for treatment of addiction.
- Moves to Algiers, LA.

JACK KEROUAC

US novelist and poet (1922-1969), best known for *On the Road* (1957), which kicked off the whole "Beat Generation" movement, described by WSB as "an absolutely unprecedented worldwide cultural revolution".

WSB appears in a fictionalised form in *On the Road* and some other Kerouac novels.

In his essay "Remembering Jack Kerouac", WSB credits Kerouac with getting him started as a writer.

They co-authored *And the Hippos Were Boiled in their Tanks*.

Kerouac provided WSB with the title *Naked Lunch*, although by some accounts he said "naked lust" and WSB misheard.

Kerouac described WSB as the "greatest satirical writer since Jonathan Swift".

WSB appears in most docos about Kerouac.

Kerouac films
- 🎬 Heart Beat 74
- 🎬 Kerouac, the Movie 119
- 🎬 What Happened to Kerouac? 130

WSB & Kerouac
- 💿 The Jack Kerouac Collection 168
- 💿 Kerouac - Kicks Joy Darkness 233
- 📖 And the Hippos. 295
- 💿 And the Hippos. (Audiobook) 302

Chronology

ALLEN GINSBERG

- US poet (1926-1997), best known for his poem *Howl* (1956) and his political activism.
- WSB originally wrote *Naked Lunch* as a series of letters to Ginsberg.
- Ginsberg tirelessly advocated for his friends' work and was instrumental in getting WSB's early work published.
- Appears alongside WSB in many docos.

collaborations with WSB
- 📖 The Yage Letters 8

film appearances
- 🎬 Chappaqua 24
- 🎬 Lunatics, Lovers and Poets 75
- 🎬 It Don't Pay to be an Honest Citizen. . 111
- 🎬 Heavy Petting 153
- 🎬 The Life & Times of Allen Ginsberg . . 214

recordings
- 💿 Holy Soul Jelly Roll 208

BONUS BEATS

- The Beat Generation refers to both the literary circle around Kerouac, Ginsberg and WSB and to their followers, derogatively called "beatniks".
- The fourth Beat is generally considered to be Gregory Corso, or maybe Neal Cassady. It depends.
- Most followers of the Beats had mutated into hippies by the late-sixties.

docos and comps
- 🎬 Fried Shoes, Cooked Diamonds 68
- 🎬 The Beat Generation 138
- 💿 The Beat Generation 186
- 📀 The Beat Experience 229
- 🎬 The Source 254
- 💿 Diggin the New Breed 280
- 🎬 Corso, the Last Beat 303

1949
- **Apr.** Arrested for drugs and firearms offences.
- Moves to Mexico City with family.
- Visits Ecuador in search of yage.

1950
- Enrols Mexico City College to study anthropology.
- Begins work on *Junkie*, mailing chapters to Ginsberg.

1951
- Six-week trip to South America with Lewis Marker.
- **6 Sep.** WSB accidentally shoots and kills wife Joan.
- Leaves Mexico City for South America.
- Bill Jr. is sent to live with grandparents Laura and Mortimer Burroughs.

1952
- Mexican shooting case is settled.
- Travels in South America and Tangier.
- *Junkie* accepted by Ace Books.
- Starts work on *Queer*, which will remain unpublished until 1985.

1953
- 📖 Junkie 1
- **Jan-Aug.** Yage voyage in South America. Later back in New York, edits letters to Ginsberg from South America later published as *The Yage Letters*.
- **Aug.** *Junkie* published under the pseudonym of William Lee in expurgated version by Ace Books.
- **Dec.** Returns to Tangier, and begins *Naked Lunch*.

1954
- In Tangier, writing *Naked Lunch*.

1955
- Visits London to undergo Dr. Dent's apomorphine treatment for the cure of heroin addiction.

1956
- "Letter from a Master Addict to Dangerous Drugs" published in *The British Journal of Addiction*.

1958
- Moves to Paris, 9 Rue Git-Le Coeur, the "Beat Hotel."
- Begins collaborations with **Byron Gysin**.

1959
- 📖 The Naked Lunch 2
- Lives at Empress Hotel, London.
- Excerpts from *Naked Lunch* published in *Chicago Review* and *Big Table #1* which is banned and seized by the U.S. Postal Service. Censorship creates a major controversy.
- *Naked Lunch* published in Paris by Olympia Press. US Customs seizes Olympia Press editions.
- **Sep.** Brion Gysin discovers the cut/up method.

1960
- 📖 Minutes to Go 3
- 📖 The Exterminator 4
- WSB meets technician **Ian Sommerville**, who will work on many WSB recordings.

1961
- 📖 The Soft Machine 5
- Meets Timothy Leary.

1962
- 📖 The Ticket That Exploded 6
- WSB Lives at Lancaster Terrace, London.
- Meets **Antony Balch** and starts film collaborations.
- Appears at International Writers' Conference in Edinburgh,

16

Chronology

organised by John Calder. His work is praised by Mary McCarthy. WSB causes outrage when he promotes the cut/up method.
- *Naked Lunch* published in US, creating heated literary debate.

1963
- Dead Fingers Talk 7
- The Yage Letters 8
- Towers Open Fire 9
- WSB settles in London.
- *Dead Fingers Talk*, an anthology drawn from the Olympia novels is published in London, provoking "The UGH! Correspondence" in the pages of the *Times Literary Supplement*.
- WSB collaborates with Terry Riley and Daevid Allen on experimental son-et-lumiere performances.

1964
- Nova Express 10
- Gysin and Balch start work on script for a film of *Naked Lunch*.
- **John Giorno** meets WSB.

1965
- Call Me Burroughs 11
- Valentine's Day Reading 12
- Returns to St. Louis then lives in New York, 210 Center Street.
- Father Mortimer P. Burroughs dies.
- *Naked Lunch* put on trial in Boston. A case against the book in Los Angeles is dropped.
- Paul McCartney sets up Ian Sommerville in a studio at 34 Montagu Sq., London, where he records WSB.

1966
- Chappaqua 13
- The Insect Trust 14
- Lives at Hotel Rushmore, London.
- *Naked Lunch* cleared by Massachusetts Supreme Court after three landmark U.S. Supreme Court decisions.
- Grove Press issues *Naked Lunch* in US with excerpts from the Boston trial and "Deposition" article.

1967
- Aspen 5+6 15
- Klacto/ 23 16
- Poem Posters 17
- Sgt. Pepper's Lonely Hearts Club Band 18
- The Cut-Ups 19
- The Mugwumps 20
- The Nude Restaurant 21
- The Velvet Underground and Nico 22
- The Cut-Ups 19
- WSB lives at 8 Duke Street, St. James, London.
- Future companion James Grauerholz, then fourteen, reads *Naked Lunch* in Coffeyville, Kansas.

1968
- Born to be Wild (Steppenwolf) 23
- Chappaqua 24
- The Soft Machine 25
- Witchcraft Through the Ages 26
- WSB covers the Democratic National Convention in Chicago for *Esquire* magazine.
- Following a phone call with WSB, John Giorno starts Dial-A-Poem out of MOMA in NYC.

1969
- Ali's Smile 27
- Cain's Film 28
- Piece of My Heart (Nova Express) 29
- Secrets of Sex 30
- **Oct.** Jack Kerouac dies in St. Petersburg FL, from massive esophageal haemorrhage caused by hepatic cirrhosis.
- David Budd working with WSB to find backers for a film version of *The Last Words of Dutch Schultz*.

1970
- Performance 31
- Prologue 32
- The Braille Film 33
- The Job 34
- The Last Words of Dutch Schultz 35
- Mother Laura Lee Burroughs dies.

BRION GYSIN

British/Canadian painter, writer, poet and performance artist (1916-1986).

- Discovered the cut/up technique in 1959. Passed on the info to WSB who used it in many books from then on, notably The Cut-Up Trilogy of *The Soft Machine*, TTTE and *Nova Express*.
- In 1961 with Ian Sommerville, Gysin invented the dreamachine, a flicker device for producing visionary states.
- Worked on unproduced screenplay of *Naked Lunch* with Antony Balch.
- Co-authored several books with WSB.

books with WSB
- Minutes To Go 3
- The Exterminator 4
- The Third Mind 56
- Re/Search 4/5 94

recordings
- OU Revuedisque 40-41 43
- The Dial-A-Poem Poets 44
- Life is a Killer 91
- The Coldspring Tape 154
- 10% File under Burroughs 226
- One Night @ the 1001 242
- The Spoken Word 322

film appearances
- Towers Open Fire 9
- The Cut-Ups 19
- Lunatics, Lovers and Poets 75
- Ghosts at no. 9 90
- The Final Academy Documents 107
- Thee Films 129
- Towers Open Fire & other films 160
- Destroy All Rational Thought 238
- The Beat Hotel 317

Chronology

IAN SOMMERVILLE

British technician/programmer (1940-1976), WSB's systems advisor during the sixties.

- Lived for a time at The Beat Hotel with WSB.
- Designed the first dreamachine to Brion Gysin's specifications.
- Worked with WSB on tape recorder experiments, notably "Silver Smoke of Dreams" and "K9 Was in Combat..." (on BTIGR).

recordings
- Nothing Here Now but the Recordings ... 81
- Break Through in Grey Room ... 124

ANTONY BALCH

English film-maker (1937-1980), now best known for the short films he made with WSB.

- First person to attempt a film of *Naked Lunch*, with Brion Gysin and Steve Lacy.
- Balch worked as a distributor of films considered controversial in the UK, including works by Russ Meyer, Kenneth Anger, Tod Browning and others.

shorts
- Towers Open Fire ... 9
- The Cut-Ups ... 19
- Bill and Tony ... 41
- Ghosts at no. 9 ... 90
- William Buys a Parrot ... 100

features
- Witchcraft Through the Ages ... 26
- Secrets of Sex ... 30
- Horror Hospital ... 46

collections
- The Final Academy Documents ... 107
- Thee Films ... 129
- Towers Open Fire & other films ... 160

1971
- Audiopoems (Chopin) ... 36
- Electronic Revolution ... 37
- Obsolete (Hedayat) ... 38
- The Pipes of Pan at Joujouka (TMMOJ) ... 39
- The Wild Boys ... 40

- WSB, Gysin and Balch cofound Friendly Films to produce a film from Gysin's *Naked Lunch* script, now as a musical with songs by Steve Lacy.

1972
- Bill and Tony ... 41
- Can't Buy a Thrill (Steely Dan) ... 42
- OU Revuedisc 40-41 ... 43
- The Dial-A-Poem Poets ... 44

- WSB corresponds with Fred Halsted about a porno film version of *The Wild Boys* but it comes to nothing.

1973
- Exterminator! ... 45
- Horror Hospital ... 46
- OU Revuedisc 42-43-44 ... 47

- **Genesis P-Orridge** meets WSB after corresponding.

1974
- Diamond Dogs (Bowie) ... 48
- Disconnected ... 49
- Gay Sunshine Reading ... 50

- **Jan.-May** Moves from London to New York to teach at CCNY.
- **Feb.** WSB first meets **James Grauerholz**.
- WSB interviews David Bowie for *Rolling Stone*.

1975
- Biting Off the Tongue of a Corpse ... 51
- Port of Saints ... 52
- Snack ... 53
- William Burroughs / John Giorno ... 54

- Reading tour across the US.
- Writers' workshop in Denver, CO.
- WSB meets with Jimmy Page and attends Led Zeppelin show for his column in *Crawdaddy* magazine.
- **Sep.** Colloque de Tanger, tribute to WSB and Gysin, held in Geneva.

1976
- The Retreat Diaries ... 55
- The Third Mind ... 56
- Totally Corrupt ... 57
- Underground and Emigrants ... 58
- William Burrito Brothers ... 59

- WSB living mainly in Boulder, CO, as adjunct faculty at the Jack Kerouac School of Disembodied Poetics of Naropa Institute, in aftermath of his son Bill Jr.'s liver transplant in Aug. 1976.
- Ian Sommerville killed in car accident.

1977
- 90 Minutes Live ... 60
- Orgasm Addict (Buzzcocks) ... 61

- Appears on *90 Minutes Live* on Canadian TV.
- WSB, Terry Southern and Dennis Hopper work on a screenplay for *Junkie* but the project stalls.

1978
- Big Ego ... 62
- Storm the Reality Studio ... 63
- Thot-Fal'N ... 64

- Moves back to NYC in autumn and lives at 222 Bowery in "the Bunker," a former YMCA one block from the junk-dealer streets of Stanton and Rivington.
- David Bowie, Patti Smith, Iggy Pop, some Rolling Stones, Lou Reed, Chris Stein, Debbie Harry, Frank Zappa and others pay court. Victor Bockris compiles *With William Burroughs* from transcripts.
- **Nov./Dec.** The Nova Convention. Three day celebration with WSB, Brion Gysin, John Giorno, Allen Ginsberg, Timothy Leary and others. Performances by John Cage, Philip Glass, Laurie Anderson, Ed Sanders, Patti Smith, Frank Zappa. Tribute "No Wave" concert with B-52s, Suicide, Stimulators, Walter Stedding,

Robert Fripp, Debbie Harry and Chris Stein.
- Massive glut of heroin hits NYC, WSB becomes re-addicted.

1979

- Ah Pook is Here and Other Texts . . . . . `65`
- Blade Runner: A Movie . . . . `66`
- Doctor Benway . . . . `67`
- Fried Shoes, Cooked Diamonds . . . . . . `68`
- Unknown Pleasures (Joy Division) . . . `69`
- Megaton for Wm. Burroughs (Mumma) . `70`
- Rabies (Naked Lunch) . . . . `71`
- Replicas (Tubeway Army) . . . . `72`
- The Nova Convention . . . . `73`
- JWG moves to Lawrence, KS.
- **16 Oct.** "Gig of the Century" in Brussels with WSB, Cabaret Voltaire and Joy Division.

1980

- Heart Beat . . . . `74`
- Lunatics, Lovers and Poets . . . . `75`
- Sugar, Alcohol & Meat . . . . `76`
- The Exterminator . . . . `77`
- **Aug.** WSB goes on methadone.
- *Naked Lunch* staged in NYC.
- Antony Balch dies (stomach cancer).

1981

- Chelsea Hotel . . . . `78`
- Cities of the Red Night . . . . `79`
- Energy and How to Get It . . . . `80`
- Nothing Here Now but the Recordings . . `81`
- On the Nova Lark . . . . `82`
- Shamans of the Blind Country . . . . . . `83`
- The Fruit of the Original Sin . . . . `84`
- The Gospel Comes [...] (23 Skidoo) . . `85`
- Saturday Night Live . . . . `86`
- With William Burroughs . . . . `87`
- You're the Guy I Want to Share My . . . `88`
- **3 Mar.** Son Bill Jr. dies.
- **Mar.-May** Red Night Tour of readings across US with John Giorno.
- WSB appears on *Saturday Night Live* watched by millions. **Hal Willner** is music director.
- **Dec.** WSB joins JWG in Lawrence, where he makes first shotgun artworks.

1982

- A William Burroughs Reader . . . . `89`
- Ghosts at no. 9 . . . . `90`
- Life is a Killer . . . . `91`
- One World Poetry . . . . `92`
- Poetry in Motion . . . . `93`
- Re/Search 4/5 . . . . `94`
- Revolutions Per Minute . . . . `95`
- The Discipline of DE . . . . `96`
- The Final Academy . . . . `97`
- The Mortal Micronotz . . . . `98`
- William Burroughs with Kathy Acker . `99`
- William Buys a Parrot . . . . `100`
- **Oct.** The Final Academy events in the UK. Five day programme of exhibitions, readings by WSB, Gysin, Giorno and others, and performances by 23 Skidoo, Last Few Days, Cabaret Voltaire and the debut of Genesis P-Orridge's Psychic TV.

1983

- Burroughs . . . . `101`
- Live at the Kabuki . . . . `102`
- Mister Heartbreak (Anderson) . . . . . . `103`
- Pirate Tape . . . . `104`
- Taking Tiger Mountain . . . . `105`
- The Dream Machine . . . . `106`
- The Final Academy Documents . . . . . `107`
- This Song for Jack . . . . `108`
- WSB and John Giorno on a reading tour through Finland, Sweden and Denmark.

1984

- Better an Old Demon Than a New God . `109`
- Decoder . . . . `110`
- It Don't Pay to Be an Honest Citizen . `111`
- Myths: Instructions 1 . . . . `112`
- The Burroughs File . . . . `113`
- The Place of Dead Roads . . . . `114`
- The Wild Boys (Duran Duran) . . . . . . `115`
- You're a Hook . . . . `116`
- First discussions with David Cronenberg re: *Naked Lunch* film.
- Elected to the American Academy and Institute of Arts and Letters. Later that year awarded the order of Commandeur de l'Ordre des Arts et des Lettres by the Ministry of Culture of France.
- **Sub Rosa Records** founded.

JOHN GIORNO

US poet and activist (b. 1936) also known as the star of Andy Warhol's celebrated 5h20m film *Sleep*.

In 1968 Giorno started the first telephone info service delivering recorded poems to callers.

Supported WSB on many readings.

GPS LPs
- The Dial-A-Poem Poets . . . . `44`
- Disconnected . . . . `49`
- Biting Off The Tongue Of A Corpse . . . `51`
- William Burroughs / John Giorno . . . . `54`
- Totally Corrupt . . . . `57`
- Big Ego . . . . `62`
- The Nova Convention . . . . `73`
- Sugar, Alcohol & Meat . . . . `76`
- You're The Guy I Want To Share . . . . `88`
- Life is a Killer . . . . `91`
- One World Poetry . . . . `92`
- Better an Old Demon Than a New God `109`
- You're a Hook . . . . `116`
- A Diamond Hidden in the Mouth . . . . `117`
- Smack My Crack . . . . `137`
- Like A Girl I Want You to Keep Coming `156`
- Cash Cow . . . . `191`
- Selections from The Best of WSB . . . `243`
- The Best of WSB for GPS . . . . `244`

GENESIS P-ORRIDGE

English musician, artist and occultist (b. 1950), best known for work with Throbbing Grsitle and Psychic TV.

WSB supported P-Orridge when s/he was prosecuted for sending indecent mail in 1976

P-Orridge was critical in raising the profile of WSB's collaborators, Balch, Gysin and Sommerville. S/he became custodian of the Balch film archives when he died in 1980

collaborations with WSB
- Re/Search 4/5 . . . . `94`
- Pirate Tape . . . . `104`
- Scared to Live (Psychic TV) . . . . `136`
- The Coldspring Tape . . . . `154`

WSB productions by G. P-O
- Nothing Here Now but the Recordings . `61`
- Thee Films . . . . `129`

G P-O film roles
- Decoder . . . . `110`
- Modulations: Cinema for the Ear . . . . `240`
- The Ballad of Genesis and Lady Jaye `316`

Chronology

JAMES GRAUERHOLZ

US writer and editor (b. 1953), assistant and business manager to WSB since the mid-seventies.

JWG was effectively WSB's Brian Epstein. He was critical in getting WSB's work exposure outside of the underground channels in which he circulated.

Some fans lament the fact that WSB's work became less formally radical after the involvement of JWG in his affairs, but there is no data to indicate that this was not a natural development of his oeuvre.

WSB's productivity and rate of citation increased continuously after meeting JWG, ending a period of decline through the seventies that had started after the *Naked Lunch* censorship controversy had blown over.

WSB's longevity was a source of plesant surprise for his fans. There is a wide concensus that this was attributable in large part to the devotion of JWG.

JWG was also a talented music producer, and worked with a number of Lawrence-based groups as well as producing most of WSB's vocal recordings.

JWG was involved in almost all of WSB's work after their meeting, making it impractical to credit him here. Please assume his involvement on all works after 1975 (50+).

JWG edited WSB books
- Cities of the Red Night 79
- The Place of dead Roads 114
- Queer 121
- The Western Lands 141
- My Education 221
- Interzone 155
- Last Words 258
- Word Virus 250

1985
- A Diamond Hidden in the Mouth [...] 117
- Artificial Intelligence (Cale) 118
- Kerouac, the Movie 119
- Ornette: Made in America 120
- Queer 121
- The Adding Machine 122
- The Elvis of Letters 123

1986
- Break Through in Grey Room 124
- Home of the Brave 125
- Major Malfunction (LeBlanc) 126
- The Cat Inside 127
- The Doctor is on the Market 128
- Thee Films 129
- What Happened to Kerouac? 130

Jul. Brion Gysin dies in Paris after long respiratory illnesses. WSB is deeply affected.

1987
- Anarchy in the UK (Proby) 131
- Jane's Addiction 132
- Minutes 133
- Code (Cabaret Voltaire) 134
- Rhythm Killers (Sly and Robbie) 135
- Scared to Live (Psychic TV) 136
- Smack My Crack 137
- The Beat Generation 138
- The Master (Haffner) 139
- The Mugwump Dance (Proby) 140
- The Western Lands 141
- The White Arcades 142

Sep. River City Reunion held in Lawrence, KS. A week long "Beat" literary festival featuring WSB, Jello Biafra, Stan Brakhage, Jim Carroll, Marianne Faithfull, Allen Ginsberg, John Giorno, Keith Haring, Ed Sanders and others.

19 Dec. First gallery show, at the Tony Shafrazi Gallery, NYC.

1988
- Action! (The Alliance) 143
- Minutes to Go 144
- Queer (Manapsara) 145
- Routine (Manapsara) 146
- Twister 147
- Uncommon Quotes 148

Authorized biography, *Literary Outlaw* by Ted Morgan.

Exhibitions in Santa Fe, London and Vancouver.

1988–90
Paintings shown at galleries in Antwerp, Amsterdam, London, and Santa Fe.

1989
- Bloodhounds of Broadway 149
- Drugstore Cowboy 150
- End of the Century Party (Clail) ... 151
- Gang of Souls 152
- Heavy Petting 153
- The Coldspring Tape 154
- Interzone 155
- Like a Girl, I Want You to Keep Coming . 156
- Seven Souls (Material) 157
- Storm the Studio (Meat Beat Manifesto) 158
- The Naked Lunch (Screenplay) 159
- Towers Open Fire & other films 160

Exhibitions in Rome, Toronto, Lisbon, Basel, Montreal, Lawrence, St. Louis.

1990
- A Short Conversation from the Grave 161
- Dead City Radio 162
- Friendly as a Hand Grenade (Tackhead) 163
- Millions of Images 164
- Rollercoaster (Jesus & Mary Chain) . 165
- The Black Rider 166
- The Black Rider (Documentary) 167
- The Jack Kerouac Collection 168

Exhibitions in Sapporo, Tubingen, Madrid, Paris, Frankfurt, LA, Tokyo.

Apocalypse gallery show with Keith Haring, London.

Black Rider tie-in show with Robert Wilson, Hamburg.

1991
- Bajo El Sol Jaguar (Reyes) 169
- Commissioner of Sewers 170
- Naked Lunch 171
- ReR Quarterly, Vol. 1 Selections ... 172
- Suicide Alley (Manic Street Preachers) 173
- A Thanksgiving Prayer 174
- The Nova Mob 175
- Wax 176

Jun. Triple bypass surgery.

Exhibitions in Basel, Amsterdam, Bilbao.

Chronology

1992
- Apocalypse Across the Sky (TMMOJ) . 177
- Burning in Water [...] (Skrew) 178
- Burroughs! 179
- Everything is Permitted 180
- Just One Fix (Ministry) 181
- Naked Lunch (Soundtrack) 182
- Naked Making Lunch 183
- Prison (Bernstein) 184
- The "Priest" They Called Him 185
- The Beat Generation 186
- The Longest Line (Nofx) 187
- Wireless Imagination 188
- *Seven Deadly Sins* (with George Condo) exhibitions in Lawrence, LA, London. WSB exhibits in Turin and Bergamo.
- *Here to Go* tribute show for WSB and Gysin in Dublin. (WSB does not attend).

1993
- Ambient- 152 minutes 33 seconds . . 189
- Beavis and Butthead: Tornado 190
- Cash Cow 191
- Even Cowgirls Get the Blues 192
- Kika 193
- Spare Ass Annie and Other Tales . . 194
- Technodon (YMO) 195
- The Black Rider (Waits) 196
- The Junky's Christmas 197
- The Operator's Manual 198
- Twelve Selves (Allen) 199
- Vaudeville Voices 200
- Words of Advice For Young People . 201
- World Turning (Trischka) 202
- **Oct.** Kurt Cobain visits WSB in Lawrence, KS.
- Exhibitions in NY, Marseilles, Madrid, Kansas City.

1994
- Ah Pook Is Here 203
- Big Hard Disk Vol. 2 204
- Dreamspeed (Fier) 205
- Glitterbug 206
- Hallucination Engine (Material) 207
- Holy Soul Jelly Roll (Ginsberg) 208
- Nowhere (Therapy?) 209
- Poetry in Motion 210
- Einstein's Brain 211
- September Songs 212
- The Greatest Show of Truth 213
- The Life & Times of Allen Ginsberg . 214
- The Myths Collection Part Two 215
- Nike Ads 216
- Exhibitions in Munich, Lawrence, Amsterdam.

1995
- Clear (Bomb the Bass) 217
- Clueless 218
- Cough it Up! 219
- In Extremis (Nirvana) 220
- **My Education** 221
- Pantopon Rose 222
- The Dark Eye 223
- The Heart/Hertz Files (Klange) 224
- The Mortal Micronotz Tribute! 225
- Exhibitions in Odense and SF.
- *Beat Culture and the New America*, a major "Beat" retrospective opens at the Whitney Museum, NY.

1996
- 10%: File under Burroughs 226
- Naked Lunch (Audiobook) 227
- Songs in the Key of X 228
- The Beat Experience 229
- The Man Who Invented Modern Sex 230
- Exhibitions in Santa Monica, Waxahachie, Seattle, Chicago, NY.
- **Jul.** *Ports of Entry* retrospective at the LA County Museum of Art.
- **Nov.** Nova Convention Revisited at Lied Center, Lawrence, KS reunites surviving members of the 1975 convention.

1997
- Communiqué (Lacy) 231
- Junky (Audiobook) 232
- Kerouac - Kicks Joy Darkness 233
- **Naked Lens** 234
- September Songs 235
- Xtrmn8mm 236
- **5 Apr.** Allen Ginsberg dies.
- **2 Aug.** WSB dies 6 pm at Lawrence Memorial Hospital.
- **7 Aug.** Buried at Bellefontaine Cemetery, St. Louis.

SUB ROSA

Belgian record label, founded in 1984 by Guy Marc Hinant and Frédéric Walheer.

WSB releases
- Break Through in Grey Room 124
- Three Allusive Tracks 307

WSB tributes
- Queer (Manapsara) 145
- Routine (Manapsara) 146
- 10% File under Burroughs 226

WSB comp appearances
- Myths: Instructions 1 112
- The Myths Collection Part Two 215
- One Night @ the 1001 242
- Hashisheen: The End of Law 252
- Up from the Archives (Malanga) . . . 265
- Rhythm Science (DJ Spooky) 279
- Noise & Electronic Music #4 287
- Sound Unbound (DJ Spooky) 299

BILL LASWELL

Prolific US bass-player and record producer (b. 1955), has made hundreds of recordings.

WSB albums
- Seven Souls (Material) 157
- The Road to the Western Lands 247

WSB with Laswell
- Mister Heartbreak (Anderson) 103
- Home of the Brave (Anderson) 125
- Rhythm Killers (Sly & Robbie) 135
- Ambient- 152 minutes 33 seconds . . 189
- Hallucination Engine (Material) 207
- 10% File under Burroughs 226
- Hashisheen: The End of Law 252
- Innermedium (Musso) 257
- Rhythm Science (DJ Spooky) 279
- Noise & Electronic Music #4 287
- Words Of Advice 294
- Sound Unbound (DJ Spooky) 299
- Incunabula (Method of Defiance) . . . 309
- Jahbulon (Method of Defiance) 311

HAL WILLNER

US producer (b. 1957), also known for his tribute projects.

First met WSB as musical director of *Saturday Night Live*.

WSB projects
- Dead City Radio 162
- Spare Ass Annie and Other Tales . . . 194
- The Operator's Manual 198
- Words of Advice for Young People . . 201
- Big Hard Disk Vol. 2 204
- September Songs 212
- Naked Lunch (Audiobook) 227
- September Songs 235
- Words of Advice 294

Posthumous releases

1998
- Cyber-Sadism Live! (Home) — 237
- Destroy All Rational Thought — 238
- Let It Come Down — 239
- Modulations: Cinema for the Ear — 240
- Negro Necro Nekros (Dälek) — 241
- One Night @ the 1001 — 242
- Selections from The Best of WSB — 243
- **The Best of WSB from GPS** — 244
- The Book of Life — 245
- The Nova Convention Revisited — 246
- The Road to the Western [...] (Material) — 247
- Venus Blue — 248
- Wising up the Marks — 249
- **Word Virus** — 250
- Zur Holle Mama #3 — 251

1999
- Hashisheen: The End of Law — 252
- **Nova Express** — 253
- The Source — 254

2000
- Beat — 255
- Condo Painting — 256
- Innermedium (Musso) — 257
- Last Words — 258
- Night Waltz — 259
- NYC Ghosts and Flowers (Sonic Youth) — 260
- Planet Rave — 261
- Stoned Immaculate — 262
- Stranglehold — 263
- The Night Watch — 264
- Up from the Archives (Malanga) — 265

2001
- Last Words: Qui Vivre Verra — 266
- Sleep in a Nest of Flames — 267
- The Last Words of Dutch Schultz — 268

2002
- Last Night on Earth (U2) — 269
- More Dub Infusions — 270
- The Wire: 20 Years 1982-2002 — 271

2003
- Elephant — 272
- New Deutsch — 273
- Portrait of a Bookstore as an Old Man — 274
- Tagebuch eines Rückzuges — 275

2004
- Post Industrial Boys — 276
- Radio Hyper-Yahoo (Sharp) — 277
- Retaking the Universe — 278
- Rhythm Science (DJ Spooky) — 279

2005
- Diggin the New Breed — 280
- Land Rush (Harrington) — 281
- Lawrence Home Movies — 282
- Newspaper Taxis — 283
- Nova Psychedelia (Clark) — 284

2006
- Absolute Wilson — 285
- MakroSoft 'Theme' (Makrosoft) — 286
- Noise & Electronic Music #4 — 287
- The Audience's Listening — 288
- The Sopranos: Members Only — 289
- The Theatre of Repetitions — 290
- Transfixiones — 291

2007
- Obscene — 292
- **Real English Tea Made Here** — 293
- **Words of Advice** — 294

2008
- And the Hippos [...] — 295
- Chelsea on the Rocks — 296
- CinemaSonics (Wimbish) — 297
- Flora Meets Fauna (Violet Halo) — 298
- Sound Unbound (DJ Spooky) — 299
- The Instrument of Control — 300
- The Japanese Sandman — 301

2009
- And the Hippos [...] (Audiobook) — 302
- Corso: The Last Beat — 303
- Eats Darkness (Apostle of Hustle) — 304
- Riding Strange Horses (Hill & Spencer) — 305
- Naked Lunch (Audiobook) — 306
- Three Allusive Tracks — 307

2010
- **A Man Within** — 308
- Incunabula (Method of Defiance) — 309
- Interzone (Zorn) — 310
- Jahbulon (Method of Defiance) — 311
- Marijuana Dreams (Dubblestandart) — 312
- Step Right Up! — 313
- The Source (TMMOJ) — 314

2011
- Nova Express (Zorn) — 315
- The Ballad of Genesis and Lady Jaye — 316
- The Beat Hotel — 317

2012
- Hell Money (Rome) — 318
- Mentallusions — 319
- Outtakes from the Life of a Happy Man — 320
- The Black Meat — 321
- **The Spoken Word** — 322

2013
- Dreamachines (Zorn) — 323
- Wanderlust (Hines) — 324

SHOW ALL YOUR CARDS

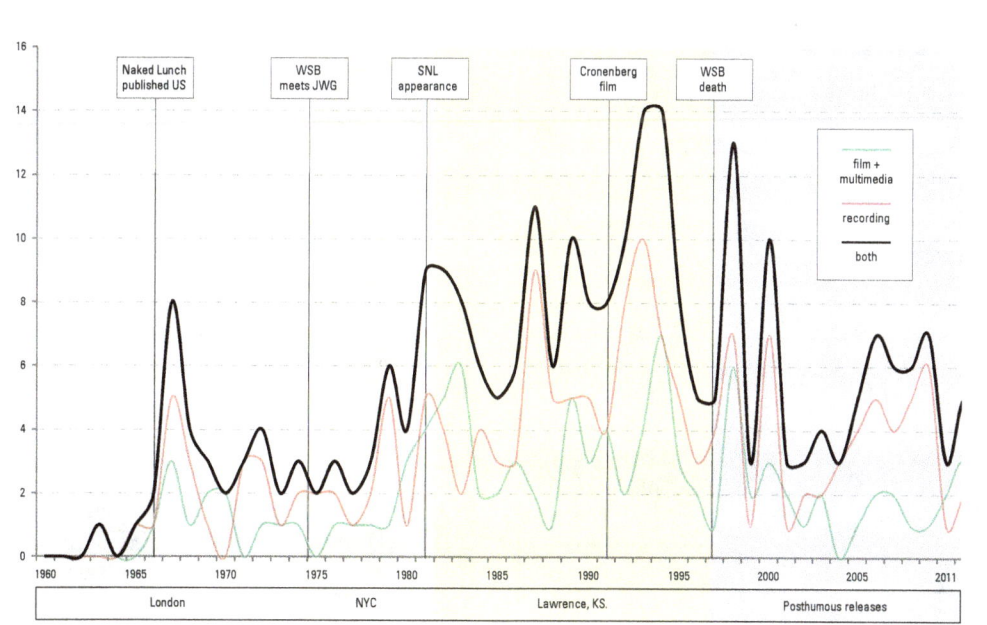

This chart shows the number of WSB-related films and recordings issued 1960-2011. Place of domicile and some representative life events are also shown. Yes, I know it should be a bar chart but that didn't look as cool.

How to read the cards

card no. / item type / genre
The range of genres varies according to the item type.

media

book	record	film	multimedia
binding type of the first edition.	formats of original release.	run time and colour b/w indicator.	media and operating system

released / created
Year created is only given if significantly earlier than release.

commerce
This field indicates the (original) mode of distribution of the artefact rather than its economic performance.

●	●●	●●●	●●●●
underground	independent	commercial	corporate

critical
This field indicates the general critical reception of the artefact. Where no information was available, I have made a subjective, or at least an arbitrary, judgement.

●	●●	●●●	●●●●
bomb	okay	good	epic

WSB quotient
This field indicates the proportion of WSB-originated or WSB-related, material in the artefact..

●	●●	●●●	●●●●
some WSB	more WSB	mostly WSB	entirely WSB

cover image
If no image is available, this space will be intentionally left blank.

book	record	film	multimedia
cover of first edition	cover of first issue, or disc label if no cover.	earliest release poster, or title frame.	image of media cover.

nationality
The national flag of the country of first issue. This book assumes a basic level of vexillological literacy.

---

1 book
fiction

JUNKIE
William Lee

media

PAPERBACK
released
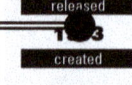
1953
created

commerce

critical

WSB quotient

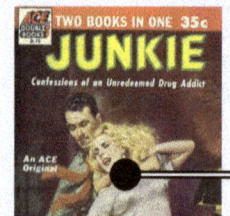

First published under a pseudonym, sixtynined with *Narcotic Agent* by Maurice Helbrant, *Junky* (sic) was reissued unexpurgated in 1977 by Penguin and for a time was the only widely-available WSB title in the UK, circulating in playgrounds alongside *Skinhead* and *Clockwork Orange*. In that year Jacques Stern optioned the book and had Terry Southern produce a screenplay for Dennis Hopper 254 to direct and star in, maybe with David Bowie 13 and Jack Nicholson, but the project stalled. WSB would release an audiobook version 232 in 1997. A definitive text, edited by Oliver Harris, was issued to mark the book's fiftieth anniversary in 2003.

blurb
Note that cross-references to other cards are not shown in all instances.

1 book — fiction 🇺🇸

JUNKIE
William Lee

- media: PAPERBACK
- released: 1953
- created:
- commerce: ●●○○○
- critical: ●●●○○
- WSB quotient: ●●●●○

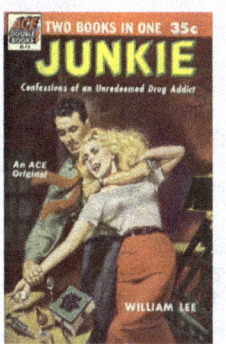

First published under a pseudonym, sixtynined with *Narcotic Agent* by Maurice Helbrant, *Junky* (sic) was reissued unexpurgated in 1977 by Penguin and for a time was the only widely-available WSB title in the UK, circulating in playgrounds alongside *Skinhead* and *Clockwork Orange*. In that year Jacques Stern optioned the book and had Terry Southern produce a screenplay for Dennis Hopper 254 to direct and star in, maybe with David Bowie 48 and Jack Nicholson, but the project stalled. WSB would release an audiobook version 232 in 1997. A definitive text, edited by Oliver Harris, was issued to mark the book's fiftieth anniversary in 2003.

2 book — fiction 🇫🇷

THE NAKED LUNCH
William Burroughs

- media: PAPERBACK
- released: 1959
- created:
- commerce: ●●●○○
- critical: ●●●●●
- WSB quotient: ●●●●●

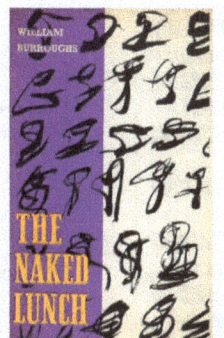

WSB's most celebrated work was too hot for the anglosphere and could only be published in Paris by Maurice Girodias of the Olympia Press, who became interested when the *Big Table* controversy exploded. On publication, Girodias prefixed the title with a definite article that stayed to this day on European versions of the book. The Spurious Article Tendency would soon climax in the nomenclature of many musical groups, although no informed person would cite, for example, The Joy Division or, indeed, Thee Psychic TV. Subsequent editions of this would accumulate forewords and afterwords in the manner of bonus tracks on "deluxe" CD reissues.

3 book — cut/ups 🇫🇷

MINUTES TO GO
Burroughs / Gysin / Beiles / Corso

- media: PAPERBACK
- released: 1960
- created:
- commerce: ●○○○○
- critical: ●●●○○
- WSB quotient: ●●●●○

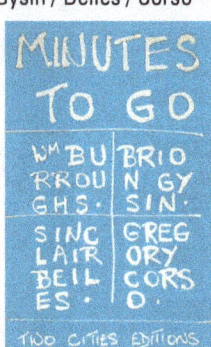

The value of Gysin's accidental discovery of the cut/up technique at the Beat Hotel in Paris was immediately recognised by WSB and cut/ups would remain prominent in his oeuvre until COTRN 79 in the early eighties. Reading here, it's easy to see how *The Naked Lunch* mutated into The Nova Trilogy via techniques that would be elaborated in *The Third Mind* 56, although they ended up having wider impact in music and film than in literature. This first collection includes Gysin's seminal titular poem alongside contributions by Sinclair Beiles, who had been WSB's secretary in the Paris years, and some equivocal prevarications by Gregory Corso 303.

4 book — cut/ups 🇺🇸

THE EXTERMINATOR
William Burroughs & Brion Gysin

- media: HARDBACK
- released: 1960
- created:
- commerce: ●○○○○
- critical: ●●○○○
- WSB quotient: ●●●●○

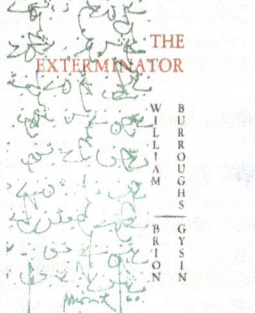

Not to be confused with the 1973 collection 45 (or film 77) his first stab at an extended cut/up like a prototype for *The Soft Machine* perhaps. It's fun to wonder whether any forward-thinking BBC employees stumbled onto this, maybe considering a futuristic sf show, leveraging new tape-recorder technologies, dealing with notions of social control under emergent technologies, thinking hey that would be a good thing for the evil robot nazi cruel-set things to shout, maybe inna metallic stylee. Well, that's what I reckon anyway.

1953

1

25

4

1960

1961

5 book — cut/ups
THE SOFT MACHINE
William Burroughs

media: PAPERBACK
released: 1961
created:
commerce: ●●●
critical: ●●●●
WSB quotient: ●●●●

The first edition, from the Olympia Press, was substantially rewritten for publication in the US by Grove in 1966, and then again for the 1968 Calder UK edition. The Olympia version is much more experimental than the subsequent versions and has not been reissued. The mutable nature of the text prefigures the cult of remixology that came to prominence in the dance scene in the UK from the mid-eighties, represented by the *Words of Advice* mini-LP [201]. This book forms the first volume of The Cut-Up (or Nova) Trilogy, followed by TTTE [6] and *Nova Express* [10]. Even as recently as 2011, a Turkish translation was charged with obscenity and suppressed.

6 book — cut/ups
THE TICKET THAT EXPLODED
William Burroughs

media: PAPERBACK
released: 1962
created:
commerce: ●●●
critical: ●●●●
WSB quotient: ●●●●

As with *The Soft Machine* [5], the Olympia Press first edition of TTTE was substantially revised for publication in the US by Grove in 1967 which text was also used for the 1968 UK Calder version. Both the later editions add the influential "Invisible Generation" essay compiled from two articles by WSB for *International Times*. A group called after this book formed in 2004, and there was a 2011 opera too, but neither of those appear here. Sorry!

1963

7 book — cut/ups
DEAD FINGERS TALK
William Burroughs

media: HARDBACK
released: 1963
created:
commerce: ●●●
critical: ●●●
WSB quotient: ●●●●

WSB's appearance at the 1962 International Writers' Conference in Edinburgh, organised by Scottish publisher John Calder, had turned him into an avant-garde celebrity with his work scorned or adored depending on viewpoint. His three Paris novels were still too hot for publication in the UK so towards the end of 1963 Calder put out this anthology drawn from the least unpalatable of those texts. Following a scalding review in the *TLS*, a furious row (the "UGH Correspondence") erupted, masterfully stoked by Calder, and enhanced WSB's reputation all the more. These exchanges were suffixed to UK editions of *Naked Lunch* [2] when it surfaced the next year.

8 book — letters
THE YAGE LETTERS
William Burroughs & Allen Ginsberg

media: PAPERBACK
released: 1963
created: 1953
commerce: ●●●
critical: ●●●●
WSB quotient: ●●●●

A collection of letters and short pieces dealing with WSB's South American travels in search of the drug Yage, aka telepathine, or more widely these days, ayahuasca. In the early nineties there was an English group called The Yage Letters who had a tenuous connection to Cliff Richard, and an episode from the book was filmed as *The Japanese Sandman* [301]. An expanded version of this book, edited by WSB scholar Oliver Harris, was issued in 2006. Bonus info! In 2009 a mysterious three-minute clip from a doco about ayahuasca, narrated by WSB and probably dating from the sixties, appeared on the internet but no further info could be located.

9 **film**	
experimental	

TOWERS OPEN FIRE
Antony Balch dir.

media: **10M B/W**
released: **1963**
created:
commerce:
critical:
WSB quotient:

Balch was responsible for filming the earliest footage of WSB and for realising filmic versions of cut/up experiments to compliment their written and audio counterparts. This was the first film that Balch completed, shot in 16mm in Paris, London and Gibraltar from Dec. 1962 to Dec. 1963 and based on episodes from *The Soft Machine* [5]. It features WSB with Ian Sommerville, Brion Gysin, Michael Portman and an uncredited Alexander Trocchi. The film played in London with Todd Browning's *Freaks* which was then being resurrected by Balch. *Towers Open Fire* was subsequently released on [107] [129] [160].

10 **book**	
cut/ups	

NOVA EXPRESS
William Burroughs

media: **HARDBACK**
released: **1964**
created:
commerce:
critical:
WSB quotient:

Given this book's heavy use of cut/ups, it's surprising that it lent itself so well to live readings, with extracts appearing on *Call Me Burroughs* [11], NHNBTR [81], *Spare Ass Annie* [194], YTGIWTSMMW [88], *Sugar, Alcohol & Meat* [76], *Klacto/23* [16] and elsewhere. WSB would spend the rest of the sixties making short cut/up texts and this would be his last novel until *The Wild Boys* [40] in 1971. Whilst David Cronenberg [171] had said that he couldn't make a direct adaptation of *Naked Lunch* [2], Alex Perkowski [253] successfully confronted the even greater challenges posed by this book with a meagre fraction of his resources.

11 **recording**	
spoken word	

CALL ME BURROUGHS
William Burroughs

media: **LP**
released: **1965**
created:
commerce:
critical:
WSB quotient:

These first recordings of WSB remained the only ones in general circulation for many years. The recordings were made by Ian Sommerville at the behest of Gaït Frogé in the basement of her English Bookshop at 42 Rue de Seine, Paris, with WSB reading extracts from his novels [2] [5] [10]. The cover design, by Tientje Louw, featured a photo by Harriet Crowther and notes by Fluxus poet Emmet Williams. Only 1,000 copies were pressed but the record had a profound impact on the elite of the emerging UK underground scene with fans including Paul McCartney and Brian Jones. It was reissued in the US on LP (1966) and finally on CD (and cassette) in 1995.

12 **book**	
fiction	

VALENTINE'S DAY READING
William Burroughs

media: **BOOKLET**
released: **1965**
created:
commerce:
critical:
WSB quotient:

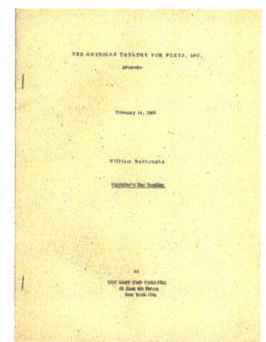

WSB turned 17 just nine days before the massacre which saw seven mobsters killed on the North Side of Chicago on 14 Feb. 1929. Exactly 36 years later he gave a reading at the American Theatre for Poets, 85 E. 4th Street, NY, but elliptically he focussed on another slain mobster, "Dutch" Schultz, who had been shot in 1935 and died a few hours later after a bizarre stream-of-consciousness monologue that was recorded by a police stenographer and is reproduced here. WSB's reading drew heavily from the text and facts surrounding the shooting and was recorded and released in *Revue Ou* [43] [47] before being reworked into his unproduced film-script [35].

1966

13 **film** drama

CHAPPAQUA
Conrad Rooks dir.

media
82M COL.
released
1966
created

commerce
critical
WSB quotient

Written, produced and directed by Conrad Rooks based on his experiences of drug addiction. The movie was photographed by Robert Frank 80 108 and features WSB (as Opium Jones), Swami Satchidananda, Allen Ginsberg, Moondog, Ornette Coleman, The Fugs, and Ravi Shankar. Rooks had commissioned Coleman to compose the soundtrack but it was deemed unsuitable so Ravi Shankar provided a replacement 24 and Coleman released his score as *Chappaqua Suite*. The film was well received, winning the Silver Lion at the Venice Film festival in 1966, but nevertheless vanished from view for many years before resurfacing in the late nineties.

14 **recording** rock

THE INSECT TRUST
The Insect Trust

media
LP
released
1966
created

commerce
critical
WSB quotient

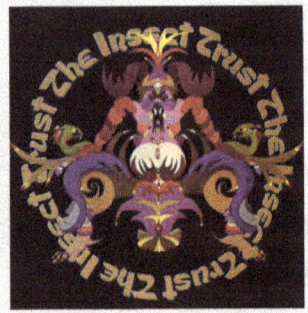

Taking their name from villains in The Nova Trilogy, this group was active for four years from 1966. The core of the group was guitarist/songwriter Luke Faust and Robert Palmer on alto sax and clarinet. They released two albums before disbanding, with music ranging from surreal folk-rock through soulful pop to full-on free jazz. Palmer went on to become a music critic and conducted one of the most celebrated WSB interviews and to supply sleeve notes to the 1971 *Joujouka* album 39. He should not be confused with Robert "Addicted to Love" Palmer.

MORE: Palmer, Robert. *Rolling Stone Interview: William Burroughs*. RS #108, 11 May 1972

1967

15 **recording** experimental

ASPEN 5+6
Various

media
8" FLEXI
released
1967
created

commerce
critical
WSB quotient

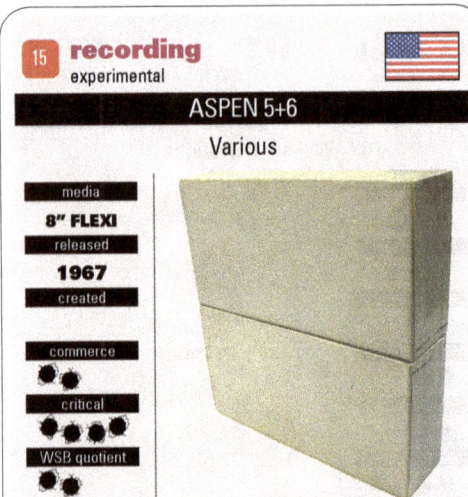

Phyllis Johnson published her multimedia magazine out of its upscale namesake NY ski resort sporadically from 1965 to 1971. Like a better-healed version of Chopin's *Ou* 43 each issue came in a customized box or folder filled of booklets, recordings, posters, postcards and even super-8 film reels. Most issues were themed and the double "minimalism" issue included an 8" 33rpm flexi of WSB reading "This, gentlemen, is a death dwarf..." (4:20) and "Mister Bradley Mister Martin..." (4:13), from *Nova Express* 10. On the flipside Alain Robbe-Grillet reads from "Jealousy" (10:07) which I mention only because he's top value and well worth checking out too.

16 **recording** spoken word

KLACTO/23
Various

media
1/4" TAPE
released
1967
created

commerce
critical
WSB quotient

This reel-to-reel tape complimented Carl Weissner's *Klactoveedsedsteen* magazine and included a recording of WSB reading "Crab Nebula" (13:30) from *Nova Express* 10 made by Weissner 93 during a visit by WSB to Germany. The tape also features selections by Harold Norse, Jeff Nuttall, Claude Pelieu, Charles Bukowski, Carol Berge, Brion Gysin, Henri Chopin and Francois Dufrene.

17 film	
documentary	🇺🇸

POEM POSTERS
Charles Henri Ford dir.

media: **24M COL...**
released: **1967**
created:
commerce: ●●
critical: ●●
WSB quotient: ●

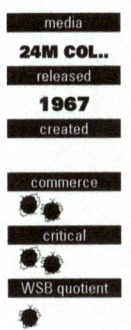

Ford (1913-2002) was an American polymath who, with Parker Tyler, co-wrote *The Young and Evil* which was published by the Obelisk (fore-runner of Olympia) Press in 1933, prefiguring the work of the "Beats". Ford also took the iconic photo of WSB in Paris for *The Paris Review* in 1965. This was Ford's first film, and documents the 1965 opening of an exhibition of Ford's work in NYC and features WSB along with Robert Indiana, Roy Lichtenstein, Gerard Malanga, Jayne Mansfield, Jonas Mekas, Claes Oldenburg, James Rosenquist, Edie Sedgwick, Jack Smith, Virgil Thomson, Andy Warhol. In 2001 Ford was the subject of *Sleep in a Nest of Flames* 267.

18 recording	
psyche	🇬🇧

SGT. PEPPER'S LONELY HEARTS CLUB BAND
The Beatles

media: **LP**
released: **1967**
created:
commerce: ●●●●●
critical: ●●●●●
WSB quotient: ●

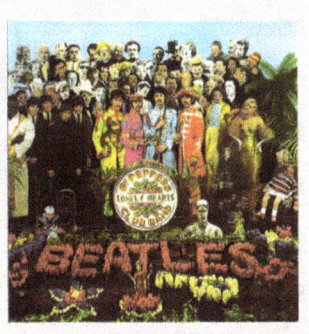

WSB is on Peter Blake's iconic cover sandwiched between Marilyn Monroe and Sri Mahavatar Babaji at the behest of Beatle Paul who was mates with WSB's pal Miles who ran the Paul-funded Indica bookshop and was intended to curate their avant-garde Zapple label. Paul also recruited Ian Sommerville as an engineer and helped him set him up a studio at 34 Montagu Place where he worked on tunes including "Eleanor Rigby". Many of WSB's early tape experiments (qv NHNBTR 81 and BTIGR 124) were made there. In 2010 Yoko Ono unveiled a plaque there signifying a building of national historical interest.

MORE: Miles, Barry. *Paul McCartney: Many Years From Now* (Secker & Warburg, 1997)

19 film	
experimental	🇬🇧

THE CUT-UPS
Antony Balch dir.

media: **19M B/W**
released: **1967**
created:
commerce: ●●
critical: ●●●
WSB quotient: ●●●●

For his second film, Balch took some footage he'd filmed for a WSB "documentary", to be called *Guerilla Conditions*, and had an assistant chop it into foot long strips, regardless of content, which were then spliced back together at "random" to create the first cut/up film. The soundtrack by Sommerville, Gysin and WSB is taken from a Scientology manual and consists of various short alternating phrases. The result is hypnotic but surprisingly coherent. The film played at a cinema on Oxford St., London, for two weeks in 1967 and audience reception was mixed, with some customers complaining loudly, reporting headaches or mislaying possessions.

20 recording	
country/folk	🇺🇸

THE MUGWUMPS
The Mugwumps

media: **LP**
released: **1967**
created: **1963**
commerce: ●●
critical: ●●
WSB quotient: ●

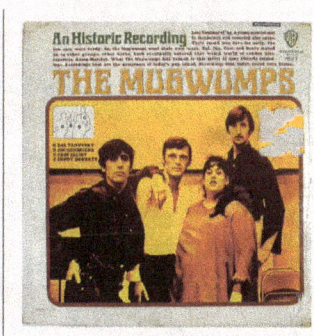

An NYC proto-folk-rock outfit that is remembered mainly for the subsequent activities of 75% of its members. Zal Yanovsky would go on to join the Lovin' Spoonful while Denny Doherty and Cass Elliot would form half of the Mamas and the Papas. Jim Hendricks would fail to achieve much in the way of rock-fame, unlike his namesake. They probably did not take their name from the creatures in *Naked Lunch* but rather from a slang term for an uncommitted person, or a supporter of the Democratic Party, having their mug (face) on one side of the fence and their wump (rump) on the other, this being manifest in the group via their folk/pop dichotomy.

1967

21 film — experimental
THE NUDE RESTAURANT
Andy Warhol dir.

media: 95M COL..
released: 1967
created:
commerce: ●●●
critical: ●●
WSB quotient: ●

The title of one of Warhol's less-celebrated feature films appears to be derived from WSB's *Naked Lunch* [5]. Alongside better-known "Superstars" Taylor Mead, Brigitte Polk, and Viva, we find one Julian Burroughs (whose real name was Andrew Dungan) playing "Man in Tub". Dungan falsely claimed to be WSB's son in real life having adopted a false name on deserting from the US military. In the final scene Dungan asks viewers to attend a forthcoming anti-Vietnam war protest in front of the Federal Building, to which we hear Viva off-screen ask "Where's the Federal Building?"

MORE: http://www.warholstars.org (20 Aug. 2013)

22 recording — psyche
THE VELVET UNDERGROUND AND NICO
The Velvet Underground

media: LP
released: 1967
created:
commerce: ●●●
critical: ●●●●●
WSB quotient: ●

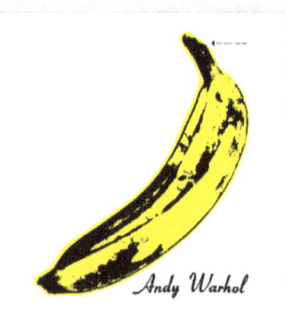

In the mid-sixties Andy Warhol, a fan of crappy novelty compilations, persuaded Lou Reed and John Cale, who were making surf and drag-racing records for Pickwick, to record an LP based on life at The Factory. They called their group the Velvet Underground after a softcore potboiler by one Michael Leigh who was obviously inspired by WSB's idiosyncratic titles. The early VU contributed to *Aspen* [15] and provided a flexidisc of cut/ups for Warhol's *Index* book. Many tracks on their debut album explored similar territory to WSB's early work. In *With William Burroughs* [87] Lou Reed claims his tune "Lonesome Cowboy Bill" is about WSB, so maybe it is.

1968

23 recording — rock
BORN TO BE WILD
Steppenwolf

media: 7"
released: 1968
created:
commerce: ●●●
critical: ●●
WSB quotient: ●

Probably the first stoner-rock classic, famous from its inclusion on the *Easy Rider* soundtrack, the lyrics includes a reference to "Heavy Metal Thunder", making it the first recontextualisation of WSB's term, first used in *The Soft Machine* [5]. The term now became synonymous with the loud fast rock movement originating in Birmingham, England. Previous to this "heavy metal" was a scientific term for a vaguely defined collection of elements exhibiting metallic properties. Numerous groups also used the term metatextual-stylee in their names but they were all shit except for Lobby Loyde's Heavy Metal Kids (1974–1977).

24 recording — jazz
CHAPPAQUA (SOUNDTRACK)
Ravi Shankar

media: LP
released: 1968
created:
commerce: ●●
critical: ●●●
WSB quotient: ●

Ravi Shankar's epic tripped-out sitar score for Conrad Rooks' film [13] has a five second sample by WSB (taken from *Nova Express* [10] on *Call Me Burroughs* [11]) on the last track "Theme" (4:19). This LP is not to be confused with Ornette Coleman's *Chappaqua Suite* which was commissioned by Rooks but not used in the film. Incidentally, "Chappaqua" is also the title of a 1958 jazz standard by Stan Getz.

25	**recording**
	psyche

THE SOFT MACHINE
The Soft Machine

- media: **LP**
- released: **1968**
- created:
- commerce: ●●●
- critical: ●●●●
- WSB quotient: ●

Originally from Canterbury, this was the first group to name itself for a WSB reference with WSB's blessing, via founding member Daevid Allen who had briefly lived in Allen Ginsberg's old room at The Beat Hotel 317 whilst WSB was based there. The Soft Machine became one of the house bands at London's UFO club along with Pink Floyd and The Crazy World of Arthur Brown. A "barely audible aphorism" by WSB appears buried in the mix on a demo mix of *She's Gone* from June 1967, making them the first group to sample WSB, even if only inaudibly and privately.

26	**film**
	documentary

WITCHCRAFT THROUGH THE AGES
Benjamin Christensen dir.

- media: **77M B/W**
- released: **1968**
- created: **1922**
- commerce: ●●●
- critical: ●●●●
- WSB quotient: ●●●

WSB masterfully narrates Balch's reworking of the much-loved and controversial silent classic. Taken alongside the new and sporadically incongruous jazz score by Daniel Humair, played by a quintet including Jean-Luc Ponty on violin, this effectively updates the film from the roaring twenties to the swinging sixties. In fact, it's so postmodern (inna Guy Madden stylee) that it got smacked with an X certificate. Bizarrely, the movie climaxes with a screed likening diagnoses of hysteria in the twenties to ancient witchmania, prefiguring Scientology propaganda by a good few years. Yikes!

MORE: Stevenson, Jack. *Witchcraft Through the Ages* (FAB Press, 2007)

27	**book**
	fiction

ALI'S SMILE
William Burroughs

- media: **HARDBACK**
- released: **1969**
- created:
- commerce: ●●
- critical: ●●●
- WSB quotient: ●●●●

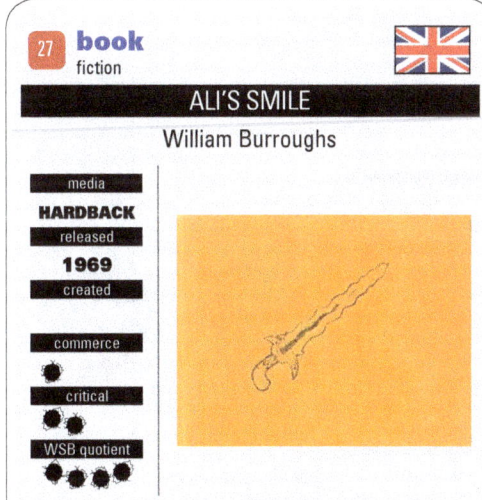

This super-deluxe buckram-bound edition was put out by Bill Butler, an ex-pat American who ran the Unicorn Bookshop and Press in Brighton, East Sussex. Limited to just 99 copies (probably to avoid purchase tax), the book came in a 40cm box with a 12 inch LP, one side of which was WSB reading the piece and the other containing technical info on the recording. The text was collected later in *Exterminator!* 45 and the recording later surfaced on *Vaudeville Voices* 200. Given that the text refers to Scientology, we could refer you here to L. Ron Hubbard's distinguished musical career... or then again not.

28	**film**
	documentary

CAIN'S FILM
Jamie Wadhawan dir.

- media: **27M B/W**
- released: **1969**
- created:
- commerce: ●
- critical: ●●
- WSB quotient: ●●

A classic short doco about Alexander Trocchi who had written porno novels for Olympia Press, collaborated with the Situationist International, and authored *Cain's Book* about his experiences with heroin, a book that WSB describes in his appearance here as "a real milestone". The film includes heaps of interesting footage including a visit to the offices of John Calder (who had published *Cain's Book* and fought its obscenity charges) and also of an event at the Arts Lab with Jim Haynes, Ronald Laing and others including Stewart Home's 237 mum Julia Callan-Thompson.

MORE: http://www.stewarthomesociety.org/luv/splinters.htm (22 Aug. 13)

29 recording / jazz

TAKE ANOTHER LITTLE PIECE OF MY HEART
Nova Express

- media: 7"
- released: 1969
- created:
- commerce: ●●●
- critical: ●●●
- WSB quotient: ●

Demonstrating WSB's disproportionate profile amongst jazz fans at the time, the third group to name themselves for a WSB reference was from Melbourne, Australia, which was hardly at the vanguard of Bohemia. This soul-jazz outfit put out just this one single before splitting. Their frontwoman Linda George, a powerful vocalist, toured for a while with showbands, including playing for Australian troops in Vietnam, before starting her solo career in 1972. She gained acclaim for her portrayal of the Acid Queen in the all-star 1973 Australian production of The Who's *Tommy*.

30 film / erotica

SECRETS OF SEX
Antony Balch dir.

- media: 85M COL..
- released: 1969
- created:
- commerce: ●●●
- critical: ●●●
- WSB quotient: ●

aka *Bizarre*. With the backing of legendary producer Richard Gordon, Balch hit paydirt with his horror-sex-comedy portmanteau film that ran for years in the UK in the early seventies. Narrated by a mummy (voiced by Valentine Dyall), the battle of the sexes takes on a Burroughsian spin, one of the characters is even reading a copy of *Nova Express* 10! Brion Gysin claimed to have written some scenes. Unfortunately, my DVD of this is faulty and shuffles the footage in a cut/up stylee which is funny but makes objective assessment problematic. It's such a shame that Balch's proposed musical of *Naked Lunch* 5 never took off. It would been a mindblast!

31 film / drama

PERFORMANCE
Donald Cammell & Nicolas Roeg dirs.

- media: 105M COL.
- released: 1970
- created:
- commerce: ●●●
- critical: ●●●
- WSB quotient: ●●●

WSB was certainly an influence on this, the most representative overground artefact of the seedier side of Swinging London. Cammell and Roeg were reportedly inspired by Balch's short films 129 and even inserted Calder editions of WSB works under the end credits. If you listen carefully, Mick Jagger makes a reference to Professor Burroughs at one point and during his tune "Memo from Turner" he refers obliquely to *The Soft Machine*. At times, other parts of the soundtrack are reminiscent of Joujouka music, and the whole movie is permeated with a generalised London-era Burroughsian vibe. Check it out.

32 film / drama

PROLOGUE
Robin Spry dir.

- media: 87M B/W
- released: 1970
- created:
- commerce: ●●●
- critical: ●●●
- WSB quotient: ●

Spry (1039–2005) was a highly-regarded Canadian film-maker with an interest in sociological themes. His debut feature was a docudrama centred round the police riot at the 1968 US democratic party convention, and includes footage of WSB who was covering the events for *Esquire* magazine.

33 book — cut/ups

THE BRAILLE FILM
Carl Weissner & William Burroughs

media: PAPERBACK
released: 1970
created:
commerce:
critical:
WSB quotient:

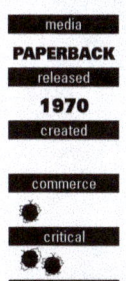

Yeah... I know this isn't by WSB but it might as well be. For my money, this is one of the great cut/up novels by anyone. Weissner (1940-2012) was a key figure in the German avant-garde, translator of WSB, and also Andy Warhol, J.G. Ballard, Allen Ginsberg, Charles Bukowski, Bob Dylan and Frank Zappa. He also wrote the (Germanophone) 1973 hörspiel *Deadline USA*, about the sixties US counterculture and featuring WSB with the other usual suspects.

34 book — interviews

THE JOB
William Burroughs & Daniel Odier

media: HARDBACK
released: 1970
created:
commerce:
critical:
WSB quotient:

Published first in French translation a year earlier, this is a highlight from the period when WSB was experimenting with new ways of producing texts. In response to questions from Odier, WSB often replies with pasted in lengthy preexisting responses, and ends up approximating a manifesto. The "Academy 23" section reads like a recipe for The Temple of Psychic Youth 136 and there's heaps here relating to the audio-visual field (e.g. ideas for groups and performances) that would have had an impact, especially on musicians. There are a few different versions of this around, some including bits or all of *Electronic Revolution* 37.

35 book — screenplay

THE LAST WORDS OF DUTCH SCHULTZ
William Burroughs

media: HARDBACK
released: 1970
created:
commerce:
critical:
WSB quotient:

WSB's treatment of "Dutch" Schultz's logorrhoeic death throes had been foreshadowed at the Valentine's Day Reading of 1965 12 and here they are reworked into the form of a film script. The film rights were bought by Dennis Hopper and there was reported interest from Francis Ford Coppola but it was never produced. There's a short piece on *Spare Ass Annie* 194 based on this work, and in 2001 a part-animated short 268 was produced in the Netherlands, inspired by the original text but once again quite different. Note that this first edition of the book is very different from the 1986 Calder edition.

36 recording — experimental

AUDIOPOEMS
Henri Chopin

media: LP
released: 1971
created:
commerce:
critical:
WSB quotient:

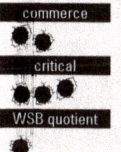
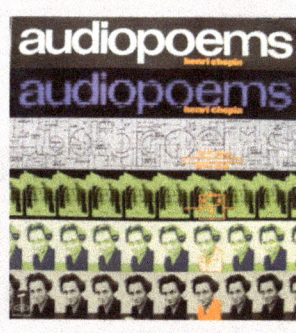

Henri Chopin (1922-2008) was a French poet, painter, graphic artist and designer, typographer, independent publisher, filmmaker, broadcaster and arts promoter, He was based in Paris until 1968 when he left following consequences of his involvement in the May uprisings. Chopin moved to Ingatetstone in Essex (UK) where he issued this LP of his own sound-poetry that features very early computer graphics and brief sleeve-notes by WSB who would go on to appear on the final two issues of Chopin's *Revue Ou* 43 47. Since there's a bit of space left here, we will use it to salute the multitalented Henri for his role in the origination of ASCII art. 8^)

1971

37 book — nonfiction 🇬🇧
ELECTRONIC REVOLUTION
William Burroughs

media: PAPERBACK
released: 1971

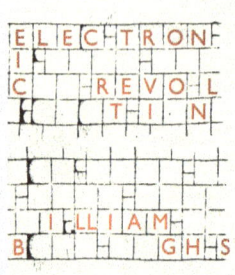

First published in Germany a year earlier, these two interconnected essays summarise WSB's theories regarding The Word as a viral technique of control and methods for its neutralisation. The book was hugely influential on the emergent Industrial scene in the North of England, qv Cabaret Voltaire [134], Throbbing Gristle (later Psychic TV [136] and Coil) 23 Skidoo [85] and many many more. One or both parts of this crop up in later editions of *The Job* [34].

38 recording — jazz 🇫🇷
OBSOLETE
Dashiell Hedayat

media: LP
released: 1971

Hedayat was a pseudonym of French novelist Jack-Alain Léger (birth name Daniel Theron) aka Melmoth. WSB provides a twelve second sample, from "Uranian Willy" on *Call Me Burroughs* [11] at the end of "Love Song for Zelda" (7:46). The tape is thought to have been supplied by Daevid Allen who played guitar backing Hedayat on vocals, keyboards and "cosmic-hedayat-rumble and cut-ups" with the rest of the *Camembert Electrique*-era line-up of Gong (a spin-off of The Soft Machine [25]). Heed the dire warning: "This record must be played as loud as possible, must be heard as stoned as impossible, and thank you everybody." Those were the days.

39 recording — joujouka 🇬🇧
THE PIPES OF PAN AT JOUJOUKA
The Master Musicians of Joujouka

media: LP
released: 1971
created: 1968

Hailing from a village in the Ahl Srif mountain range in Morocco, this traditional Sufi trance music was much enjoyed by WSB and Brion Gysin when they encountered it on their North African travels in the fifties. Gysin, and his friend Hamri, brought Brian Jones to record a performance (on 29 Jul. 1968) which Jones edited and finished mixing shortly before his death in 1969. The record came out on Rolling Stones Records in 1971 featuring artwork by Hamri. WSB recorded some radio spots with DJ Kenny Everett and Beatles aide Derek Taylor for the LP. Having become a collector's item, a 1995 reissue proved controversial. See also [177] [314].

40 book — fiction 🇺🇸
THE WILD BOYS: A BOOK OF THE DEAD
William Burroughs

media: HARDBACK
released: 1971

Immortalised in the pop canon by Duran Duran [115], we can only speculate why no group has called themselves this when other less obvious names (e.g. The Ticket That Exploded) have been snapped up. I mean, just off the top of my head, we've had The Soft Boys, The Dead Boys, The Zero Boys, The Jerky Boys, etc. Maybe groups are scared peeps would think they're named for the Duran Duran tune but isn't there such a thing as ironic consumption? In 2011, there was an Australian tv series called this but it was about (heterosexual) bushrangers. Actually, forget it, wasn't Heinz's backing group called the Wild Boys?

41 film — experimental 🇬🇧
BILL AND TONY
Antony Balch dir.

media: 5M COL..
released: 1972
created:
commerce: ●●
critical: ●●●
WSB quotient: ●●●●

aka "Who's Who". A short film, this time in colour, based on experimental performances with projections by Gysin and Sommerville with Domain Poetique in Paris from 1960-64. The film alternates shots of WSB and Balch's heads with each other's voices over-dubbed and/or face superimposed over a soundtrack of those old favourites, extracts from Tod Brownings *Freaks* and a Scientology manual. The film wasn't intended for release but as a private experiment. Recently some contemporaneous video footage from the same sessions has surfaced on the internet.

MORE: Sargeant, Jack. *Naked Lens: Beat Cinema* (Creation, 1997)

42 recording — jazz 🇺🇸
CAN'T BUY A THRILL
Steely Dan

media: LP
released: 1972
created:
commerce: ●●●
critical: ●●●
WSB quotient: ●

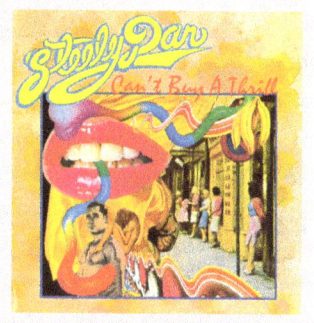

Steely Dan is (still) an American jazz-rock combo formed by Donald Fagen and Walter Becker. They appear here because they took their name from a dildo mentioned in *Naked Lunch* [2]. WSB wasn't much of a fan though, in *New Times* magazine (18 Feb. 1977) he states: "These people are too fancy… To write a bestseller, you can't have too much going on. You take *The Godfather*, the horse's head. That's great. But you can't have a horse's head on every page. These people tend to have too many horses' heads." Nevertheless, Donald Fagen would go on to work with his hero on *Dead City Radio* [162].

43 recording — experimental 🇬🇧
OU REVUEDISQUE 40-41
Various

media: 10"
released: 1972
created:
commerce: ●●
critical: ●●
WSB quotient: ●●

Edited and produced by Henri Chopin (1922–2008) [36], *Revue Ou* was a multimedia poetry magazine consisting of a folder of artwork often accompanied by a record. Besides WSB, its distinguished contributors included Gil J. Wolman, François Dufrêne and Raoul Hausmann. The March 1972 issue included the first of two parts (10:15) of a recording of WBS's Valentine's Day Reading [12]. The tape has been cut/up (perhaps by Ian Sommerville) with various unpleasant noises. Also featured are Brion Gysin, Bernard Heidsieck, J.A. Da Silva and Chopin himself. Around 75 copies of the record were available separately in a plain bag.

44 recording — spoken word 🇺🇸
THE DIAL-A-POEM POETS
Various

media: 2LP
released: 1972
created: 1963–
commerce: ●
critical: ●●
WSB quotient: ●●●

John Giorno started Dial-A-Poem out of MOMA in New York in 1968. It was one of the first telephone information services, with twelve lines from which callers received a randomly allocated two-and-a-half minute recorded poem. The service ran for six months, taking 800,000 calls for thirty poets, before being shut down by a disgruntled parent. After the service was discontinued Giorno started releasing LPs of readings on his GPS label, to which WSB contributed over the next twenty-five years. This disc features WSB reading an extract from *The Wild Boys* [40] (6:53) recorded by Giorno in WSB's Duke St. flat in London on 19 Nov. 1971.

1973

45	**book**
	fiction

EXTERMINATOR!
William Burroughs

media: **HARDBACK**
released: **1973**
created:

commerce: ●●○○○
critical: ●●●○○
WSB quotient: ●●●●○

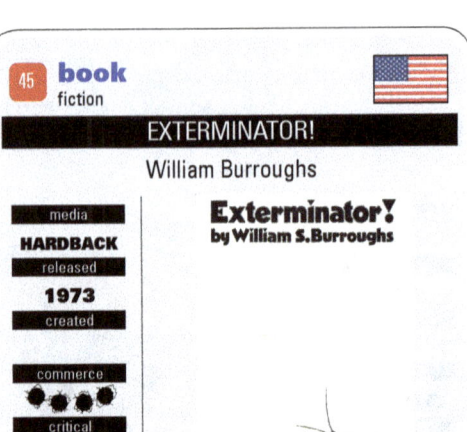

Self-evidently a collection of short stories, and waggishly the only one of WSB's works to be sub-titled "a novel". Many of the pieces would be used for readings or form the basis of sound or video works: *The Discipline of DE* [96], "Ali's Smile" [27], "Twilight's Last Gleamings" [86], "What Washington? What Orders?" [49], "The 'Priest' They Called Him" [185]. Material from the title story was incorporated into Cronenberg's film of *Naked Lunch* [171]. Of interest here also is the story "The Lemon Kid" which uses lyrics from the 1927 smash "Ain't She Sweet" recorded by many artists including uh The Beatles [18].

46	**film**
	horror

HORROR HOSPITAL
Antony Balch dir.

media: **91M COL..**
released: **1973**
created:

commerce: ●●●○○
critical: ●●○○○
WSB quotient: ●○○○○

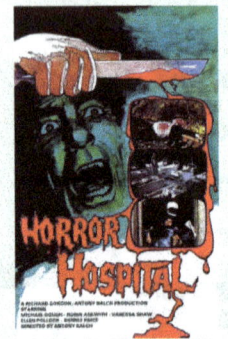

Balch's second feature is firmly in the mold of British seventies horror but still manages to evoke a whiff of WSB for those in the know. Herein stressed-out pop star Robin Askwith takes a "hairy holiday" at a purported health farm where, as is customary, his fellow patients turn out to be victims of sporadically gory mind-control experiments. Apparently intended as a black comedy, there are plenty of laughs to be had but it's difficult to know whether they're intentional or not. The spooky mansion in question is Knebworth House, Herts, where the heavy metal festivals were held and where *Sir Henry at Rawlinson End*, and other films, were filmed.

45

36

48

1974

47	**recording**
	experimental

OU REVUEDISQUE 42-43-44
Various

media: **10"**
released: **1973**
created:

commerce: ●●○○○
critical: ●●●○○
WSB quotient: ●●●○○

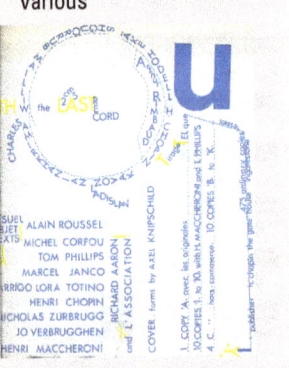

The final edition of Henri Chopin's [36] sound-poetry journal features a second extract from WSB's *Valentine's Day Reading* [12] (8:15), this time lacking the unpleasant noises that punctuated the first [43]. In fact, this piece is virtually a greatest hits of WSB tropes and phrases that will recur over the next forty years. The record also features: Åke Hodell, Charles Amirkhanian, Ladislav Novak, Arthur Rimbaud and *OU* supremo Henri Chopin himself. As with the previous disc around 75 copies were available without the accompanying journal.

48	**recording**
	rock

DIAMOND DOGS
David Bowie

media: **LP/CC**
released: **1974**
created:

commerce: ●●●●○
critical: ●●●●○
WSB quotient: ●●●○○

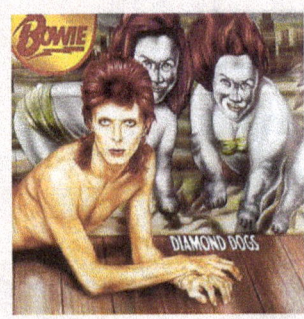

Bowie has acknowledged WSB's influence on aspects of his vast oeuvre in several interviews. His most overtly Burroughsian work is *Diamond Dogs*, an ambitious concept album cross-pollinating Orwell's *1984* with WSB-inspired imagery and sounds. The contemporaneous BBC 1974 *Cracked Actor* doco shows the glam-rock icon cutting up texts inna Gysin stylee, and furthermore on the subsequent tour (released as the *David Live* album) the show was introduced with snatches of Joujouka-ish music. Bowie now admits he was off his noodle on charlie at the time.

MORE: Copetas, Craig. *Beat Godfather meets Glitter Mainman.* RS #155. 28 Feb. 1974

49 recording
spoken word
DISCONNECTED
Various

- media: 2LP
- released: 1974
- created: 1965–
- commerce: ●●○○○
- critical: ●●●●○
- WSB quotient: ●●●○○

The second Giorno Poetry Systems comp features not only photos of Giorno apparently wanking, but also instructions (with costings) on how to set up you own Dial-A-Poem service in an early open source idiom. WSB contributes "What Washington, What Orders?" (7:01) from *Exterminator!* [45] recorded at GPS on 1 Apr. 1974. Others featured include GPS regulars John Cage, Jim Carroll, Gregory Corso, Robert Creeley, Diane Di Prima, Ed Dorn, Allen Ginsberg, John Giorno, Gerard Malanga, Peter Orlovsky, Ed Sanders, Trungpa Rinpoche, Diane Wakowski, Anne Waldman, Philip Whalen, John Wieners.

50 film
spoken word
GAY SUNSHINE READING
William Burroughs

- media: 36M COL..
- released: 1974
- created:
- commerce: ●●○○○
- critical: ●●●○○
- WSB quotient: ●●●○○

THIS SPACE
INTENTIONALLY
LEFT BLANK

The library of University of California at Berkeley (UCB Media Ctr VIDEO/C 1220) holds a videocassette filmed off-air at the First Unitarian Church, SF, on 4 Nov. 1974. In an event cosponsored with the newspaper *Gay Sunshine*, Leland Winston introduces WSB and John Giorno. WSB reads "Sexual Conditioning" (later collected in *The Adding Machine* [122]) and "What Washington? What Orders?", "From Here to Eternity" and "Virus B-23" (all from *Exterminator!* [45]). As far as I know, this film has not been circulated.

51 recording
spoken word
BITING OFF THE TONGUE OF A CORPSE
Various

- media: LP
- released: 1975
- created: 1966–
- commerce: ●●○○○
- critical: ●●●○○
- WSB quotient: ●●●○○

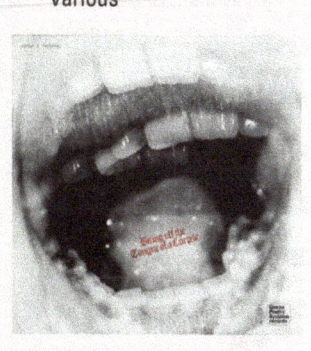

Another GPS release. WSB provides "A Top Level Conference is in Progress" (6:00) from *The Wild Boys* [40], recorded at St. Marks Church, NYC, 24 April 1974. The LP also features Gary Snyder, John Giorno, Charles Olson, Ted Berrigan, Ed Sanders, Edwin Denby, Helen Adam, Diane Di Prima, John Wieners, Robert Duncan, John Cage, Denise Levertov, Frank O'Hara, Kenneth Koch, John Ashbery, Charles Stein. Cover photo and design, as usual, are by Les Levine.

52 book
fiction
PORT OF SAINTS
William Burroughs

- media: HARDBACK
- released: 1975
- created:
- commerce: ●●○○○
- critical: ●●●○○
- WSB quotient: ●●●●○

Actually released in 1973 but I fucked up there. The first edition was reworked for wider publication in 1980 and forms a bridge between *The Wild Boys* [40] and COTRN [79]. This book is notable as the least read from novel in WSB's canon, with only "Firecracker (excerpt)" (3:51) from the University of Chicago on 9 Mar. 1975, surfacing posthumously on *The Best of WSB at GPS* comp [244].

1975

53 book — interviews
SNACK: TWO TAPE TRANSCRIPTS
William Burroughs & Eric Mottram

media: **BOOKLET**
released: **1975**
created: **1964–73**
commerce:
critical:
WSB quotient:

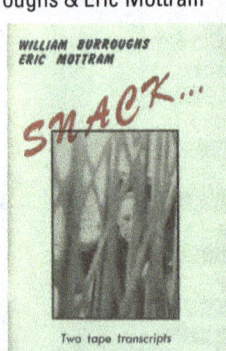

Transcriptions of two tape recordings: "William Burroughs and The Algebra of Need", a BBC Third Programme radio broadcast (8:00–8:30pm, 9 Mar. 1964), and an interview between WSB and Mottram recorded at WSB's flat in London in 1973. Mottram was one WSB's first advocates in the UK, defending him in the UGH! Correspondence [2] and authoring the first book length study, *The Algebra of Need*, published in 1977.

54 recording — spoken word
WILLIAM BURROUGHS / JOHN GIORNO
William Burroughs & John Giorno

media: **2LP**
released: **1975**
created:
commerce: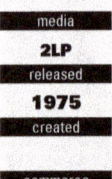
critical: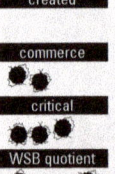
WSB quotient:

Aka "A D'Arc Press Selection". Disc one features Giorno and the second is all WSB: (1) "The Chief Smiles" (6:50) from *The Wild Boys* [40] recorded by KPFA, Berkley Barb Reading, UC, 7 Nov. 1974. (2) "The Green Nun" (3:32) from *The Wild Boys* [40] recorded at St. Mark's Church, NY, 24 Apr. 1974. (3) From *Ah Pook Is Here* [65] (12:00) recorded at Columbia University, NY, 17 Apr. 1975. (4) From (then unpublished) COTRN [79] (10:00), details as #3. (5) "103rd Street Boys" (7:29) from *Junkie* [1], recorded at WBAI, NY, 5 Mar. 1975. (6) From *Naked Lunch* [2] (20:28) details as #5. (7) "From Here to Eternity" (3:40) from *Exterminator!* [45] details as (1).

1976

55 book — journals
THE RETREAT DIARIES
William Burroughs

media: **PAPERBACK**
released: **1976**
created:
commerce:
critical:
WSB quotient:

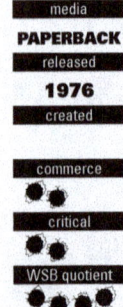
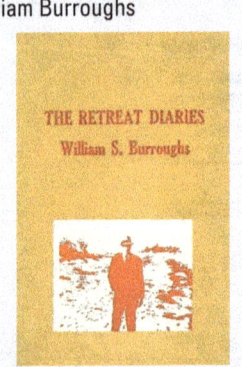

WSB's journal of a two week Buddhist retreat at Chogyam Trungpa's Vermont ranch. Mostly comprised of dream notes, prefiguring *My Education* [221] by several years, the text was collected in *The Burroughs File* [113] and formed the basis of a posthumous hörspiel [275].

56 book — nonfiction
THE THIRD MIND
William Burroughs & Brion Gysin

media: **HARDBACK**
released: **1976**
created: **1960–73**
commerce:
critical:
WSB quotient:

As with *The Job* [34], this was first published in French translation, not appearing in the UK until 1979. This collects documentation and examples of WSB and Gysin's collaborative experiments with cut/ups and permutations, with cameos from Ian Sommerville, Antony Balch and Sinclair Beiles. One of the best bits is WSB's reworking of the UGH! Correspondence [2], and it also includes a short extract from the aborted Gysin/Balch *Naked Lunch* musical.

57 recording
spoken word
TOTALLY CORRUPT
Various

media: **2LP**
released: **1976**
created:
commerce: ●●
critical: ●●
WSB quotient: ●●

Another GPS comp with WSB contributing "When Did I Stop Wanting to Be President" (7:07). Also here are Allen Ginsberg, John Giorno, Anne Waldman, John Cage who, with WSB, formed the Board of GPS as shown on the cover. Also present are Charles Bukowski, Sylvia Plath, Michael McClure, Ed Sanders, Imamu Amiri Baraka, Ken Kesey, Jackson Mac Low, Charles Amirkhanian, William Carlos Williams, Frank O'Hara, Taylor Mead, Jackie Curtis, Charles Olson, Jerome Rothenberg, Ted Berrigan, Susan Howe, Rochelle Owens, Bill Knott, Tony Towle, Bernard Heidsieck, Peter Orlovsky and more.

58 film
documentary
UNDERGROUND AND EMIGRANTS
Rosa von Praunheim

media: **89M COL..**
released: **1976**
created:
commerce: ●
critical: ●
WSB quotient: ●

THIS SPACE
INTENTIONALLY
LEFT BLANK

This badly-reviewed doco was too hard to track down, but reportedly it includes interviews with members of the New York "underground" fraternity including WSB (who doesn't say anything), together with Andy Warhol (off in the distance) and Fernando Arrabal (interviewed in Spanish). The emigrants of the title are notable Germans, such as Greta Keller and Grete Mosheim, who left their country before World War II.

59 recording
country/folk
WILLIAM BURRITO BROTHERS
William Burrito Brothers

media: **LP**
released: **1976**
created:
commerce: ●
critical: ●
WSB quotient: ●

To my knowledge, there has never been a group called the William Burrito Brothers, not in 1976 or any other year. What a shame.

60 film
documentary
90 MINUTES LIVE
William Burroughs & Peter Gzowski

media: **90M COL..**
released: **1977**
created:
commerce: ●●●
critical: ●●●
WSB quotient: ●●

90 Minutes Live was a Canadian late-night tv talk show, hosted by the much-loved Peter Gzowski, which aired from 1976 to 1978. This is the first WSB tv appearance that I've managed to find and his demeanour here is somewhat less theatrical it would later become. WSB talks (for about ten minutes) about his early connections to the Beats, experiences with addiction and the apomorphine cure.

61 recording — punk 🇬🇧
ORGASM ADDICT
Buzzcocks

media: 7"
released: 1977
created:
commerce: ●●●●
critical: ●●●●
WSB quotient: ●

Formed in Manchester in 1975 by Pete Shelley, Howard Devoto, Steve Diggle and John Maher. Devoto left early on to form Magazine and the band shuffled instruments to accommodate Gart Smith on bass. Clocking in at two minutes exactly, their second single takes its title from a WSB quote and wanks alongside The Undertones' "Teenage Kicks" as one of the greatest masturbation anthems. The Buzzcocks recorded four albums before they broke up in 1981, going on to become one of the most feted of all punk groups, influencing everyone from Nirvana to Hüsker Dü and loads in between. The group reformed in 1989 and AFAIK they're are still at it.

62 recording — spoken word 🇺🇸
BIG EGO
Various

media: 2LP
released: 1978
created:
commerce: ●●●
critical: ●●●
WSB quotient: ●●●

Another year, another bulletin from GPS. WSB contributes an excerpt from Naked Lunch 2, "The Laboratory has been Locked for Three Hours Solid" (2:14) from St. Marks Church, NYC, 9 Apr. 1977. Others present include: Laurie Anderson, Robert Ashley, Jim Brodey, The Fugs, John Giorno, Philip Glass, Bernard Heidsieck, Robert Lowell, Meredith Monk, Frank O'Hara, Claes Oldenburg, Ron Padgett, Ishmael Reed, Ed Sanders, Patti Smith, Anne Waldman, Robert Wilson & Christopher Knowles, and others.

63 recording — punk 🇬🇧
STORM THE REALITY STUDIO
Dead Fingers Talk

media: LP
released: 1978
created:
commerce: ●●
critical: ●●●
WSB quotient: ●●●●

Formed in Hull, Yorks., in 1975 by Tony Carter (Drums), Andy Linklater (Bass), Jeff Parsons (Guitar) and Bobo Phoenix (Vocals). Despite being mates with Genesis P-Orridge 136, they weren't big WSB fans but thought the name sounded cool. They had a strong following in nearby Sheffield amongst fans of Cabaret Voltaire 134 and 23 Skidoo 95 and their only LP is acclaimed as a lost classic. With strident tunes like "Nobody Loves You When You're Old and Gay" and "Can't Think Straight", they may have been the first queercore outfit but I'm not sure if they were gay. In Yorkshire in the seventies, your choice was to hedge your bets or get stabbed.

64 film — experimental 🇺🇸
THOT-FAL'N
Stan Brakhage dir.

media: 9M COL..
released: 1978
created:
commerce: ●●
critical: ●●●
WSB quotient: ●●

Stan Brakhage (1933-2003) is considered to be one of the most important figures in 20th century experimental film. In *Bomb Culture*, Jeff Nuttall describes WSB and Balch's fascination with Brakhage's subliminal techniques and his celebrated 1959 film *Window Water Baby Moving* which depicts the birth of his daughter. The short piece here is an abstract study in Brakhage's usual fragmented style and features brief shots of WSB along with Allen Ginsberg, Peter Orlovsky and Philip Whalen and others.

65 book — pictorial 🇬🇧
AH POOK IS HERE AND OTHER TEXTS
William Burroughs

- media: HARDBACK
- released: 1979
- created: 1970–
- commerce: ●●●
- critical: ●●
- WSB quotient: ●●●●

A compilation, with *The Book of Breeething* and *Electronic Revolution* 37, of texts which were functionally impossible to find in the UK. The title story had started as a collaboration between WSB and artist Malcolm McNeill in 1970 to produce what would now be called a "graphic novel" but the project was aborted when no publisher could be found. Readings from the title story would be recorded on several GPS LPs and on *Dead City Radio* 162, from which it formed the basis of an animated short 203. Trainspotters! In the 2007 Ian Curtis 69 biopic *Control*, a copy of this is on Ian's bookshelf in 1973, despite the fact it wasn't put out until after he suicided.

66 book — screenplay 🇺🇸
BLADE RUNNER: A MOVIE
William Burroughs

- media: PAPERBACK
- released: 1979
- created:
- commerce: ●●
- critical: ●●
- WSB quotient: ●●

This short treatment was liberally recycled, with WSB's permission, for Tom Huckabee's *Taking Tiger Mountain* 105. It has nothing to do with Ridley Scott's massively over-rated film, *Blade Runner*, which sits in relation to Philip K. Dick's epic novel *Do Androids Dream of Electric Sheep?* as Cronenberg's *Naked Lunch* 171 does to its own source. Rudy Wurlitzer 80 had suggested to Scott that he use WSB's title, which was itself drawn from the work of top sf novelist Alan E. Nourse. Scott's film has been subsequently re-cut and re-issued in a style derived from WSB's own cult of remixology.

67 book — fiction 🇺🇸
DOCTOR BENWAY
William Burroughs

- media: HARDBACK
- released: 1979
- created:
- commerce: ●●
- critical: ●●
- WSB quotient: ●●●●

A variant of the passage from *The Naked Lunch* 2, published in a limited edition. Dr Benway is probably WSB's most famous character, played by Roy Scheider in Cronenberg's film 171, but otherwise by WSB himself 101. There have been a few other filmic tribute nods to the character, in Alex Cox's classic *Repo Man* and in the 2008 medical horror *Autopsy*, and on tv in a 2004 ep of the body-trauma soap *CSI*.

68 film — documentary 🇺🇸
FRIED SHOES COOKED DIAMONDS
Costanzo Allione dir.

- media: 55M COL..
- released: 1979
- created:
- commerce: ●●
- critical: ●●
- WSB quotient: ●●

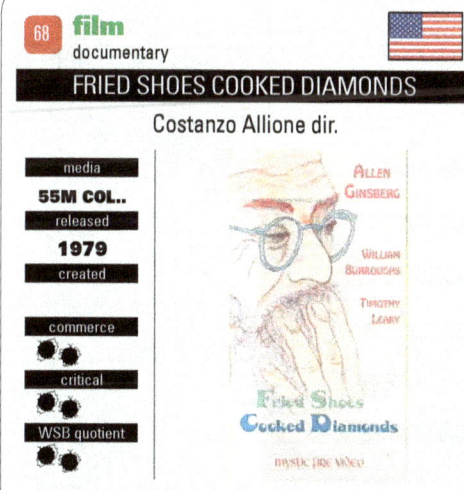

Fascinating doco on the Naropa Institute in Boulder, CO. Narrated by Allen Ginsberg and featuring Gregory Corso, Diane Di Prima, Timothy Leary, Meredith Monk, Miguel Pinero, Peter Orlovsky, Miguel Algarin, Anne Waldman, Chogyam Trungpa Rinpoche and a dynamite reading by Amiri Baraka. It's nice to see all the talk counterpointed by some direct action at Rocky Flats. The film is also notable in having the only known footage of WSB sitting next to a girl in a bikini by a swimming pool.

69 recording — punk 🇬🇧
UNKNOWN PLEASURES
Joy Division

media: **LP**
released: **1979**
created:
commerce: ● ● ●
critical: ● ● ● ● ●
WSB quotient: ●

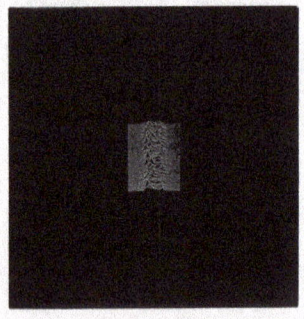

The originators of Glum Rock, as exemplified by groups like Echo and the Bunnymen and reaching apotheosis with Morrissey and the Smiths. This can be seen as an introspective humanised Lancastrian response to Sheffield's sociopolitical industrial movement as epitomised by Cabaret Voltaire [134]. Both those groups had supported WSB at the Gig of the Century in Brussels (16 Oct. 1979) where, if you choose to believe the unverifiable, WSB told Curtis to "get lost". On this LP, the track "Interzone" is (probably) the first use of the WSB reference that would go on to be used for numerous tunes.

70 recording — experimental 🇺🇸
MEGATON FOR WM. BURROUGHS
Gordon Mumma

media: **LP**
released: **1979**
created: **1963**
commerce: ● ● ●
critical: ● ● ●
WSB quotient: ●

Gordon Mumma (b. 1935) is an American composer known for electronic musique-concrète style compositions, often performed on homebrew equipment. In 1963 his "Megaton For Wm. Burroughs" (22:34) was performed by The Once Group, comprised of George Manupelli, Harold Borkin, Joseph Wehrer, Milton Cohen and Robert Ashley, at the Cooperative Studio for Electronic Music in Ann Arbor, Michigan. The recording was issued on Lovely Music in 1979 and on the "Electronic Music of Theatre and Public Activity" CD in 2005.

71 recording — electro 🇬🇧
RABIES
Naked Lunch

media: **7"**
released: **1979**
created:
commerce: ● ●
critical: ●
WSB quotient: ●

The first Naked Lunch I've been able to track down is this synthpop outfit from the late seventies. Based in London but also popular on the Sheffield scene they put out two more singles in 1984 before folding. The name has been taken up by several outfits with varying degrees of unsuccess: a German new wave outfit from the early eighties, a US industrial group and an Australian and/or New Zealand metallic combo from the mid-nineties. The first group so named to break through was an Austrian alt-rock outfit who've been going almost twenty years and put out several records. There are also reports of a SF-based latin/psyche group c.1969.

72 recording — electro 🇬🇧
REPLICAS
Tubeway Army

media: **LP/CC**
released: **1979**
created:
commerce: ● ● ● ●
critical: ● ●
WSB quotient: ● ●

As a child excited more by the flash of a spotlight on Hank Marvin's guitar than by music, Gary Numan (the first cyberpunk) derived much of his early imagery from the oeuvre of WSB, alongside Philip K. Dick and J.G. Ballard. "Wind Die. You Die. We Die" (a piece in *Exterminator!* [45]) was truncated to "I Die: You Die" for a 1980 single, on the sleeve of which Numan appears to be crawling through some kind of futuristic sewer with Steely Dan (the vibrator rather than the pop group) strapped to his back. Numan's groundbreaking electropop was hugely influential but snobbery from the music press denied him his critical due for several decades.

73 recording — spoken word

THE NOVA CONVENTION
Various

- media: 2LP/2CC
- released: 1979
- created:
- commerce: ●●
- critical: ●●●●
- WSB quotient: ●●

Organized by Sylvère Lotringer, John Giorno, and JWG, the Nova Convention ran from 30 Nov. to 2 Dec. 1978 at various locations in NYC. The event included readings from Terry Southern, Allen Ginsberg, Patti Smith, and Frank Zappa; panel discussions with Timothy Leary and Robert Anton Wilson; and concerts from Philip Glass, The B-52's, Suicide, and Debbie Harry & Chris Stein. The convention was documented and released by GPS, the cassette edition includes an extra track "Matriarchly" (7:40) by Anne Waldman. On 26 Nov. 1996, many of the original cast reunited in Lawrence for "The Nova Convention (Revisited)" 246 .

74 film — drama

HEART BEAT
John Byrum dir.

- media: 110M COL..
- released: 1980
- created:
- commerce: ●●
- critical: ●
- WSB quotient: ●

Based on Carolyn Cassady's autobiography, WSB is comprehensively written out of this poorly received biopic about the menage-a-trois between Kerouac (Nick Nolte), Jack (John Heard) and Carolyn Cassady (Sissy Spacek). Despite this, he reported generously on the film for *Rolling Stone* having visited the set. Obviously, he is a much better writer than what I am since I found it impossible to find anything positive to say about this uh daytime soap opera.

MORE: Burroughs, William. *Heart Beat: Fifties Heroes as Soap Opera*. RS #309. 24 Jan. 1980.

75 film — documentary

LUNATICS, LOVERS AND POETS
Andrea Andermann dir.

- media: 90M COL..
- released: 1980
- created:
- commerce: ●●
- critical: ●●
- WSB quotient: ●●

Aka "Castelporziano, ostia dei poeti", this doco records the first International Festival of Poetry given in Ostia, the beach resort near Rome where Pier Paulo Pasolini was killed. The crowd is very lively and punters get naked and throw things. On the last night, Ginsberg MCs and we get to see him, Brion Gysin, Amiri Baraka and others reading to a warm reception. Unfortunately WSB's performance doesn't make the cut and he only appears peripherally.

76 recording — spoken word

SUGAR, ALCOHOL & MEAT
Various

- media: 2LP
- released: 1980
- created:
- commerce: ●
- critical: ●●
- WSB quotient: ●●

WSB contributes "I was traveling with The Intolerable Kid on the Nova Lark" (8:15) from *Nova Express* 10 , recorded at The Mudd Club, NYC, 4 Apr. 1979. The sleeve features a colour shot of WSB by Robert Mapplethorpe. This record is of special interest as it includes a rare reading by William S. Burroughs Jr., who contributes "Translucent Boy / An Excellent Time / For Neal Cassidy" (5:15) recorded at JKS, Naropa Institute, 15 Aug. 1979. WSB Jr is a grossly underrated writer, and his books *Speed* and *Kentucky Ham* are well worth your attention, as is David Ohle's autobiographical compilation.

Burroughs Jr, William (Ohle, David ed.) *Cursed from Birth* (Soft Skull, 2006)

77 **film**	
drama	

THE EXTERMINATOR
James Glickenhaus dir.

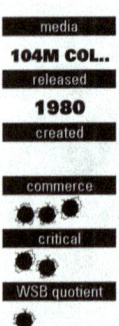
media: **104M COL..**
released: **1980**
created:
commerce:
critical:
WSB quotient:

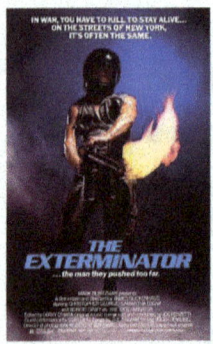

Banned in Norway! This was nothing to do with either book by WSB 4 45 but still spawned a sequel, imaginatively called *Exterminator 2*, which was also banned in Norway. Be careful not be confuse this with the 1945 Terrytoon of the same name, or with *Lady Exterminator* (Hong Kong, 1977) or *Mouse Exterminator* (a Krazy Kat cartoon from 1940). And don't miss *Ninja Exterminator* (1972), not to be confused with *Shaolin Exterminator*, or indeed *Steel and Lace* (1990) which is known in Hungary as *Final Exterminator* ("She's tough. She's tender. She's all woman. And all machine!") or the odd-sounding Spanish short *Harlequin Exterminator* (1991) and so on.

78 **film**	
documentary	

CHELSEA HOTEL
Nigel Finch dir.

media: **56M COL..**
released: **1981**
created:

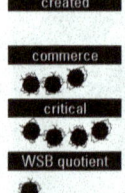
commerce:
critical:
WSB quotient:

Broadcast as an ep of *Arena* on the BBC on 3 Jan. 1981, Nigel Finch's doco is still remembered as an all-time classic. Interviewees include Virgil Thompson (composer of *Tubby the Tuba*), artist Alphaeus Cole, singer Jobriath and Quentin Crisp. There's also the legendary dinner party sequence with WSB and Andy Warhol, who keeps his headphones on when he eats exactly like teens would go on to do in the 21st century. There have been a few movies about the Chelsea, including Abel Ferrara's effort 296, and heaps of books but the one below gets hyped coz it's from the guys at Headpress.

Joe Ambrose *Chelsea Hotel Manhattan* (Headpress, 2007)

79 **book**	
fiction	

CITIES OF THE RED NIGHT
William Burroughs

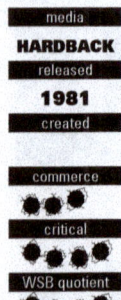
media: **HARDBACK**
released: **1981**
created:
commerce:
critical:
WSB quotient:

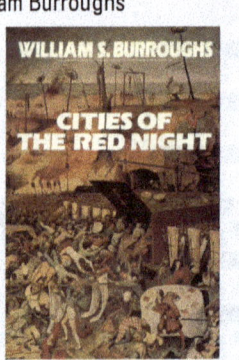

WSB's epic first part of The Final Trilogy had been a feature of readings since at least 1975 54, but its print publication had been delayed as the manuscript was re-edited to conform to the requirements of his new major publishers. When it came out, JWG organised a mammoth international reading tour (with John Giorno supporting) to promote the book. Recordings surfaced on a number of LPs, mainly GPS comps, including 1.33 sides of YTGIWTSMMW 88. The 2007 Danish doco *Words of Advice* 294 deals comprehensively with the tour.

80 **film**	
drama	

ENERGY AND HOW TO GET IT
Robert Frank dir.

media: **30M B/W**
released: **1981**
created:
commerce:
critical:
WSB quotient:

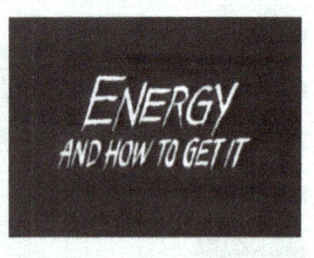

Written by Rudy Wurlitzer, this started out as a documentary about Robert Golka, a scientist conducting research into lightning (thanks! – *Ed*), but was turned into a parody of the documentary form with the casting of WSB as an Energy Czar, and Giorno as his henchman. Dr John (the Night Tripper) puts in a musical number. An edited (14:20) version appears on the GPS *It's Clean, It Just Looks Dirty*... A VHS comp whose other contributors include Psychic TV 136, Cabaret Voltaire 134, Hüsker Dü, John Giorno, John Waters and extracts of Howard Brookner's 101 last film (about Robert Wilson 285).

81 recording
experimental
NOTHING HERE NOW BUT THE RECORDINGS
William Burroughs

- media: LP
- released: 1981
- created: 1959-78
- commerce: ●●○○○
- critical: ●●●●○
- WSB quotient: ●●●●○

WSB, Brion Gysin and Ian Sommerville had been fooling around with these tapes in hotels for years but it was Peter Christopherson and Genesis P-Orridge who persuaded them that their private experiments were worthy of a public release. They compiled this LP with the assistance of JWG and it became the final release on their Industrial Records label, occupying the same place in the emergent industrial/electro scene as *Call Me Burroughs* 11 had in the psychedelic underground of the sixties. Tracks would be sampled mercilessly through the years and the LP would change hands for stupid money until its reissue on *The Best of WSB from GPS* 244.

82 recording
spoken word
ON THE NOVA LARK
William Burroughs

- media: 6" FLEXI
- released: 1981
- created:
- commerce: ●○○○○
- critical: ●●○○○
- WSB quotient: ●●●○○

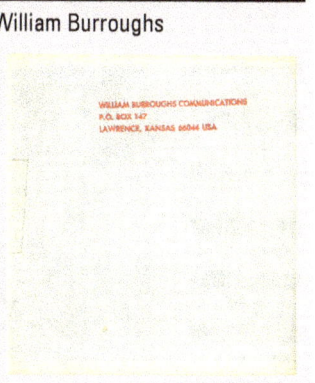

This oddity was available only with *Talk Talk* magazine, which had a cover by, and feature on, WSB. "On The Nova Lark" (3:03) is a text from *Nova Express* 10 and was recorded in the early sixties in London or Tangiers, and here has backwards weird sounds overdubbed. "Abandoned Artifacts" (3:09) overlaps three readings from TPODR 114 (The Edge, Toronto, Tuts, Chicago, and Keystone Corner, SF) with a rhythm track by Martin Olsen 112. Recorded At Ramona Recording Studios (Lawrence, KS) by James Grauerholz and Karl Hoffmann. The tracks were later included on *Minutes To Go!* 144.

83 film
documentary
SHAMANS OF THE BLIND COUNTRY
Michael Oppitz dir.

- media: 221M COL..
- released: 1981
- created:
- commerce: ●○○○○
- critical: ●●○○○
- WSB quotient: ●●○○○

WSB provides the (English language) narration for this very hard-to-find documentary epic about the Magar people of Nepal, a pre-literate mountain tribe living in the vicinity of the Dhaulagiri range of the Himalayas who practice a shamanistic religion.

84 recording
industrial
THE FRUIT OF THE ORIGINAL SIN
Various

- media: 2LP
- released: 1981
- created:
- commerce: ●○○○○
- critical: ●●○○○
- WSB quotient: ●○○○○

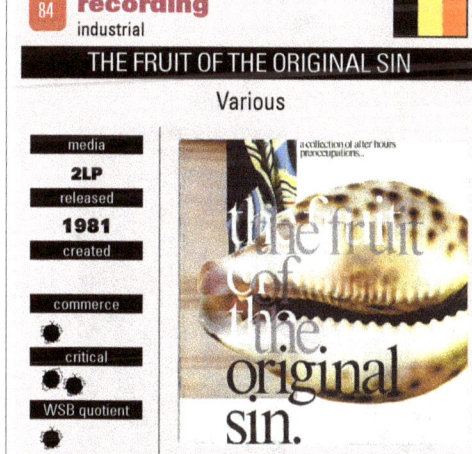

"Twilight's Last Gleamings" (4:27) from the Red Night tour at Keystone Corner, SF, 16 May 1981, "a mixing experience reading recorded both from the audience and from the dressing room, produced by James Grauerholz."

85 recording — industrial
THE GOSPEL COMES TO NEW GUINEA
23 Skidoo

- media: 12"
- released: 1981
- created:
- commerce: ●●●
- critical: ●●●
- WSB quotient: ●

An industrial outfit formed 1978 in Sheffield, England, who worked with Cabaret Voltaire [134] and members of Throbbing Gristle, they took their name from a piece in *The Old Movies* chapbook (collected in *The Burroughs File* [113]), or maybe a Julian Biggs' 1964 short film, or a 1930 Arthur Hurley silent short, or from a pre-depression US slang term roughly translating as "fuck off". WSB is cited by Robert Anton Wilson as the discoverer of The 23 Enigma, a belief that the number occurs disproportionately and/or mysteriously influences events.

86 film — spoken word
SATURDAY NIGHT LIVE
William Burroughs

- media: 6M COL..
- released: 1981
- created:
- commerce: ●●●
- critical: ●●●
- WSB quotient: ●●●

The 7 Nov. 1981 ep of "Saturday Night Live" featured host Lauren Hutton introducing WSB to 100 million viewers as "America's greatest living writer". WSB read "Twilight's Last Gleamings" to NBC stock music from SNL's musical director, Hal Willner, who was so impressed that he went out and bought several WSB books and subsequently worked with WSB on recording projects including *Dead City Radio* [162], *Spare Ass Annie* [194] and the *Naked Lunch* audiobook [227]. It was WSB's last NYC engagement before moving to Lawrence to meet up with JWG.

87 book — interviews
WITH WILLIAM BURROUGHS
Victor Bockris

- media: PAPERBACK
- released: 1981
- created: 1974-80
- commerce: ●●
- critical: ●●●
- WSB quotient: ●●●●

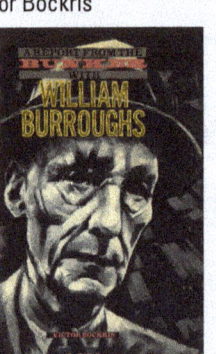

Victor Bockris' compilation of transcripts of recorded discussions at WSB's NYC "bunker" came out just as WSB was getting ready to blow the gaff and move to Kansas. Dinner guests include: Andy Warhol, Debbie Harry, Lou Reed, Joe Strummer, Susan Sontag, Christopher Isherwood, Nicholas Roeg, Allen Ginsberg, Tennessee Williams, Barry Miles, David Bowie, Richard Hell, Mick Jagger and many many more. Portions of the talks appeared in magazines from *Screw* to *The New Review*, and led to mentions of WSB in NYC gossip columns.

88 recording — spoken word
YOU'RE THE GUY I WANT TO SHARE MY MONEY WITH
Giorno / Burroughs / Anderson

- media: 2LP
- released: 1981
- created:
- commerce: ●●●
- critical: ●●●
- WSB quotient: ●●●

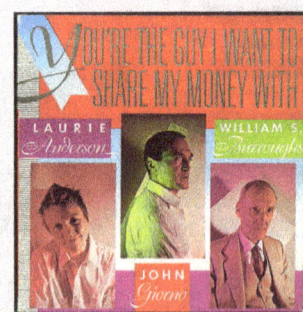

WSB contributes all of side three and one track on the triple-grooved side four. WSB tracks, from *Nova Express* [11], *Ah Pook is Here* [203], COTRN [79] and TPODR [114], were recorded on The Red Night Tour, in Los Angeles on 9 May 1981, Santa Cruz on 13 May, San Fransisco on 16 May and Toronto on 31 May. Also contributing a side and a third each are John Giorno and Laurie Anderson [103], who wasn't on the tour but was riding high after her #1 pop smash hit "O Superman". It was reissued on CD in 1993 omitting one track by Giorno.

89 book — critical
A WILLIAM BURROUGHS READER
John Calder (ed)

- media: PAPERBACK
- released: 1982
- created: 1956–82
- commerce: ●●●
- critical: ●●●
- WSB quotient: ●●●

A significant work in WSB's disoccultation in the UK, launched the same time as the paperback of COTRN 79, these were WSB's first works to reach British High Street bookshops. This important collection was edited and annotated by WSB's consistent ally, John Calder (organiser of the 1962 Edinburgh Writer's Conference). Calder also published Alex Trocchi (the Scottish Burroughs), Samuel Beckett (the Irish Burroughs) and brought many other outstanding European experimental works into English including Alain Robbe-Grillet (the French Burroughs) and many many more.

MORE: Calder, John. *Pursuit* (Calder, 2001)

90 film — experimental
GHOSTS AT NO. 9
Antony Balch dir.

- media: 45M B/W
- released: 1982
- created: 1963
- commerce: ●●
- critical: ●●
- WSB quotient: ●●●

Jack Sargeant's book 234 tells the story of how Genesis P-Orridge 316 rescued several dozen cans of film from Antony Balch's garbage following his death. Seventeen of the cans contained footage, intended for the aborted *Guerilla Conditions* film, which was edited by P-Orridge into *Ghosts at No. 9 (Paris)* with a soundtrack compiled from his archive of related material, in time for the Final Academy event 97. The other cans contained the footage for *William Buys a Parrot* 100 and a so-far unreleased film, titled *Transmutations* by P-Orridge, that has only been rarely screened.

MORE: Sargeant, Jack. *Naked Lens: Beat Cinema* (Creation, 1997)

91 recording — various
LIFE IS A KILLER
Various

- media: LP
- released: 1982
- created:
- commerce: ●
- critical: ●
- WSB quotient: ●

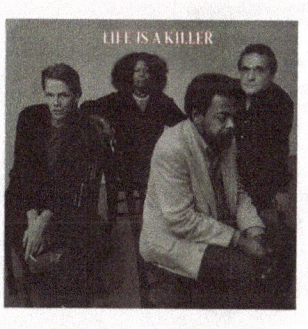

By this release, GPS albums had an increasingly musical orientation but WSB continued to contribute purely vocal tracks. Here he provides "The Mummy Piece" (3:55) from *The Western Lands* 141 recorded at Market St. Cinema, SF, 17 Sep. 1981. The LP also features John Giorno, Amiri Baraka*, Jim Carroll*, Jayne Cortez*, Ned Sublette, Rose Lesniak, Four Horsemen* and Brion Gysin doing 'Junk' (3:21) with musical backing recorded in Paris, 1982. The starred contributors were recorded in Toronto and their pieces are also featured in Ron Mann's film *Poetry in Motion* 93.

92 recording — spoken word
ONE WORLD POETRY
Various

- media: 2LP
- released: 1982
- created:
- commerce: ●
- critical: ●
- WSB quotient: ●

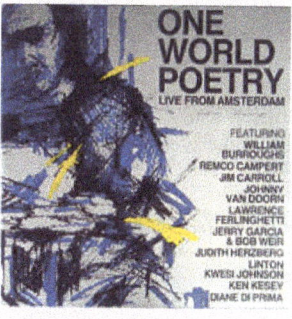

WSB provides "Cold Hearted Bastard" (3:22) to this GPS comp of tracks recorded at the fourth annual One World Poetry Festival, held in 1981 at the Melkweg in Amsterdam. The festival attracted a record 12,000 visitors to see 63 poets from all over the world. To my knowledge, it's the only time that WSB shared a stage with LKJ, the UK's leading performance poet.

1982

93 film — documentary
POETRY IN MOTION
Ron Mann dir.

- media: 91M COL..
- released: 1982
- created:
- commerce:
- critical:
- WSB quotient:

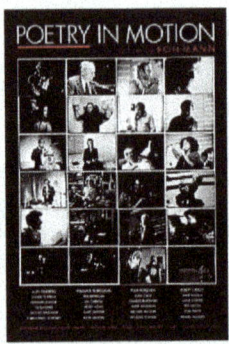

GPS, the Movie! A Bukowski interview frames readings by heaps of beat poets, sometimes with music and/or interview fragments. WSB reads a couple of skits from TPODR 114 (3:48), recorded at The Edge in Toronto, 31 May 1981, and to be frank it's not the highlight of the film because that just has to be Helen Adam's "Cheerless Junkie's Song". Amiri Baraka, John Giorno and Ginsberg's punked out "Captitol Air" are good too. Some of the recordings appeared on *Life is a Killer* 91 and it was later issued as an interactive CD-Rom 210.

94 book — critical
RE/SEARCH 4/5
Burroughs / Gysin / Throbbing Gristle

- media: PAPERBACK
- released: 1982
- created:
- commerce:
- critical:
- WSB quotient:

Based in SF, Re/Search had started out as punk rock zine *Search and Destroy* originally bankrolled by Ginsberg and Ferlinghetti and edited by V. Vale, before mutating into a broader-based counter-culture tabloid, co-edited by Andrea Juno, and then, with this special issue, a large format paperback journal. This is effectively a compliment to NHNBTR 81, issued around the same time, and providing context for the recordings with a host of unpublished excerpts, interviews, listings and photos. The many highlights include extracts from *The Revised Boy Scout Manual* and G.P-O and Peter Christopherson's interview with Gysin.

95 recording — experimental
REVOLUTIONS PER MINUTE
Various

- media: 2LP
- released: 1982
- created:
- commerce:
- critical:
- WSB quotient:

Produced by Ronald Feldman Fine Arts, NYC, to allow some of their clients, primarily visual artists, a sonic outlet. Piotr Kowalski contributes a version of WSB's "You Only Call the Old Doctor Once" (4:45). Kowalski (1927-2004) was an artist, sculptor, and architect who was known for his work in non-traditional media such as earthworks, explosions and electronic or mechanical devices. Here he treats WSB's piece here with his time machine, a digital audio processor that reverses sound in real time, but personally I don't see the point. Also here are Joseph Beuys, R. Buckminster Fuller, and GPS art director Les Levine. I hope their tracks are a bit less wanky.

96 film — drama
THE DISCIPLINE OF DE
Gus Van Sant dir.

- media: 9M B/W
- released: 1982
- created:
- commerce:
- critical:
- WSB quotient:

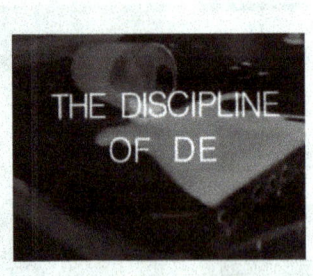

From the very start of his career, Gus Van Sant (b. 1952) was WSB's biggest advocate in the overground movies. His first short was based on a piece from *Exterminator!* 45 that offers a Burroughsian slant on the self-help genre. Van Sant had visited WSB on a trip to NYC to ask for permission and characteristically WSB and JWG consented even though there was no money in the deal. Van Sant went on to make a record using WSB samples 123, to cast him in his first feature *Drugstore Cowboy* 150, to direct the promo for *A Thanksgiving Prayer* 174 and a couple of other things too.

MORE: Fuller, Graham. *Interview with Gus Van Sant* (Apr. 1993)

97 book — critical 🇬🇧
THE FINAL ACADEMY
Roger Ely (ed)

- media: BOOKLET
- released: 1982
- created:
- commerce: ●●
- critical: ●●●
- WSB quotient: ●●●●

Designed by Neville Brody (who did the first edition of *With William Burroughs* 87) this was the programme for a series of events organised by David Dawson, Roger Ely and Genesis P-Orridge that ran from 29 Sep. to 2 Oct 1982 in the UK. The Ritzy Cinema in Brixton had the and shows by 23 Skidoo 85, Cabaret Voltaire 134, Psychic TV 136 and others, while an exhibition of Gysin's work ran at the B2 Gallery in Wapping and there was a signing session at Compendium Books in Camden. Outside the capital WSB played Manchester on 4 Oct., Liverpool on 5 Oct. and Heaven, back in Charing Cross, on 7 Oct. See also *The Final Academy Documents* 107.

98 recording — punk 🇺🇸
THE MORTAL MICRONOTZ
The Mortal Micronotz

- media: LP
- released: 1982
- created:
- commerce: ●
- critical: ●●
- WSB quotient: ●

aka The Micronotz, these guys were an American punk group from Lawrence, KS, formed in 1980. They came to the attention of Bill Rich, a local promoter who had put out WSB's *Talk Talk* flexi 82, and he signed them to his label. JWG did the production on this, their first LP, which featured lyrics by WSB on the track "Old Lady Sloan". There's plenty to like on this if you like this kind of slop (like I do). If you need bonus portent, there's a mental cover of The Hombré's "Let it All Hang Out", which is always a good sign.

99 film — spoken word 🇺🇸
WILLIAM BURROUGHS WITH KATHY ACKER
Fenella Greenfield dir.

- media: 45M COL..
- released: 1982
- created:
- commerce: ●●
- critical: ●●●
- WSB quotient: ●●●●

Produced for the ICA's "Writers in Conversation" series, this is arguably the greatest WSB interview on camera. Filmed at the October Gallery, London, Kathy Acker, herself a towering writer and self-admittedly indebted to WSB, discusses issues including comparing montage in painting with the cut/up method, verbal vs. visual thinking, WSB's connections with the early beat "movement", the historical context of *Junkie* 1, *Queer* 121 and *Naked Lunch* 2, WSB's unpublished novel on the life of Christ, the relationship between word and control and political ramifications of the cut/up method. Phew!

100 film — documentary 🇬🇧
WILLIAM BUYS A PARROT
Antony Balch dir.

- media: 2M COL..
- released: 1982
- created: 1963
- commerce: ●
- critical: ●●
- WSB quotient: ●●●●

Filmed by Balch in the early sixties but released (and titled) posthumously when the footage was re-examined by Genesis P-Orridge. This could be the earliest surviving colour film of Burroughs and, presumably due to the bright sunlight, he is wearing an especially impressive hat. The two minute (silent) film punches over its weight in terms of semiotic disassociation: it's a cockatoo and it's not for sale. The film is analysed at amusing (but not tedious) length in Timothy Murphy's interesting book 249.

MORE: Murphy, Timothy. *Wising Up the Marks* (UC Press, 1997)

1983

101 film — documentary
BURROUGHS
Howard Brookner dir.

media: 86M COL..
released: 1983
created:
commerce:
critical:
WSB quotient:

Produced by Alan Yentob for BBC's *Arena* series and shown on 22 Feb. 1983, for my money Howard Brookner's first film is still the greatest WSB doco. It has illuminating appearances by his brother Mortimer, pals JWG, Allen Ginsberg, Terry Southern, John Giorno and Lucien Carr, and some painful-to-watch footage of William Burroughs Jr. following his liver transplant. On the lighter side, there's a hilarious skit with WSB as Dr Benway and Warhol/Makavejev superstar Jackie Curtis as a nurse. The documentary was issued on VHS by GPS but is currently very hard to track down.

102 recording — spoken word
LIVE AT THE KABUKI
William Burroughs

media: CC/CD
released: 1983
created:
commerce:
critical:
WSB quotient:

This recording, from the Kabuki Theatre, SF, on 25 Feb. 1983, circulated on cassette before being issued by Sound Photosynthesis on CD some years later. A cut showed up on the GPS *You're a Hook* comp 116. The reading (46:44) is all from TPODR 114.

103 recording — electro
MISTER HEARTBREAK
Laurie Anderson

media: LP
released: 1983
created:
commerce:
critical:
WSB quotient:

Plugging in nicely to the Talking Heads fuelled NYC art-school hype of the time, GPS regular Anderson's second LP (produced by Bill Laswell) crossed over in a big way and laid the groundwork for her *Home of the Brave* movie 125. Following on from their co-billing on their YTGIWTSMMW LP 88, WSB provides guest voice here on "Sharkey's Night" (2:29), a track that was later used as the b-side to 'Sharkey's Day' single, and with an extended version (3:58) to make a promo 12" for this album.

104 film — experimental
PIRATE TAPE
Derek Jarman dir.

media: 15M COL..
released: 1983
created:
commerce:
critical:
WSB quotient:

Derek Jarman is unquestionably one of the most original English film-makers. This is one of his Super-8 diary films, in which WSB shows up with Peter Christopherson 81 and FM Einheit 110 at the October Gallery in Sep. 1982 for The Final Academy event 97. The soundtrack, by Psychic TV, based on a loop of WSB saying "Boys! Schools, showers and swimming pools full of 'em..." (from *Disconnected* 49) would invariably generate fits of barely-suppressed embarrassed giggles when the film was shown in straight company. The short is included in several collections of Jarman's work and more of the footage crops up in *Glitterbug* 206.

105 film — sf
TAKING TIGER MOUNTAIN
Tom Huckabee dir.

media: **81M B/W**
released: **1983**
created:
commerce:
critical:
WSB quotient:

Based on material from *Blade Runner: A Movie* 66, WSB's only produced screenwriting credit is this experimental feature directed starring Bill Paxton. "Militant feminist scientists brainwash research subject to assassinate the Welsh Minister of Prostitution. Meanwhile World War III is being fought and the USA has been invaded." Filmed on leftovers from Dustin Hoffman's Lenny Bruce biopic in Wales and with (for the time) explicit sex scenes! It's nothing to do with the Chinese opera or the Eno LP of the same name.

106 film — experimental
THE DREAM MACHINE
Derek Jarman dir.

media: **35M COL..**
released: **1983**
created:
commerce:
critical:
WSB quotient:

Man. This has completely stumped me. Cannot find a copy of this or significant reference anywhere. It supposedly has something to do with Gysin's dreamachine (sic) and includes WSB footage, probably from the Final Academy 97 events. GAH! Youse will all have to buy the second edition of this. BWAH!

107 film — spoken word
THE FINAL ACADEMY DOCUMENTS
Antony Balch / Malcolm Whitehead dirs.

media: **2VHS/2BETA**
released: **1983**
created:
commerce:
critical:
WSB quotient:

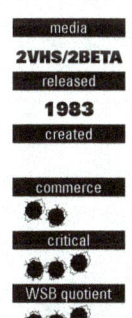
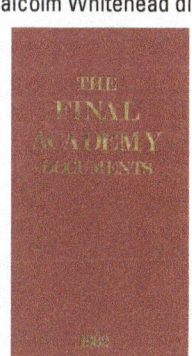

A slip-cased set of two videocassettes documenting an event at the Hacienda Club in Manchester on 4 Oct. 1982 as part of The Final Academy events 97. The first tape contains the first video release of Balch's films *Ghosts at No. 9* 90 and *Towers Open Fire* 9, which were screened on the evening. The second tape has readings from the Hacienda by WSB (from TPODR 114 and *The Western Lands* 141) and John Giorno (~50 min.). It's a shame that the footage is poorly lit and the sound is low quality but much better than not having it at all. The tapes were reissued on DVD in 2006.

108 film — experimental
THIS SONG FOR JACK
Robert Frank dir.

media: **26M B/W**
released: **1983**
created:
commerce:
critical:
WSB quotient:

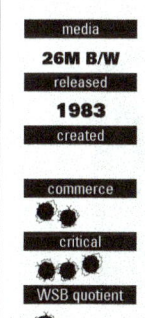

Robert Frank is best remembered for his 1972 Rolling Stones doco *Cocksucker Blues* and his 1959 short *Pull My Daisy* which featured pretty much all the beatnik megastars of the time except WSB. This short film, shot mostly on the porch of the Columbia Lodge, Chautaugua Park, documents the 1982 *On The Road* Conference at Boulder, CO, celebrating the 25th anniversary of its publication. It features WSB, with Ginsberg, Orlovsky, Ken Kesey, Carl Soloman and others. Frank had worked also with WSB on *Energy and How to Get It* 80.

MORE: Sargeant, Jack. *Naked Lens: Beat Cinema* (Creation, 1997).

109 recording
various

BETTER AN OLD DEMON THAN A NEW GOD
Various

media: LP
released: 1984
created:
commerce: ●●
critical: ●●●
WSB quotient: ●●

This transitional GPS release sees the series moving in a more music-oriented wider appeal direction. WSB contributes "Dinosaurs" (5:57) an unpublished performance text, recorded at Re/Search Video, SF, 20 Mar. 1984. Others here include Psychic TV, Richard Hell, Lydia Lunch, David Johansen, John Giorno, Meredith Monk, Jim Carroll, Anne Waldman, Arto Lindsay. I was able to ascertain that Lydia Lunch did not take her name from *Naked Lunch* as a WSB tribute, but rather from her work as a waitress.

110 film
sf

DECODER
Klaus Maeck dir.

media: 87M COL..
released: 1984
created:
commerce: ●●
critical: ●●●
WSB quotient: ●●

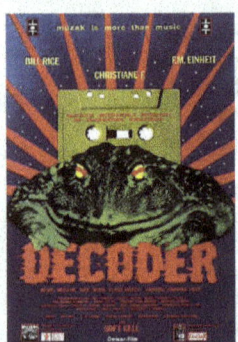

From the guy who would bring us *Commissioner of Sewers* [170], this is a bilingual German film starring F.M. Einheit, from Einstürzende Neubauten, as a dude who uses *Electronic Revolution* [37] techniques to overcome muzak programming. There's a brief WSB cameo (filmed during The Final Academy events) and a more substantial cameo by Genesis P-Orridge. The film was obviously produced on a shoestring, calling in favours from pals, and it's pretty good and still in circulation today. WSB samples (from *Call Me Burroughs* [11]) appear on the soundtrack CD on the Dave Ball/G.P.O. track "Dream" (2:32).

111 film
drama

IT DON'T PAY TO BE AN HONEST CITIZEN
Jacob Burckhardt dir.

media: 78M COL..
released: 1984
created:
commerce: ●●
critical: ●●
WSB quotient: ●●●

Based on a real-life experience of the director, Warren (Reed Bye) is robbed of a can of film and spends the film trying to track it down. WSB has a small but funty role as a mafiosi don. Allen Ginsberg also pops up as a dodger lawyer. The film is mainly notable as the feature debut of Vincent D'Onofrio, whose next role, in Kubrick's *Full Metal Jacket*, established his career. This movie isn't widely distributed but was released on VHS in Australia and Japan. I found a secondhand copy in Chopper Read's mate's shop in Collingwood.

112 recording
industrial

MYTHS: INSTRUCTIONS 1
Various

media: LP
released: 1984
created:
commerce: ●●
critical: ●●●
WSB quotient: ●●

An early Sub Rosa release. WSB contributes "The Five Steps" (8:10) with Martin Olsen on percussion and electronics, recorded in Lawrence, KS, Jun. 1983. Also here are tracks by Camberwell Now and Martyn Bates/Peter Becker (from Eyeless in Gaza), and Mark Stewart and the Maffia with "The Wrong Name & The Wrong Number" (9:26) which includes a substantial sample of WSB reading from "Last Words of Hassan I Sabbah" off NHNBTR [81]. That track would crop up in its "Original Version" (12:00) as a bonus cut on the CD of Stewart's *Learning To Cope With Cowardice*, and as a "DJ Battle" version (5:04) on the Director's Cut version thereof.

| 113 **book** | 114 **book** |
| fiction | fiction |

THE BURROUGHS FILE
William Burroughs

media: PAPERBACK
released: 1984
created: 1960-76
commerce: ●●●
critical: ●●●
WSB quotient: ●●●●

A compilation of small press booklets: *The White Subway*, *The Old Movies*, *The Retreat Diaries* 55 and *Cobblestone Gardens*, with pages from scrapbooks and short essays by JWG, Paul Bowles and Alan Ansen. The first two booklets were themselves compilations from underground mags and the pieces in *The Old Movies* contain much of audio-visual interest. *Cobblestone Gardens* unfortunately omits the photographs from the original edition here.

THE PLACE OF DEAD ROADS
William Burroughs

media: HARDBACK
released: 1984
created:
commerce: ●●●
critical: ●●●
WSB quotient: ●●●●

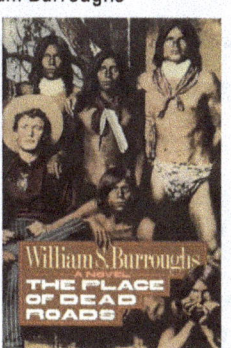

Oh shite. I fucked up. This was 1983 not 1984. Sorry about that. Probably WSB's signature work and the most-read from book in the canon, first appearing on the *The Nova Convention* 73, then *YTGIWTSMMW* 88, *You're a Hook* 116, *Smack My Crack* 137, *Live at the Kabuki* 102 and *Instrument of Control* 300. Video of readings is in *Poetry in Motion* 93, *The Final Academy Documents* 107, *Commissioner of Sewers* 170 and *Words of Advice* 294. There appear to be variant editions of the text, including a "special overseas edition" from 1986.

| 115 **recording** | 116 **recording** |
| electro | various |

THE WILD BOYS
Duran Duran

media: 7"
released: 1984
created:
commerce: ●●●●
critical: ●●
WSB quotient: ●●

The biggest group in Britain from 1982–84, the teen-idol standard bearers of the new romantic movement, were at the zenith of their fame when they released "Wild Boys", with a lyric broadly, but not profoundly, influenced by WSB's text 40. The single reached number two in the UK and the US and boasted a video directed by Russell (*Razorback*) Mulcahy. Surprisingly the clip is quite true to the spirit of WSB's novel, with bellhops, 1910 elevators and lizard boys, but omitting any unsavoury sex 'n' drugs elements. It was reportedly a teaser for an aborted feature film, and self-evidently an influence on Cronenberg's *Naked Lunch* 171.

YOU'RE A HOOK
Various

media: LP
released: 1984
created:
commerce: ●●
critical: ●●●
WSB quotient: ●●●

A best-of comp to mark the fifteenth anniversary of Dial-A-Poem. WSB contributes an unreleased recording "Old Man Bickford" (2:08) from TPODR 114 at the Kabuki Theatre, SF, 25 Feb. 1983 102. The LP also includes Laurie Anderson, Patti Smith and Frank Zappa tracks from the *Nova Convention* 73 LP and Jim Carroll, Allen Ginsberg, John Giorno, Philip Glass and Lenny Kaye from other GPS comps.

117 recording — various
A DIAMOND HIDDEN IN THE MOUTH OF A CORPSE
Various

- media: LP
- released: 1985
- created:
- commerce: ●●
- critical: ●●
- WSB quotient: ●●

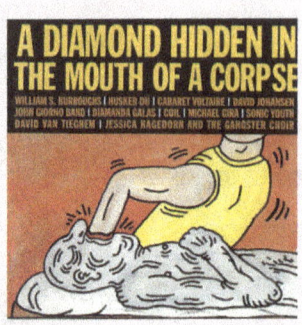

This was the first of three new-look GPS comps, with newer bigger and more rockist names than the Dial-A-Poem comps had previously carried. WSB provides "The President / Colonel Bradfield / Every Man A God" (5:36) from *The Western Lands* 141, recorded at the Naropa Institute, 28 Jul. 1985. Also appearing are Hüsker Dü, David Johansen, John Giorno Band, Sonic Youth, Cabaret Voltaire, Diamanda Galas, Coil, Michael Gira, David Van Tieghem, Jessica Hagedorn & The Gangster Choir.

118 recording — electro
ARTIFICIAL INTELLIGENCE
John Cale

- media: LP/CC/CD
- released: 1985
- created:
- commerce: ●
- critical: ●
- WSB quotient: ●

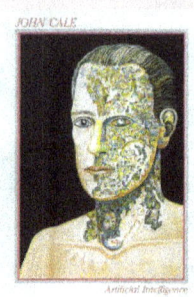

After leaving the Velvet Underground 22, John Cale pursued a solo career with varying degrees of critical acclaim and consistent commercial disappointment. In the mid-eighties, the Velvets experienced a resurgence following the breakthrough of the derivative Jesus and Mary Chain 165, the release of suppressed VU recordings, and a government ad campaign for smack. Cale's new album included "Dying on the Vine" (5:18) with a reference to "a William Burroughs playing for lost time.". The track was later reworked for the *10%* comp 226 although the booklet for that claims he says "praying for lost time".

119 film — documentary
KEROUAC, THE MOVIE
John Antonelli dir.

- media: 78M COL..
- released: 1985
- created:
- commerce: ●●
- critical: ●●
- WSB quotient: ●●

aka *Jack Kerouac's America* or *Kerouac, King of the Beats*. This award-winning Peter Coyote-narrated doco is the prime canonical biopic, sitting alongside *The Life and Times of Allen Ginsberg* 214 and *WSB: A Man Within* 308 as The Definitive Statement. No surprises here, the beatnik royal flush cast includes Allen Ginsberg, Lawrence Ferlinghetti, Carolyn Cassady, Joyce Johnson, Herbert Huncke, Michael McClure, John Clellon Holmes and WSB, who relates how the title of *And The Hippos...* 295 came over on a radio broadcast during composition; a portent of later cut/up techniques. See also *What Happened to Kerouac?* 130.

120 film — documentary
ORNETTE: MADE IN AMERICA
Shirley Clarke dir.

- media: 85M COL..
- released: 1985
- created:
- commerce: ●●
- critical: ●●●
- WSB quotient: ●

Pioneering documentarian Shirley Clarke's final film was a portrait of Ornette Coleman that she had spent more than twenty years working on. WSB is interviewed here, along with others including Buckminster Fuller and Robert Palmer 14. Coleman had worked with WSB on *Chappaqua* 13, travelled to Morocco to record with the Master Musicians of Jajouka 39 for his 1976 *Dancing in Your Head* LP and also contributed the *Naked Lunch* soundtrack 182. The film was restored for theatrical and DVD release in 2012.

121 book — fiction

QUEER
William Burroughs

- media: HARDBACK
- released: 1985
- created: 1955
- commerce: ●●●○○
- critical: ●●●○○
- WSB quotient: ●●●●○

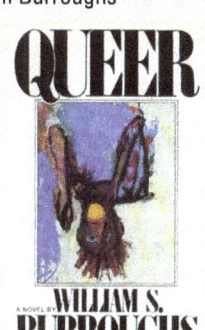

Issued thirty years after composition as part of a major publishing deal, WSB's new introduction is, in my opinion, the most interesting thing here, and appears intended to downplay any sensationalism or exploitation of the much-speculated-on circumstances of its composition. The book inspired an authorised soundtrack LP 145 but I cannot find any reference to it ever being performed at readings. In 2011, news started circulating about a film adaptation by Steve Buscemi, but at time of writing, this is still in production.

122 book — nonfiction

THE ADDING MACHINE
William Burroughs

- media: HARDBACK
- released: 1985
- created: various
- commerce: ●●●○○
- critical: ●●●○○
- WSB quotient: ●●●●○

Comprised mainly of book reviews but called "collected essays" in the UK and "selected essays" in the US, which is odd since the UK edition omits the seminal "Bugger the Queen" piece, understandably given the poisonous climate in the UK at the time. That piece had been part of *The Revised Boy Scout Manual* extracted in *Re/Search 4/5* 94 which was easier to locate than any Calder title in any case. WSB had sent a message of support along similar lines to the Sex Pistols when they released "God Save the Queen" in 1977. This book also includes WSB's important essay "It belongs to the cucumbers" about the Raudive Voice phenomena (EVP).

123 recording — electro

THE ELVIS OF LETTERS
William Burroughs & Gus Van Sant

- media: 12"
- released: 1985
- created:
- commerce: ●●○○○
- critical: ●●●○○
- WSB quotient: ●●●●○

Film-maker Gus Van Sant glues together WSB samples (from a number of sources) with guitar, sound effects and drum programming for this four-track maxi-single. It's a rare example of WSB's voice being chopped and manipulated effectively. It was the first release on T/K Records, who went on to do the Cobain collaboration 185, and was available on blue or standard black vinyl, then two tracks were used for a seven inch 164 in 1990 before the whole thing was issued on CD in 1991. We all know that the next step was for Van Sant to cast WSB in *Drugstore Cowboy* 150.

124 recording — experimental

BREAK THROUGH IN GREY ROOM
William Burroughs

- media: LP
- released: 1986
- created:
- commerce: ●●●○○
- critical: ●●●○○
- WSB quotient: ●●●●○

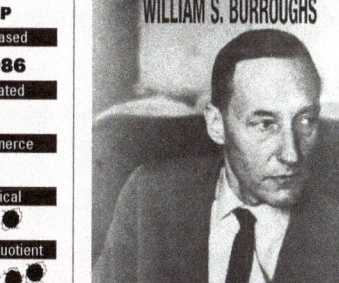

Issued on Sub Rosa, this is the classic compilation of lectures, performances, permutations, cut/ups, drop-ins, and live recordings of Joujouka spanning the sixties. Imaginative sequencing makes this the most accessible intro to these kind of recordings. See also NHNBTR 81 and *Real English Tea Made Here* 293. It's practical too, and there's nothing better for getting rid of recalcitrant dinner guests at the end of a tiring evening. The LP was issued on CD in 1993, and three tracks were put out as a limited seven-inch 307 in 2009.

125 film — music
HOME OF THE BRAVE
Laurie Anderson dir.

media: **90M COL..**
released: **1986**
created:
commerce:
critical:
WSB quotient:

A concert film of her *Mister Heartbreak* 103 tour, which was presumably bankable after the massive success of Jonathon Demme's *Stop Making Sense*. The film has a couple of WSB cameos, including the only known footage of him dancing (a tango with Laurie Anderson). It also includes a WSB-free version of "Sharkey's Night" and the WSB-derived "Language Is A Virus from Outer Space" which became a single from the soundtrack.

126 recording — industrial
MAJOR MALFUNCTION
Keith LeBlanc

media: **CD/CC**
released: **1986**
created:
commerce:
critical:
WSB quotient:

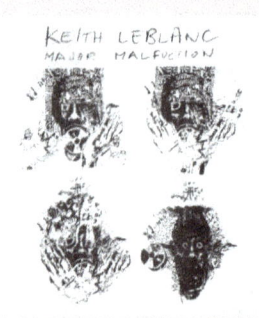

Drummer Keith LeBlanc teamed up with fellow Sugarhill players Doug Wimbish 297 and Skip McDonald for his first solo LP to follow his groundbreaking "No Sell Out" (under the name Malcom X) which had been the first electronic dance track to use cut/up samples as vocals. On this one he worked with On-U founder Adrian Sherwood 163 and the whole crew would go on to wear out their copy of NHNBTR 81 with samples from WSB's "Last Words of HiS" appearing on many of their releases. Here the clips come on the track "Major Malfunction" (3:31) alongside bits of the Challenger disaster commentary and Reagan's eulogy thereof.

127 book — nonfiction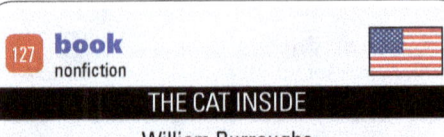
THE CAT INSIDE
William Burroughs

media: **HARDBACK**
released: **1986**
created:
commerce:
critical:
WSB quotient:

There's a potential goldmine for someone who turns this into a West End musical like they did with T.S. Eliot's cat book. He was from St. Louis too. Hmmmm. Readings from this short text appeared on *Dead City Radio* 162 and *The Best of WSB from GPS* 244.

128 recording — spoken word
THE DOCTOR IS ON THE MARKET
William Burroughs

media: **LP**
released: **1986**
created:
commerce:
critical:
WSB quotient:

Based on a bootleg cassette, this LP was first issued (with permission from WSB Comms) on James Nice's LTM records. It was well-reviewed in the UK music press and reached no. 17 in the indie charts. The LP was followed by the *Fruit of the Original Sin* comp 84 before being reissued on Interior Music in 1988 and going on to sell a total of 3,000 copies. Unfortunately, it turned out that the originating cassette had been compiled from cuts on GPS albums, which upset John Giorno and led to the LP being deleted. Around fifty copies were mispressed with Crispy Ambulance on side one.

MORE: http://home.planet.nl/~frankbri/ltmstory.html (31 Aug. 2013)

129 film	
experimental	🇬🇧

THEE FILMS
Antony Balch dir.

media: **VHS / PAL**
released: **1986**
created: **1962-63**
commerce: ●●●
critical: ●●●
WSB quotient: ●●●●●●

W.S. BURROUGHS
BRION GYSIN
IAN SOMERVILLE

This was issued by Genesis P-Orridge and Thee Temple ov Psychick Youth. Strangely it credits everyone (even if spelling their names wrong) above Antony Balch, who only rates a mention on the back. This was the first issue of *William Buys a Parrot* 100 and *The Cut-Ups* 19.

130 film	
documentary	🇺🇸

WHAT HAPPENED TO KEROUAC?
Richard Lerner & Lewis MacAdams dirs.

media: **96M COL..**
released: **1986**
created:
commerce: ●●●
critical: ●●●
WSB quotient: ●

Redundancy is not much appreciated these days and this doco overlaps a fair bit with *Kerouac, the Movie* 119. It's years since I saw this and the two have fused in my mind. I do recall that the interview segments are mostly different in each but that the same subjects say much the same things. This one maybe has more of a focus on Kerouac's latter decline into alcoholism and reaction, and includes funny and/or sad tv footage of the old pissed Kerouac sniping left (Ed Sanders) and right (William Buckley) on *The Firing Line*.

1986

131 recording	
industrial	🇬🇧

ANARCHY IN THE UK
P.J. Proby

media: **12"**
released: **1987**
created:
commerce: ●
critical: ●
WSB quotient: ●

Proby's follow-up to the *Mugwump Dance* 140 now extends the WSB references to a ten second sample (from "The Do-Rights" 88) in the company T.S. Eliot and H.D. Thoreau. It sounds not a million miles from how it would if William Shatner did it, and I mean that in a good way. I'm not sure if the tabloid references to Proby's wife-shooting on the front cover are intended to also invoke WSB. I hope not.

132 recording	
industrial	🇺🇸

JANE'S ADDICTION
Jane's Addiction

media: **LP**
released: **1987**
created:
commerce: ●●●
critical: ●●●
WSB quotient: ●

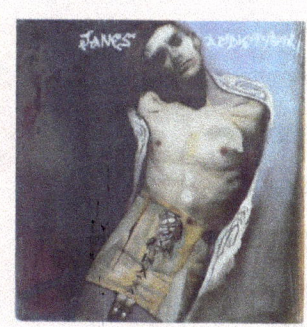

Formed in LA in 1985 by Perry Farrell. Their debut LP includes an acknowledgement in tiny writing to WSB "sitting on his skinny white ass more important than the vice president whose name I don't even know".

1987

133 recording — various
MINUTES
Various

- media: LP
- released: 1987
- created:
- commerce: ●●
- critical: ●●
- WSB quotient: ●●●

A comp from LTM, who had put out the *The Doctor is on the Market* LP [126]. Herewith WSB contributes both cuts from the *Talk Talk* flexi [82] alongside cuts by Jean Cocteau, Winston Tong, Jacques Derrida, Richard Jobson, The Monochrome Set and Louis Phillippe. The sleeve is by Thomi Wroblewski, who had done book covers for a number of WSB's UK editions.

134 recording — electro
CODE
Cabaret Voltaire

- media: LP/CD/CC
- released: 1987
- created:
- commerce: ●●●
- critical: ●●●
- WSB quotient: ●

The Cabs were probably the first group to seriously attempt implementation of WSB's sonic theories. Formed in Sheffield in 1973 by Richard H. Kirk, Stephen Mallinder and Chris Watson, they started as a performance art outfit and didn't release anything until 1978. They were instrumental in kick-starting the Sheffield-based industrial scene that gave us Clock DVA, 23 Skidoo [85], Dead Fingers Talk [63] etc. This LP is listed in the WSB *Ports of Entry* catalogue as their most WSB-influenced work but it's a tough call as his tropes are all over their whole oeuvre. My advice: start anywhere.

Wood, Eve. *Made in Sheffield*. (2001 documentary film).

135 recording — reggae
RHYTHM KILLERS
Sly and Robbie

- media: LP
- released: 1987
- created:
- commerce: ●●●
- critical: ●●
- WSB quotient: ●

The law of averages dictates that the world's most prolific musicians must have made a WSB reference and here it is – in the form of their biggest UK hit "Boops (Here to Go)" If this seems a bit far-fetched, keep in mind the song was co-written and the album was produced by Bill Laswell. Tru dat.

136 film — music
SCARED TO LIVE
Psychic TV

- media: 5M COL..
- released: 1987
- created:
- commerce: ●
- critical: ●
- WSB quotient: ●●●

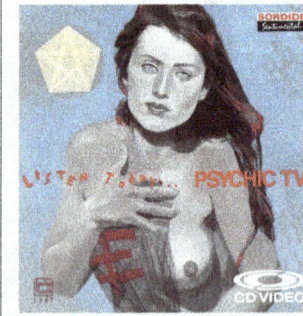

This clip for Genesis P-Orridge's group includes shots of WSB from *Bill and Tony* [41], and was issued on their *Listen Today* EP as the video component on the mini-CDV (a stillborn format). P-Orridge was instrumental in moving WSB into the multimedia field, issuing NHNBTR [81], co-convening The Final Academy [97], saving Antony Balch's films [129] and generally representing WSB's oeuvre at every opportunity via his Temple of Psychic Youth. More info on their intersections can be found in *Re/Search 4/5* [94].

137 recording — various
SMACK MY CRACK
Various

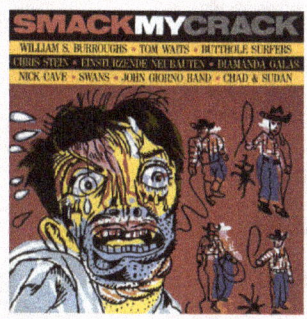

- media: LP/CD
- released: 1987
- created:
- commerce:
- critical:
- WSB quotient:

Another GPS release. WSB contributes "Worlds Of Advice / Kim Like The Great Gatsby" (4:48) from a draft of TPODR. Also includes: Tom Waits, Butthole Surfers, Chris Stein, Einstürzende Neubauten, Diamanda Galas, Nick Cave, Swans, John Giorno Band, Chad & Sudan. Cover by Gary Panter. The CD adds tracks by Hüsker Dü, David Johansen and Cabaret Voltaire from the ADHITMOAC LP 117, not then on CD.

138 film — documentary
THE BEAT GENERATION: AN AMERICAN DREAM
Janet Forman dir.

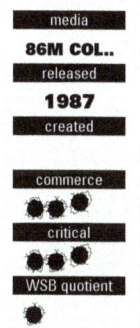

- media: 86M COL..
- released: 1987
- created:
- commerce:
- critical:
- WSB quotient:

The first comprehensive survey of the "Beats" drafts in everyone you'd expect including WSB who makes his usual statements on the topic. There's nothing surprising here as the purpose is simply to establish the canon and present the material, presumably, for an audience of literature majors who are taking the Beat module. It situates the "Beats" squarely against the enforced conformity of the Eisenhower era, and, with a typical national solipsism, appears to assume that no other nation produced bohemian youth cultures before or since. Not nearly as funty as 1999's *The Source* 254 but it was there first.

139 recording — psyche
THE MASTER
Nick Haeffner

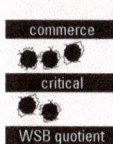

- media: 12"
- released: 1987
- created:
- commerce:
- critical:
- WSB quotient:

Another forgotten hero of the popsike revolt of the eighties, when a generation of disgusted young brits turned their back on the present day and tried to find a way back. This came out on the legendary Bam Caruso reissue label, and uses WSB samples from *Call Me Burroughs* 11 in the version of ex-Soft Machinist 25 Kevin Ayres' "Song From the Bottom of a Well" (6:08). The track is included on the CD reissue of his classic LP *The Great Indoors*. Nick also played guitar on Psychic TV's 136 version of "Eve of Destruction".

140 recording — industrial
THE MUGWUMP DANCE
P.J. Proby

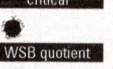

- media: 12"
- released: 1987
- created:
- commerce:
- critical:
- WSB quotient:

The Savoy empire is one of the most enduring English counter-cultural institutions. Born of the *New Worlds* SF milieu of the sixties (deeply inspired by WSB) Dave Britton and Michael Butterworth have put out swathes of books and discs to confound and confront. It's hard to speak of the relative oddness of their artefacts but their relaunch of the career of sixties icon P.J. Proby was amongst their most quixotic and poetic gestures. His fourth single for them is a hi-energy funk riot and I'm pretty sure he's talking about Burroughsian mugwumps here, not the other sort 20. See also 131.

David Britton and Michael Butterworth on WSB www.realitystudio.org (15 Sep. 2013).

141	**book**
	fiction

THE WESTERN LANDS
William Burroughs

media: **HARDBACK**
released: **1987**
created:
commerce:
critical:
WSB quotient:

Third volume of The Final Trilogy and WSB's last major novel, readings from this provided the basis for Material's *Seven Souls* LP 157 and its remix follow-up 247. The novel had been road-tested at readings over many years, with extracts featured on a number of GPS comps starting with 1982's *Life is a Killer* 91 then ADHITMOAC 117 and *Smack My Crack* 137, and also on *Dead City Radio* 162 and *Spare Ass Annie* 194. Film of readings appears in *Commissioner of Sewers* 170 and probably elsewhere too.

142	**recording**
	ambient

THE WHITE ARCADES
Harold Budd

media: **LP**
released: **1987**
created:
commerce:
critical:
WSB quotient:

Harold Budd (b. 1936) is a US contemporary classical composer, mainly working for piano in an ambient idiom. This, probably his best-known LP, uses a WSB text on the track "Algebra of Darkness" (6:32) but it must be mixed low. I couldn't hear it. The track has been used in a couple of early nineties US tv docos, *The Dinner Party* and *Coney Island*. His 1991 follow-up *By The Dawn's Early Light*, had a track called "The Place Of Dead Roads" too.

143	**recording**
	hip hop

ACTION!
The Alliance

media: **12"**
released: **1988**
created:
commerce:
critical:
WSB quotient:

Early cut/up groove inspired by artists like M/A/R/R/S and Bomb The Bass 217, the first track here "Action (extended version)" (6:30) samples "K9 Was in Combat With the Alien Mind Screens" from BTIGR 124. Not surprising really since they sample pretty much everything here. I picked up Prince, Trouble Funk, Afrika Bambaataa, The Incredible Bongo Band, Sugarhill Gang, Herbie Hancock, Beastie Boys, Harold Faltermeyer and the mighty 2 Live Crew. Try it! It's funty!

144	**recording**
	industrial

MINUTES TO GO
Various

media: **LP**
released: **1988**
created:
commerce:
critical:
WSB quotient:

Subtitled "Hommage à William S. Burroughs" and "Respectfully dedicated to William Seward Burroughs and his CutUp method of composition". Includes the *Talk Talk* flexi tracks 82 plus "Towers Open Fire" (2:01) from TDIOTM 128 and "Twilight's Last Gleamings" [6:53], a longer version of the track on *The Fruit of the Original Sin* comp 84. Also has variably-WSB-relevant contributions by Cabaret Voltaire (who do "Baader-Meinhof", one of their most overtly Burroughsian cut/ups) plus The Anti Group, Tuxedomoon, Jean Cocteau, Jacques Derrida and Winston Tong. Put out by Interior Music, who were reissuing TDIOTM 128 (with a different cover).

145 recording	
electro	

QUEER
Manapsara

- media: **LP**
- released: **1988**
- created:
- commerce: ● ● ●
- critical: ● ● ●
- WSB quotient: ● ● ●

An authorised "Soundtrack to the Novel" that came out on Sub Rosa, the work of Bradley Koehler and Christopher Hartman. Beyond the fact it was recorded in San Francisco, I can find no other info. Apparently some copies had a printed insert but I haven't seen it. The LP wasn't issued on CD but three tracks were included on Sub Rosa's 1992 industrial CD comp *Deadheads and Roses*. It's effective in a brooding ethnic electro way but to my old ears sounds kinda dated like a lot of that eighties industrial stuff. As far as I know, these guys didn't issue anything else, except the following.

146 recording	
electro	

ROUTINE (EXTENDED MIX)
Manapsara

- media: **12"**
- released: **1988**
- created:
- commerce: ● ●
- critical: ● ●
- WSB quotient: ● ● ●

Maxi-single extended remixes from the *Queer* OST 145 in that eighties stylee not a million miles from Duran Duran's Wilder Than Wild Boys Extended Mix of "The Wild Boys" 115. On the plus side, at times the bassline sounds a bit like the one from The Human League's *The Lebanon*. The flipside is the Common Market Mix of "Marketplace".

---

147 film	
comedy	

TWISTER
Michael Almereyda dir.

- media: **94M COL..**
- released: **1988**
- created:
- commerce: ● ● ●
- critical: ● ●
- WSB quotient: ● ●

This off-beat comedy shouldn't be confused with the 1996 disaster movie of the same name, as has happened in at least one online interview with WSB that turned out funnier than this movie. WSB has a small but worthwhile cameo as "Man in Barn" and says "Jim? ... Jim got kicked in the head by a horse back in February. He went around killing horses for a while... Then one day he ate the insides of a clock and died." Almereyda went on to direct quite a few films and tv episodes, the best-known probably being his version of *Hamlet* (2000). For extra windsploitation action see *Beavis and Butthead* 190 or check out WSB's 1989 book *Tornado Alley*.

148 recording	
spoken word	

UNCOMMON QUOTES
William Burroughs

- media: **CC**
- released: **1988**
- created:
- commerce: ● ● ●
- critical: ● ● ●
- WSB quotient: ● ● ● ●

A live recording of WSB's performance at the Caravan of Dreams, Fort Worth, TX, on 11 Sep. 1986. Came in a clamshell pack with an essay "William Burroughs: A Shift in Vision" by Robert Palmer 14. Taking its name from a Brion Gysin reference, the Caravan of Dreams was a performing arts complex including a night club, theatre, recording studio and geodesic dome. It opened on 29 Sep. 1983 with concerts by Fort Worth native Ornette Coleman, whose biopic 120 was released on the same label. The complex closed in 2001 but there was an unofficial (?) but classy CD reissue of this in 2010.

1989

149	**film**
	comedy

BLOODHOUNDS OF BROADWAY
Howard Brookner dir.

media
93M COL..
released
1989
created

commerce
critical
WSB quotient

After his WSB doco 101, Brookner's first feature was a star-studded adaptation of Damon Runyan stories. He cast WSB in a brief two-line role as a butler (co-starring with a parrot again 100) which synchronicitally appears at exactly 23 minutes into the film. Amongst a glut of big names, the film also features Matt Dillon 150, Steve Buscemi 277, Rutger Hauer 268 and Madonna who has a big *Western Lands* 141 themed production number. Sadly, Brookner died just months before the film was released, cutting short his short but promising career.

150	**film**
	drama

DRUGSTORE COWBOY
Gus Van Sant dir.

media
102M COL..
released
1989
created

commerce
critical
WSB quotient

Gus Van Sant based his first studio feature on a then unpublished autobiographical novel by James Fogle, who was in jail for robbing pharmacies to support his drug habit. Fogle died in jail in 2012, aged 75, having been sentenced the year before for a similar crime. Alongside Matt Dillon 149 and Kelly Lynch, WSB has his most substantial film role here, as Tom the Priest, for which he provided much of his own dialogue. It's a powerful and poignant performance. And it doesn't hurt that the soundtrack features top tunes such as The Count Five's *Psychotic Reaction* and Desmond Dekkers' *The Israelites*.

151	**recording**
	industrial

END OF THE CENTURY PARTY
Gary Clail

media
LP/CD
released
1989
created

commerce
critical
WSB quotient

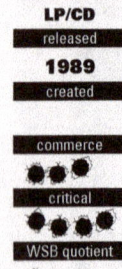

Gary Clail was associated with the On-U Syndicate (qv Mark Stewart 112, Doug Wimbish 297) and fronted the Tackhead Sound System, whose 1987 *Tackhead Tape Time* LP is still arguably the best example of Sommerville-inspired tape cut/ups. Where Cabaret Voltaire 134 had tried to get funkier, they came over a bit cheesy, but Tackhead were anything but that! Clail's debut album includes a sample from "Curse Go Back" from BTIGR 124 on the track "Toes Tapping" (5:54).

152	**film**
	documentary

GANG OF SOULS
Maria Beatty dir.

media
60M COL..
released
1989
created

commerce
critical
WSB quotient

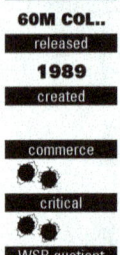
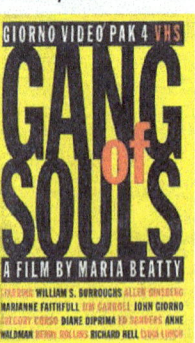

The feature doco debut by the NYC-based director and one-time resident of the Chelsea Hotel 78 who has more recently specialised in explorations of female sexuality. Here she links interviews with WSB, Ginsberg, Corso, Di Prima, Waldman, Giorno and others with commentary from contemporary musicians, Marianne Faithfull, Richard Hell, Lydia Lunch and Henry Rollins to capture the ongoing influence of the Beat megastars.

153 film
documentary

HEAVY PETTING
Obie Benz dir.

media: 78M COL..
released: 1989
created:
commerce: ●●
critical: ●
WSB quotient: ●●●

Lightweight but entertaining and good-natured doco compiled from lots of old sex education clips mixed with various folks talking about their early sexual experiences and coming of age in the fifties. WSB says very little whilst looking uncomfortable next to a more relaxed Allen Ginsberg, Also here are David Byrne, Ann Magnuson, Spalding Gray, Laurie Anderson, Abbie Hoffman and others. Hal Willner was music producer, which may help explain the familiarity of the line-up.

154 recording
spoken word

THE COLDSPRING TAPE
Gysin / Burroughs / P-Orridge

media: CC
released: 1989
created: 1960–
commerce: ●
critical: ●
WSB quotient: ●●●

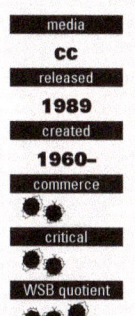

Compiled by Genesis P-Orridge from his archives, this is an interesting comp of cut/ups, radio broadcasts, permutations, taped interviews and music. A counterpart to NHNBTR 81 and BTIGR 124. Issued in a limited edition of 100 by an offshoot of G.P-O's Temple of Psychic Youth. Highlights include a live reading of "Junk is no good baby" by Gysin, and recollections of The Beat Hotel. Can you find the hidden bars of Hawkwind's "Hassan i Sabbah"? They are there!

155 book
fiction

INTERZONE
William Burroughs

media: HARDBACK
released: 1989
created: 1953-58
commerce: ●●●
critical: ●●
WSB quotient: ●●●●

Interzone was the title of the uncompleted novel that WSB started after *Junkie* and which mutated into *Naked Lunch*. This collection brings together writing from that transitional period, some of which had appeared in *Early Routines*. Also here is the longer piece "Word" which was mostly omitted from *Naked Lunch* and represents a compositional technique abandoned by WSB upon discovery of the cut/up method. The term "Interzone" has been referenced by countless groups, including: Joy Division 69, Psychic TV 136, John Zorn 310, and at least a dozen groups that have called themselves it.

156 recording
various

LIKE A GIRL, I WANT YOU TO KEEP COMING
Various

media: LP/CD/CC
released: 1989
created:
commerce: ●●
critical: ●●
WSB quotient: ●●

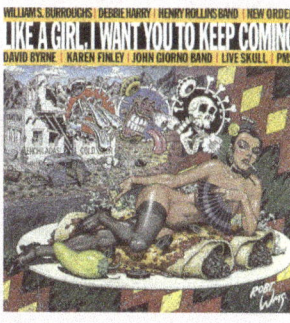

The final GPS comp to feature new material was issued on World Service records and received much wider distribution than previous GPS releases. With a line-up boasting big names such as Debbie Harry, New Order, David Byrne, Live Skull, PMS, Karen Finley, John Giorno Band and the Henry Rollins Band, and striking cover is by Robert Williams, it became virtually mandatory amongst the young cognoscenti in my part of the UK. WSB contributed "Just Say No To Drug Hysteria (excerpt) / Dead Souls" (8:15) recorded at Wichita Art Assoc. Theatre, KS on 10 Apr. 1987. Oh... and the inside sleeve features a hilarious Gary Panter comic strip too.

157 recording
electro
SEVEN SOULS
Material

media: CD/LP/CC
released: 1989
created:
commerce:
critical:
WSB quotient:

Based on WSB's readings from *The Western Lands*, Bill Laswell assembled a stellar cast (Sly Dunbar, Rammellzee, Shankar, and Nicky Skopelitis just for starters) to record this highly-rated album. Two tracks ("Equation"/"Ineffect") were issued as a single. The album was re-released on Triloka Records in 1997 with a new cover and three bonus re-mixes (featuring Jah Wobble, DJ Spooky 279 and Tim Simenon of Bomb the Bass 217) followed by a 1998 album of seven new mixes, *The Road to the Western Lands* 247. Like this if *The Sopranos* 289 brought you here.

158 recording
industrial
STORM THE STUDIO
Meat Beat Manifesto

media: 2X12"
released: 1989
created:
commerce:
critical:
WSB quotient:

First track "God O.D. (Part 1)" opens with a three second eponymous sample from "Towers Open Fire" on the TDIOTM 128. Another WSB ref is on track four, entitled "I got the fear", which is a phrase from WSB's "Letter from a Master Addict to Dangerous Drugs" which is found in UK editions of *Naked Lunch* 2 and *A William Burroughs Reader* 89 and would probably make a good title for a tune in itself. Originally from Swindon, Meat Beat Manifesto would be credited with influencing the sound of the UK's Big Beat scene in the mid-late nineties but I can't hear it myself.

159 book
screenplay
THE NAKED LUNCH (SCREENPLAY)
David Cronenberg

media: LOOSE-LEAF
released: 1989
created:
commerce:
critical:
WSB quotient:

Unpublished commercially but typescript copies circulate underground. Cronenberg's screenplay interestingly retains the definite article from the Olympia and UK editions of *Naked Lunch* 2, which was dropped from the film's 171 title upon production. Reading this back several years after seeing the film (which I didn't like) I'm struck at the skilful mashing-up of fragments and motifs from the novel with material from *Exterminator!* 45 and Morgan's bio. Maybe the best WSB mash-up since Philip José Farmer's "The Jungle Rot Kid on the Nod". If I could just persuade Mr Cronenberg to put quotation marks around his title, maybe we could call it quits?

160 film
experimental
TOWERS OPEN FIRE & OTHER FILMS
Antony Balch

media: VHS / NTSC
released: 1989
created: 1962-63
commerce:
critical:
WSB quotient:

A comp including *Towers Open Fire*, *The Cut-Ups*, *Bill and Tony* and *William Buy a Parrot* but not, apparently, *Ghosts at No. 9*. This was put out by Mystic Fire (thanks for that! – *Ed*) which was run by William Breeze who would later play with Psychic TV 136. It's a small world... but I wouldn't want to have to paint it.

161 film — drama
A SHORT CONVERSATION
Patti Podesta dir.

media: 20M COL..
released: 1990

Full title: *A Short Conversation from the Grave with Joan Burroughs*. The creator of this short piece is a highly-regarded production designer who worked on films like *Memento* and *Love and other Drugs*. I haven't been able to catch it. I have avoided reference, other than here and in the chronology, to the death of WSB's spouse as this seems an inappropriate forum for such a serious and sensitive topic. I appreciate that this is a cop-out but it strikes me as the least worst option in that regard.

162 recording — spoken word
DEAD CITY RADIO
William Burroughs

media: LP/CC/CD
released: 1990

Producer Hal Willner recruited an all-star cast to work with WSB on his first full LP of original recordings since 1965's *Call Me Burroughs* [11] and ended up with what is probably WSB's most accessible release. Amongst the acolytes are John Cale [22], Donald Fagen [42], Sonic Youth [260], but more surprisingly (perhaps) we also have much-maligned prog-rockers Yes helping out. *A Thanksgiving Prayer* would become a promo clip [174] for the LP, and *Ah Pook is Here* [65] would be animated. Alongside WSB's own texts, he reads from the Bible and delivers a (drunken?) version of *Falling in Love Again* that has become an underground standard.

163 recording — electro
FRIENDLY AS A HAND GRENADE
Tackhead

media: LP/CD
released: 1990

 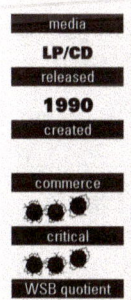 

Formed when the Sugarhill Records rhythm section of bassist Doug Wimbish [297], guitarist Skip McDonald and drummer Keith LeBlanc [126] met On-U kingpin Adrian Sherwood in 1984. Tackhead were massively influential in their own right (not least on US group Ministry [181]) as well as backing Mark Stewart [112] and Gary Clail [151]. Their debut LP has a couple of WSB samples on the track "Ticking Time Bomb" (4:23).

164 recording — electro
MILLIONS OF IMAGES
William Burroughs & Gus Van Sant

media: 7"
released: 1990

  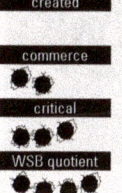 

WSB's first 7" single was taken from *The Elvis of Letters* [123] for Bob (ex-Hüsker Dü) Mould's Singles Only Label. there are reports of pressings on clear, red, yellow and finally black vinyl. The track would be used on the soundtrack Ben Meade's short film *Seratonin* [319].

1990

165 recording — rock 🇬🇧
ROLLERCOASTER
The Jesus and Mary Chain

- media: CD
- released: 1990
- created:
- commerce
- critical
- WSB quotient

aka the Scottish Velvet Underground Show, the eighties' leading exponents of junk rock were supposedly banned from wearing "Heroin Thrills" T-shirts on their first Top of the Pops appearance. The third track of this ep, "Lowlife" (3:25), opens with a WSB sample from *Last Words of HiS* on NHNBTR [81] "I bear no sick words, no junk words, no forgive words from Jesus..." Actually, it's pretty rockin'. Fess up time. Guilty pleasure, I loved em back in the day.

166 film — music 🇦🇹
THE BLACK RIDER
Robert Wilson dir.

- media: 136M COL..
- released: 1990
- created:
- commerce
- critical
- WSB quotient

WSB wrote the libretto (based on a German folktale called *Der Freischütz*) for Robert Wilson's [285] production with music by Tom Waits [196]. It premiered at Hamburg's Thalia Theatre on 31 March 1990, before transferring to Theater an der Wien, Vienna, Austria, 12-16 Jun. 1990, where it was filmed and broadcast on Austrian tv. Its English-language premiere wasn't until 1998, when it opened at the Edmonton International Fringe Festival in Canada before travelling to NYC and further afield.

167 film — documentary 🇩🇪
THE BLACK RIDER (DOCUMENTARY)
Theo Janssen & Ralph Quinke dir.

- media: 30M COL..
- released: 1990
- created:
- commerce
- critical
- WSB quotient

German WDR tv made a doco about the production of Robert Wilson's opera [166], but it is sometimes unclear if parts pertain to the Thalia premiere or the Viennese production. The doco includes some great interviews with WSB, along with Tom Waits [196] and Robert Wilson [285], and it includes the only known footage of WSB taking a curtain call.

168 recording — spoken word 🇺🇸
THE JACK KEROUAC COLLECTION
Jack Kerouac

- media: 4LP/4CC/3CD
- released: 1990
- created:
- commerce
- critical
- WSB quotient

This boxed set on Rhino became the prototype for spoken word deluxe retrospectives including *The Beat Generation* [186], *Holy Soul, Jelly Roll* [208], and *The Best of WSB from GPS* [244]. Here WSB provides liner notes, "A Historic Memoir of America's Greatest Existentialist", a revised version of "Remembering Jack Kerouac" from *The Adding Machine* [122].

169 **recording**	
ambient	

BAJO EL SOL JAGUAR
Jorge Reyes

media: **CD**
released: **1991**
created:
commerce:
critical:
WSB quotient:

Jorge Reyes (1952-2009) was a Mexican multi-instrumentalist specialising in ambient ethnic fusion style tunes. This release features WSB narration on the track "Viaje al Sitio de Los Violines de Flores" (3.21) taken from an interview in *Commissioner of Sewers* `170`, which is only fair since Reyes contributed to the soundtrack.

---

170 **film**	
documentary	

COMMISSIONER OF SEWERS
Klaus Maeck dir.

media: **60M COL..**
released: **1991**
created:
commerce: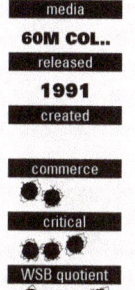
critical:
WSB quotient:

From the director of *Decoder* `110`, this film is built around (a) a Burroughs reading at Filmkunst 66 in Berlin on 9 May 1986, which includes spirited versions of "When Did I Stop Wanting to be President?" and "Old Man Bickford". (b) an interview by Jürgen Ploog, covering diverse aspects of WSB's thought including brief discussion of J.W. Dunne's theories. `169` (c) short clips from *Towers Open Fire* `9`, *A Thanksgiving Prayer* `174` etc. (d) the only known footage of WSB looking at tigers in a zoo. I like this doco a lot, not least because the emphasis is very much on WSB's work rather than his biography.

---

171 **film**	
drama	

NAKED LUNCH
David Cronenberg dir.

media: **115M COL..**
released: **1991**
created:
commerce:
critical:
WSB quotient:

 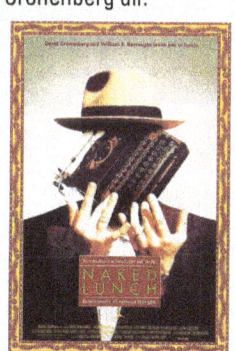

Cronenberg has done nicely out of asset-stripping the postmodern canon but I don't really dig his shit. It must be dull inside his skull if this is the best that he can do with WSB. If it had been called something else I might have liked it better. The poster, trailer, credits and soundtrack `182` are pretty cool and it's even got Roy Scheider in it! As it stands it just reminds me of the Duran Duran clip `115`. Tim Murphy's book `249` includes a good overview of the film's shortcoming and I made a response film in 2008 but I forgot to include it in this book. There's also a "making of" book `160` and doco `183` that help put the bloody thing in a WSB context.

---

172 **recording**	
experimental	

ReR QUARTERLY, VOL. 1 SELECTIONS
Various

media: **CD**
released: **1991**
created:
commerce:
critical:
WSB quotient:

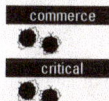 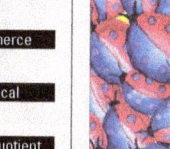 

I haven't been able to discern WSB's contribution to this comp from the Chris Cutler edited avant-garde review that ran from 1985-97. I suspect the most likely candidate for samples is "Mystery Tapes" (6:07) by John Oswald. Oswald (b. 1950) is best-known for his Plunderphonics project (1988) which he directly attributes to WSB's cut/up experiments.

| 173 **recording** 🇬🇧
| punk |

SUICIDE ALLEY
Manic Street Preachers

media: 7"
released: 1991
created:
commerce: ●●●
critical: ●
WSB quotient: ●

These Welsh lads were the first group to shamelessly hark back to the punk sound of 1976 and did very well out of it, with one exception, becoming one of the biggest groups in the UK for a while. They were very fond of putting WSB quotes on their covers and this, their debut release, has an (uncredited) quote from *The Job*. Although the follow-up *New Art Riot* (on Damaged Goods records – one of the greatest labels of all time) featured an (uncredited) quote by Andy Warhol, they returned to WSB on some subsequent releases. I'd like to make a joke here about "the biggest twats of the pro-Chinese Welsh" but I'm too polite. Oh go on then...

| 174 **film** 🇺🇸
| spoken word |

A THANKSGIVING PRAYER
Gus Van Sant dir.

media: 3M COL..
released: 1991
created:
commerce: ●●●
critical: ●●●●
WSB quotient: ●●●●

Gus Van Sant made this promo clip for the track from *Dead City Radio* 162. It's stirring stuff but terribly literal, which given its target demographic is perhaps forgivable. It received wide circulation when it was featured on U2's *Zoo TV* world tour and aired on the TV special thereof on MTV and Fox in 1992. Indeed, WSB's last creative gesture would be a role in a U2 promo 269.

68

| 175 **recording** 🇺🇸
| rock |

THE NOVA MOB
The Nova Mob

media: LP/CC/CD
released: 1991
created:
commerce: ●●
critical: ●
WSB quotient: ●

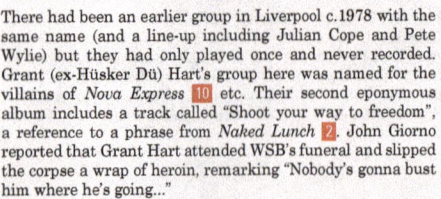

There had been an earlier group in Liverpool c.1978 with the same name (and a line-up including Julian Cope and Pete Wylie) but they had only played once and never recorded. Grant (ex-Hüsker Dü) Hart's group here was named for the villains of *Nova Express* 10 etc. Their second eponymous album includes a track called "Shoot your way to freedom", a reference to a phrase from *Naked Lunch* 2. John Giorno reported that Grant Hart attended WSB's funeral and slipped the corpse a wrap of heroin, remarking "Nobody's gonna bust him where he's going..."

| 176 **film** 🇺🇸
| experimental |

WAX
David Blair dir.

media: 85M COL..
released: 1991
created:
commerce: ●●
critical: ●●●●
WSB quotient: ●●●

or "The Discovery of Television Among the Bees". This film was groundbreaking in a few ways. NY-based experimental film-maker David Blair used a cheap digital video editor to combine computer graphics, stock footage and original material into a feature length exploration of weapons technology, postmortal survival, spirit photography and apiary. His techniques would prefigure the DIY film culture of the 21st century. It was also the first feature-film to be streamed online (1993) over the internet. WSB took the brief but critical role of James 'Hive' Maker here but only appears peripherally as animated stills.

177 recording	
joujouka	

APOCALYPSE ACROSS THE SKY
The Master Musicians of Jajouka

- media: CD
- released: 1992
- created:
- commerce:
- critical:
- WSB quotient:

1989 had been a big year for the Master Musicians, what with guesting on the Rolling Stones' *Steel Wheels* LP and touring with Ornette Coleman. They followed through with this LP, recorded on their home-turf in the Rif Mountains of Morocco on 8-10 Nov. 1991, produced by Bill Laswell and with notes by WSB. It was followed by a re-issue of their 1971 LP `39` but a schism had opened between two factions. This one ("Jajouka") led by Bachir Attar, son of the group's leader in the sixties was more prolific in terms of recordings (qv *The Source* `314`). The other ("Joujouka") was associated with Hamri the Painter, appeared at Here to Go `238` and recorded for Sub Rosa.

178 recording	
metal	

BURNING IN WATER DROWNING IN FLAME
Skrew

- media: CD/LP/CC
- released: 1992
- created:
- commerce:
- critical: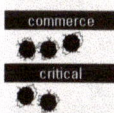
- WSB quotient: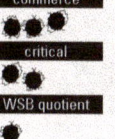

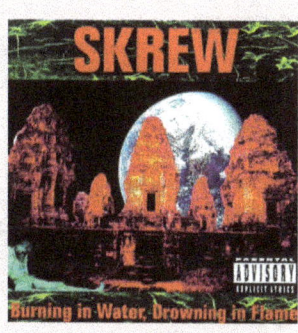

Skrew were an influential industrial metal band from Austin, TX, not a million miles from Ministry `181`. Their debut LP includes the track "Poisonous" (4:36) concludes with a WSB sample "Sometimes I think some junkie nurse may be skimping on my medication".

179 film	
spoken word	

BURROUGHS!
Graham Duff

- media: N/A
- released: 1992
- created:
- commerce:
- critical:
- WSB quotient:

I was quite clear I wasn't going to cover unfilmed stage productions here but Graham is an old mate. Wouldn't you? His one man show, based on WSB's life and texts from *Exterminator!* `45`, premiered at Brighton Festival in May 1992 and went on to tour for over a hundred performances including stints at the Edinburgh Festival and Glastonbury. Graham went on write the underrated *Dr Terrible's House of Horrible* for the BBC in 2001 then 53 episodes (2005-2011) of the classic sitcom *Ideal* starring Johnny Vegas, at the same time he was script editing for Radio 4's *Count Arthur Strong's Radio Show*. But wait! There's more...

180 book	
critical	

EVERYTHING IS PERMITTED
Ira Silverberg (ed)

- media: PAPERBACK
- released: 1992
- created:
- commerce:
- critical: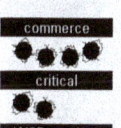
- WSB quotient:

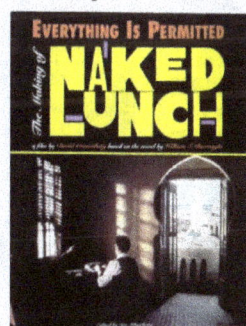

This lavish illustrated account of the making of Cronenberg's *Naked Lunch* `171` is worth it for the uh diplomatic introduction by WSB alone. It also has an intro by Cronenberg, an essay on their intersections by Chris Rodley `183`, a useful intro to WSB by Gary Indiana, a look at the special effects by Jody Duncan, along with a production diary and lots of stills, including some of WSB on set. This book can usefully be seen as a damage limitation exercise. I got mine for two quid in a remainder shop years ago. Did anyone else notice that WSB appears to be smoking a joint on the back cover? Dude!

1992

181 recording
industrial

JUST ONE FIX
Ministry

media: **12"/CD**
released: **1992**
created:
commerce:
critical:
WSB quotient:

Ministry was a US industrial band started in 1981 by Al Jourgensen. They hit mainstream paydirt with their 1991 LP *Psalm 69* and put out this maxi-single. The tracks are alternate mixes of with added samples of WSB., who also provided the cover art, entitled "Last Chance Junction And Curse On Drug Hysterics". The promotional video, directed by Peter Christopherson (ex-TG), featured a cameo by WSB and went on to be acclaimed on *The Beavis and Butthead Show* 190.

---

182 recording
jazz

NAKED LUNCH (SOUNDTRACK)
Howard Shore / Ornette Coleman / LPO

media: **CD/CC**
released: **1992**
created:
commerce:
critical:
WSB quotient:

I reckon the soundtrack was the best thing about Cronenberg's movie 171 if you don't count the end credits which I was very glad to see. Mixing film-noir tropes with be-bop and joujouka nods here, Shore includes new (extracted) recordings of Ornette Coleman's 120 historical pieces "Ballad" (from 1965's *Ornette Coleman In Europe, Vol. 2*) and "Midnight Sunrise" (from *Dancing in Your Head*) recorded in 1973 with the master Musicians of Jajouka in the company of WSB. The album was re-released in a remastered edition in 2005.

1992

183 film
documentary

NAKED MAKING LUNCH
Chris Rodley dir.

media: **52M COL..**
released: **1992**
created:
commerce:
critical:
WSB quotient:

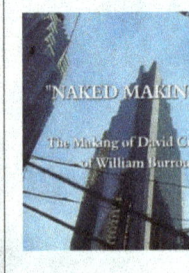

First-rate doco on the making of *Naked Lunch* 171 which must make it the film of *Everything is Permitted* 180. Includes copious new interview footage of WSB including the 1991 Toronto press conference, featuring a nonplussed Cronenberg being damned with faint praise, if that, and the famously idiotic "Mr Burroughs, have you ever done anything you regret?" sequence. Bonus interview with Barry Miles, who afaik didn't have anything to do with Cronenberg's film. The end title theme, Peter Blegvad's version of "I've Got You Under My Skin", is omitted from some prints.

Chris Rodley ed. *Cronenberg on Cronenberg* (Faber, 1992)

---

184 recording
spoken word

PRISON
Steven Jesse Bernstein

media: **CD**
released: **1992**
created:
commerce:
critical:
WSB quotient:

Steven "Jesse" Bernstein (1950 – 1991) was an American poet based in Seattle. His poetry and performances were highly regarded and acknowledged as an influence by many groups, some of which he would open for, including Big Black, Nirvana and Cows. Following WSB's successful recordings, particularly the Cobain collaboration 185, Sub-Pop suggested that Bernstein too should make a record. Sadly, before it was complete, Bernstein's personal problems overwhelmed him and he committed suicide. Bernstein was an admirer and friend of WSB and a photo of the two of them graces the sleeve of this, his only recording, which was issued posthumously.

185 recording
industrial
THE "PRIEST" THEY CALLED HIM
William Burroughs & Kurt Cobain

media: 10"/CD
released: 1992
created:
commerce: ●●●
critical: ●●●
WSB quotient: ●●●●

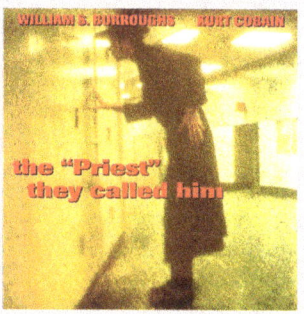

One-sided vinyl of WSB reading the piece from *Exterminator!* 45 recorded at Red House Studios, Lawrence, KS on 25 Sep. 1992 with guitar (an improvisation on *Silent Night*) by Cobain recorded in Nov. at Laundry Room Studios, Seattle, WA. Cobain was a big WSB fan and often used the cut/up method to generate lyrics. He'd visited WSB in Lawrence and asked if he'd like to play the part of the crucifixee in the video for "Heart-Shaped Box". WSB declined but if you squint you can almost see it. There was a later picture disc version of this release limited to 5000 copies, and it was remixed on the unofficial *In Extremis* CD 220.

186 recording
various
THE BEAT GENERATION
Various

media: 3CD
released: 1992
created:
commerce: ●●
critical: ●●
WSB quotient: ●

Rhino Word-Beat's deluxe follow-up to their *Jack Kerouac Collection* 168 includes all the usual suspects plus fellow travellers like Ken Nordine and Lord Buckley and music from Bob McFadden's iconic "I Belong to the Beat Generation" to Slim Gaillard and, my personal fave, the Charles Mingus / Jean Shepherd track "The Clown". WSB contributes "Naked Lunch (Excerpt)" (6:26), which is the full track "Bradley the Buyer" from *Call Me Burroughs* 11. The accompanying booklet briefly mentions WSB and reproduces the cover of the Ace edition of *Junkie* 1, erroneously noting it as "complete and unabridged".

187 recording
punk
THE LONGEST LINE
NOFX

media: 12"
released: 1992
created:
commerce: ●●●
critical: ●●
WSB quotient: ●●●

NOFX were/are a band from LA formed in 1983. They played an undemanding but unassuming style of punk that has made them one of the most successful independent groups ever. A caricature of WSB appears on the back cover sleeve of the vinyl only of this five song mini-LP. The cover art was done by Dan Sites. Others queuing include Jimi Hendrix, Salvador Dali, Jesus, Elvis, Divine, Chas Manson, The Furry Freak Bros, Venus De Milo, Tutenkhamen, Fidel Castro, Patty Hearst. Actually, their cover of "Leaving on a Jet Plane" on an earlier obscure B-side was kinda rockin'.

188 book
critical
WIRELESS IMAGINATION
Douglas Kahn & Gregory Whitehead (eds)

media: HARDBACK
released: 1992
created:
commerce: ●●●
critical: ●●●
WSB quotient: ●

This collection from MIT Press on the topic of "Sound, Radio, and the Avant-Garde" includes Robin Lydenberg's essay "Sound Identity Fading Out", a short but informed overview of WSB's tape recorder experiments. The book also has pieces on Raymond Roussel, Antonin Artaud, Marcel Duchamp, André Breton, John Cage, Hugo Ball and Kurt Weill, thus situating WSB's tape works in a historical milieu. Notwithstanding any reservations regarding the academic paradigm in general, this book has some useful applications.

189 recording
ambient

AMBIENT - 152 MINUTES 33 SECONDS
Various

- media: 2CD
- released: 1993
- created:
- commerce: ●●●
- critical: ●●
- WSB quotient: ●

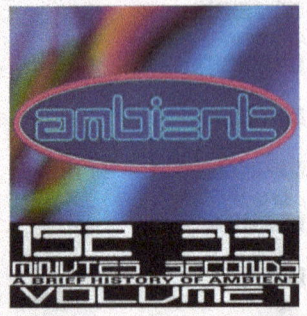

Citing John Cage, this comp attempts to contextualise the genre by associating it with cool groups like Hawkwind, Gong, Faust and Tangerine Dream alongside more expectable sources such as Harold Budd, both Enos (Brian and Roger) and Robert Fripp. For WSB fans, it has an edit of Material's "The End of Words" (3:46) from *Seven Souls* [157]. WSB's adoption by the ambient kids comes as no surprise... with hindsight.

190 film
comedy

BEAVIS AND BUTTHEAD: TORNADO
Mike Judge dir.

- media: 10M COL..
- released: 1993
- created:
- commerce: ●●●
- critical: ●●
- WSB quotient: ●

First aired 10 Sep. 1993, this episode opened with Ministry's 'Just One Fix' [181] to approving comments including "Even the old dude is cool". This show was, of course, MTV's staging of Beckett's *Waiting for Godot*, and the arrival of a clip that doesn't suck is equivalent to Godot showing up. This episode is now usually shown edited of its original pyromantic references. Also included are videos of "Balls to the Wall" (Accept), "Naughty Girls Need Love Too" (Samantha Fox), "50 ft Queenie" (P.J. Harvey).

191 recording
various

CASH COW
Various

- media: CD
- released: 1993
- created:
- commerce: ●●
- critical: ●●●
- WSB quotient: ●●●

A CD comp of the most viable tracks from GPS from 1965 to 1993, this has WSB reading "The Do Rights / The Laboratory Has Been Locked for 3 Hours Solid" (5:58) from YT-GIWTSMMW [68] and *Big Ego* [62]. Also contributions from earlier volumes by Cabaret Voltaire, Debbie Harry, Buster Poindexter, John Giorno, Hüsker Dü, Laurie Anderson, Philip Glass, Patti Smith, Coil, Diamanda Galas, Glenn Branca and Frank Zappa. The booklet features many photos of WSB with the other contributors.

192 film
comedy

EVEN COWGIRLS GET THE BLUES
Gus Van Sant dir.

- media: 95M COL..
- released: 1993
- created:
- commerce: ●
- critical: ●

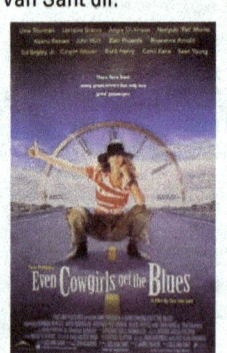

Van Sant had followed his debut *Drugstore Cowboy* [150] with the even bigger hit *My Own Private Idaho* but bombed relatively with this all-star adaptation of Tom Robbin's lauded novel which has WSB's last albeit tiny big screen cameo. Van Sant returned to the limelight with 1997's oscar-winning *Good Will Hunting* which was dedicated to WSB and Allen Ginsberg, both of whom had recently died.

193	**film**
	comedy

KIKA
Pedro Almodóvar dir.

media	
114M COL..	
released	
1993	
created	

commerce
critical
WSB quotient

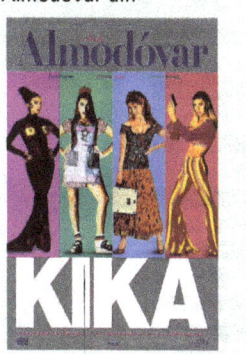

Given the polymorphous transgressive nature of Almodóvar's films, it's odd there aren't more WSB references beyond the one near the start of this film here where one of the characters makes a reference to the death of Joan Vollmer.

194	**recording**
	hip hop

SPARE ASS ANNIE AND OTHER TALES
William Burroughs

media	
CD	
released	
1993	
created	

commerce
critical
WSB quotient

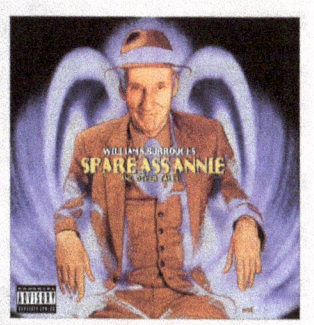

Hal Willner followed up the success of *Dead City Radio* `162` by getting Michael Franti's outfit The Disposable Heroes of Hiphoprisy to drop some beats over WSB readings. What seemed like an ace idea unfortunately rendered patchy results, not least as WSB's voice has been chopped to match the beats and his distinctive meter is lost. The LP includes a version of "Words of Advice" (4:41), a piece that had appeared on *Smack my Crack* `137` and in *Decoder* `110`. Now it would be remixed for *The Operator's Manual* `198` and the *Words of Advice* 12" `201` in a desperate attempt to give WSB a college radio hit that kinda worked. Oh... and the cover is awful.

195	**recording**
	electro

TECHNODON
Yellow Magic Orchestra

media	
CD	
released	
1993	
created	

commerce
critical
WSB quotient

Seminal Japanese electro outfit, comprising of Haruomi Hosono, Yukihiro Takahashi and Riyuichi Sakamoto, that formed in 1977 and went on influence the development of synthpop, ambient, j-pop, techno, hip-hop etc. This is regarded as their most accessible disc and WSB samples can be heard on the tracks "Be a Superman" and "I Tre Merli". Apropos of nothing, there's a famous photo of TG where Genesis P-Orridge is wearing a YMO shirt. See?

196	**recording**
	leide

THE BLACK RIDER
Tom Waits

media	
LP/CD	
released	
1993	
created	

commerce
critical
WSB quotient

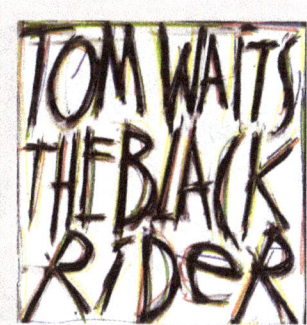

Tom Waits recorded versions of tunes from his musical collaboration `166` with Robert Wilson and WSB, who contributes guest vocals to "'T' Ain't No Sin" (2:35), and co-wrote three others. This official issue had been preceded by bootlegs of Waits' 1990 demos (including WSB's track) on Alka Seltzer records. Bootleg vinyl copies of the official release also surfaced after it was deleted.

197 film — animation
THE JUNKY'S CHRISTMAS
Nick Donkin & Melodie McDaniel dir.

- media: 21M B/W
- released: 1993
- created:
- commerce:
- critical:
- WSB quotient:

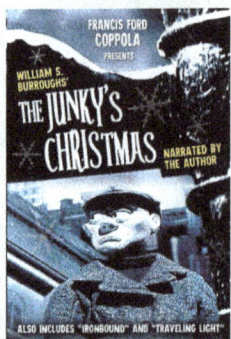

First aired on VH-1, Xmas Eve, 1993, this wonderful claymation promo for the track from *Spare Ass Annie* 194 (originally in *Interzone* 155) is probably as close to Frank Capra as WSB ever got. The film opens in a classic "Ghost Story at Christmas" fashion with live footage of WSB at home in his Xmas decorated pad and closes with him celebrating with a bunch of friends, and the only known footage of WSB carving a turkey. Poignant as all fuck.

198 recording — hip hop
THE OPERATOR'S MANUAL
William Burroughs

- media: CD
- released: 1993
- created:
- commerce:
- critical:
- WSB quotient:

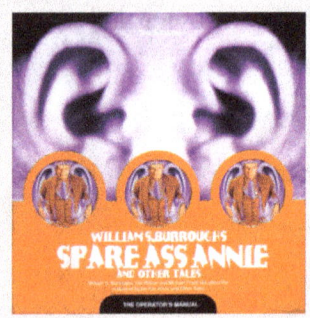

A radio promo for the *Spare Ass Annie* LP 194. Hal Willner, Michael Franti and WSB talk about the making of the album over extracts of tunes for about an hour, then there are three radio jingles followed by two remixes of "Words of Advice...", the Pete Arden "Round the World" mix (8:37) (check content before airing!) and the "Interzone Radio Edit" (4.28).

199 recording — psyche
TWELVE SELVES
Daevid Allen

- media: CD
- released: 1993
- created:
- commerce:
- critical:
- WSB quotient:

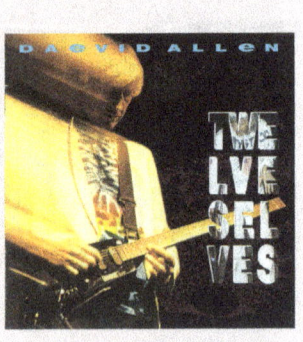

Daevid Allen (b. 1938), aka Divided Alien, had been a resident of the Beat Hotel 317 and got to know WSB in London in the early sixties, performing parts of *The Ticket That Exploded* 6 on stage before cofounding the Soft Machine 25 and going on to form the Gong collective in 1970. In 1981 Allen returned to his native Melbourne (Australia) and went on to make heaps more records. The one here includes the cut "Collage Patafisico / Divided Alien Manifesto" (5:39) which apparently has a WSB sample but I haven't been able to track it down.

200 recording — spoken word
VAUDEVILLE VOICES
William Burroughs

- media: CD
- released: 1993
- created: 1965
- commerce:
- critical:
- WSB quotient:

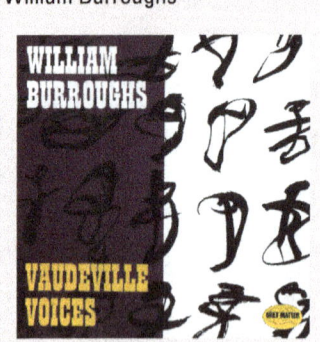

A probably unofficial CD reissue of the then-unavailable *Call Me Burroughs* LP 11 along with *Ali's Smile* 27. Some track names are incorrect and it sounds like it was mastered from a vinyl copy but at least the packaging is neat, reproducing several photos including the Mapplethorpe shot.

201 recording
hip hop
WORDS OF ADVICE FOR YOUNG PEOPLE
William Burroughs

media: 12"
released: 1993
created:
commerce: ●●●
critical: ●●●
WSB quotient: ●●●●

"From the Beat Generation to the generation of big big beats", this disc collects six (count em) remixes from the *Spare Ass Annie* LP 194. All tracks remixed by Bill Laswell except "(Round The World Mix)" remixed by Pete Arden, which crops up on *Big Hard Disk 2* 204. Ingredients: Interzone Radio Edit (4:28) / Mutatis Mutandis Radio Edit (3:43) / Round the World Mix (8:01) / Interzone Extended Mix (6:14) / Mutatis Mutandis Lemurs in the Mist Interzone Mix (8:37) / Mutatis Mutandis Mix (4:34)

202 recording
country/folk
WORLD TURNING
Tony Trischka

media: CD
released: 1993
created:
commerce: ●●
critical: ●●
WSB quotient: ●

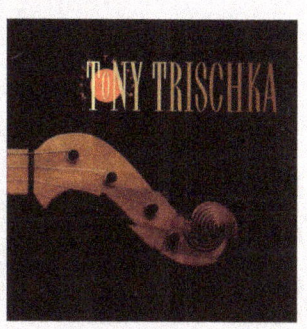

Tony Trischka (b. 1949) is a US banjo-player, widely seen as its leading exponent. This LP explores the divergent potential of this misunderstood instrument and WSB provides a suitably poignant narration on the track "The Boatman's Dance/Over the Mountains" (3.13).

203 film
animation
AH POOK IS HERE
Philip Hunt dir.

media: 6M COL..
released: 1994
created:
commerce: ●●
critical: ●●●
WSB quotient: ●●●●

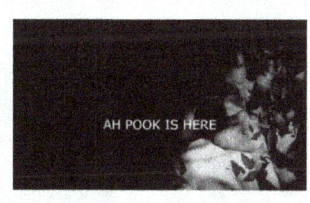

There's some amazing stop-motion work in this clip derived from the John Cale 22 scored track off *Dead City Radio* 162, originally from the aborted Malcolm McNeill graphic novel 65. the film puts me in mind of a goth or industrial take on Oliver Postgate's groundbreaking work, especially *The Clangers*, but I reckon Vernon Sullivan's music wins hands down. I understand that others may feel differently.

204 recording
electro
BIG HARD DISK VOL. 2
Various

media: CD/CC
released: 1994
created:
commerce: ●●●
critical: ●●●
WSB quotient: ●

Any hacker worth their salt will spew over the oxymoronic title of this comp: "disk" being an abbreviation of "diskette", a flexible magnetic medium, rather than a mere alternate spelling of "disc". The purpose of the comp appears to be to collect 12 inch mixes into a CD format, and here WSB fans get "Words of Advice for Young People (Pete Arden Mix)" (8:04) from *Words of Advice* 201 plus tracks from Sheep on Drugs, Yello, Grace Jones, The Orb and a remix of a non-WSB Material track "Mantra" from *Hallucination Engine* 207.

205 recording — psyche
DREAMSPEED
Anton Fier

- media: CD
- released: 1994
- created:
- commerce: ●●
- critical: ●●
- WSB quotient: ●

Anton Fier (b. 20 Jun. 1956) is an American drummer, composer and band leader. He was an early member of The Lounge Lizards and The Feelies, worked with Pere Ubu, was briefly in the Voidoids with Richard Hell, and founded The Golden Palominos. Fier has toured and recorded with Bob Mould (ex-Hüsker Dü), and played drums on Laurie Anderson's 'Sharkey's Night' 103. This record, executive produced by John Zorn and featuring Fier's frequent collaborator Bill Laswell, opens with a short WSB quote "I'm all turned around you know" on the title track.

206 film — experimental
GLITTERBUG
Derek Jarman dir.

- media: 60M COL..
- released: 1994
- created: 1970s–
- commerce: ●●
- critical: ●●
- WSB quotient: ●●

Derek Jarman (1942-1994) was an English writer, activist and film-maker, best known for *Sebastianne* (1976), *Jubilee* (1977) and *Caravaggio* (1986). He ranks amongst the most radical film-makers England has produced. This was his final film, a compilation of Super 8 diary footage set to a soundtrack by Brian Eno, It includes brief fragments shot at The Final Academy 97 and not found on *Pirate Tape* 104, including the only known shots of WSB signing an autograph for someone other than Andy Warhol.

207 recording — electro
HALLUCINATION ENGINE
Material

- media: CD
- released: 1994
- created:
- commerce: ●●●
- critical: ●●
- WSB quotient: ●

This predominantly instrumental LP, recorded with a similar line-up to *Seven Souls* 157 but this time with Bootsy Collins (!) on "space bass", includes yet another version of WSB's 'Words of Advice' (3:58). The cover features nice mylar photography by Ira Cohen.

208 recording — spoken word
HOLY SOUL JELLY ROLL
Allen Ginsberg

- media: 4CD/4CC
- released: 1994
- created:
- commerce: ●●●
- critical: ●●●
- WSB quotient: ●●

This deluxe four-disc set is the Ginsberg analogue of WSB's GPS box 244. Another release in Rhino's Word Beat series, following their Kerouac 160 and Beat Generation 186 boxes, WSB again provides notes for the booklet.

209 recording — metal 🇬🇧
NOWHERE
Therapy?

- media: 7"/CC/CD
- released: 1994
- created:
- commerce: ●●
- critical: ●●
- WSB quotient: ●

A heavy metal group formed in Belfast in 1989. The b-side (or primary supporting track) on this single is a song called "Pantopon Rose", which takes its title from an addict mentioned in *Junkie* and *Naked Lunch* The song contains no obvious WSB reference and it may be surmised that the group were mainly interested in tapping into the WSB heroin-chic current. It also seems likely that another of the group's tunes, "Junkie Nurse", is a reference to the WSB quote "some junkie nurse is skimping on my medication."

210 multimedia — spoken word 🇺🇸
POETRY IN MOTION
Ron Mann

- media: CD-ROM
- released: 1994
- created:
- commerce: ●●
- critical: ●●
- WSB quotient: ●●

An interactive version of Ron Mann's 1982 film 93, allowing the viewer to view a reading or interview together with the text of the relevant poem at the same time. Given that (a) performing poets generally annunciate adequately, and (b) poetry is a textual medium with one spatial axis, there seems little advantage to this random-access approach beyond that the playlist can be shuffled, which is in any case a feature of the DVD version. Potentially exploitable in a classroom context. There's also a volume 2 with the other poets from the movie who aren't on this one. This was released by Voyager Interactive who also did *The Beat Experience* CD-Rom 229.

211 film — documentary 🇬🇧
EINSTEIN'S BRAIN
Kevin Hull dir.

- media: 65M COL..
- released: 1994
- created:
- commerce: ●●
- critical: ●●
- WSB quotient: ●●

The literally mind-boggling story of Kenji Sugimoto, professor in Maths and Science history at Kinki University in Japan, and his pilgrimage to the US to locate Einstein's brain. This turns out to be harder than might be expected and the resulting quest is incredible and poignant. It hits its zenith of oddness when Prof. Sugimoto winds up in Lawrence and has a nice chat with WSB who coincidentally happens to be watching the nukesploitation movie *The Day After*. Actually the film does get even odder after that, ending with a cerebral serenade (a cerebrade?) in a karaoke bar. The film is so strange it is sometimes taken as a hoax, but it probably isn't.

212 film — music 🇨🇦
SEPTEMBER SONGS
Larry Weinstein dir.

- media: 91M COL..
- released: 1994
- created:
- commerce: ●●
- critical: ●●
- WSB quotient: ●●

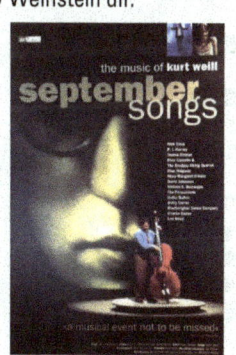

Hal Willner had put together 1985's *Lost in the Stars* Kurt Weill tribute album, and here reprises his role as music supervisor for this award-winning feature-length musical tribute to the German composer. Performers here include Elvis Costello, Lou Reed, David Johansen, Nick Cave, P.J. Harvey, Teresa Stratas, Lotte Lenya, Betty Carter, The Persuasions, Stan Ridgway, and WSB doing "What Keeps Mankind Alive?" (2:45). His vocal sits nicely with the Weill-style instrumentation and I like to think of this as a postscript to his tv spot for Nike 216. A CD version 235 was issued a few years later.

213 recording — electro
THE GREATEST SHOW OF TRUTH
The Sacred Sawdust Ring

media: CD
released: 1994
created:
commerce: ●●
critical: ●
WSB quotient: ●

Put together by producer Ken Thomas, who had worked with groups including Psychic TV, Clock DVA and David Bowie, this disc included WSB samples (from "Twilights Last Gleamings") on "The Wicker Man Song" (4:25) by WSB and Coco which is, as might be expected, a version of "Willow's Song" from the film *The Wicker Man*. The disc was limited to 888 copies and also had contributions from Katie Jane Garside & Crispin Gray, David Tibet & Harry Oldfield, Von Magnet, Coco, Jayne County, Patti Palladin (Snatch), Francois Testory, Jolyon Thomas, and Samuel Mills.

214 film — documentary
THE LIFE & TIMES OF ALLEN GINSBERG
Jerry Aronson dir.

media: 82M COL..
released: 1994
created:
commerce: ●●●
critical: ●●●
WSB quotient: ●●

Twenty-five years in the making, Aronson's comprehensive doco is hard to fault. Ginsberg apparently liked it. As well as archive material there's a fair bit of original footage of WSB, recorded 1984, talking with and about Ginsberg. It was reissued in 2007 as a two-disc set including extra interviews (including WSB) and extra footage of Ginsberg and WSB..

215 recording — industrial
THE MYTHS COLLECTION PART TWO
Various

media: CD
released: 1994
created:
commerce: ●
critical: ●
WSB quotient: ●

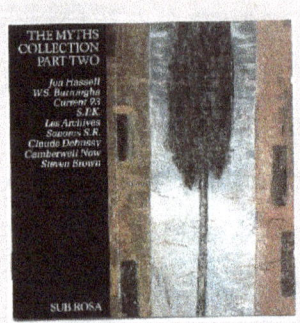

Another entry in Sub Rosa's *Myths* series 112 includes "Burroughs Called the Law" (1:30) from their BTIGR CD 124. Plus Steven Brown, SPK, Current 93, Camberwell Now, Jon Hassell, Claude Debussy, and Sub Rosa Mixed Archives.

216 film — advert
NIKE ADS
Wieden & Kennedy Agency

media: 60S COL..
released: 1994
created:
commerce: ●●●●
critical: ●●
WSB quotient: ●●●

There were two different spots for Nike Corp, both using "The Things That I Used to Do" by G-Love and Special Sauce as a backing track and featuring sweaty athletic jock types. The ads caused a degree of internet angst amongst some WSB fans who saw them as a corporate sell-out. Well, WSB had warned us several years before that "all agents defect and all resistors sell out" but coming so soon after Cronenberg's lame film 171, the ads helped me kick my oil-burner WSB habit. Although WSB never publicly commented on them, I like to take his contemporanous Kurt Weill cover 212 as a comment.

217	**recording**
	hip hop

CLEAR
Bomb The Bass

- media: LP/CD
- released: 1995
- created:
- commerce: ●●
- critical: ●●
- WSB quotient: ●

Nom-de-guerre of Tim Simenon who exploded into the UK charts in 1987 with "Beat Dis", one of the most influential sample-based records of the time. With a title straight outta Scientology, his third LP could almost qualify as a WSB concept album, riddled as it is with more or less tenuous WSB connections. "Bug Powder Dust" samples Cronenberg's film 171 and Justin Warfield's masterful rap declaims all kinds of Burroughsian excess. Personnel on the album include Keith LeBlanc 126, Doug Wimbish 297 and it samples from Mark Stewart's "The Wrong Name And The Wrong Number" 112. I could go on. It's pretty cool.

218	**film**
	comedy

CLUELESS
Amy Heckerling dir.

- media: 97M COL..
- released: 1995
- created:
- commerce: ●●●
- critical: ●●●
- WSB quotient: ●

WSB was a big Jane Austen fan. It would be interesting to know what he would have made of this teen adaptation of *Emma* set in modern-day Beverly Hills. Not much WSB here, although in one scene a character is seen reading a copy of *Junky*. I was gobsmacked that I kinda didn't entirely hate it, and didn't storm out or puke once. Weird but there you go. The tradition of putting WSB books in films started in 1969 with Antony Balch's *Secrets of Sex* 30, continued in *Performance* 31 and reached apotheosis in my own *The Naked Lunch and the Naked The Naked Lunch* in 2008.

219	**recording**
	rock

COUGH IT UP! THE HAIRBALL STORY
Various

- media: CD
- released: 1995
- created:
- commerce: ●●
- critical: ●●
- WSB quotient: ●●

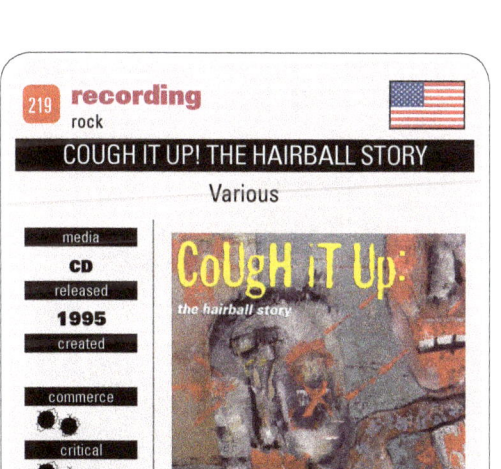

Interesting! A comp of tunes recorded by JWG at his Hairball home-studio, where *Dead City Radio* 162 was recorded. JWG was a decorated veteran of the punk wars, having lived next to CBGB's in NYC and produced The Mortal Micronotz LP 98. He found willing subjects amongst the college-punk kids when he moved back to Lawrence and, outside of KS, the biggest name here would be the Eudoras 225, but there's also half of Manapsara 145 and JWG's own group Tank Farm. WSB provides "Mr Rich Parts" (6:02) outside broadcast recorded from Terra Nova Bookstore, Lawrence, early 1995. The copious notes by JWG are prophetic; I paid A$5 for my copy.

220	**recording**
	electro

IN EXTREMIS (THE REMIXES)
Nirvana

- media: CD
- released: 1995
- created:
- commerce: ●
- critical: ●
- WSB quotient: ●

Awesomely genius example of the unofficial trance remix CD scene of the mid-nineties, book-ended between the Great KLF Deletion and *The Grey Album*. WSB appears on two tracks here: "They Called Him The Priest / Come as You Are (Radio Dog's Reservoir Mix)" (5:51) which is self-explanatory, and on "In Bloom (Stupid Fucking Club Mix)" (9:29) sampled from *Call Me Burroughs* 11. Guaranteed to get any party moving twenty years ago. You could see peeps roll their eyes when they thought it was a straight Nirvana disc you'd put on, and then, as one, let out a rousing collective "What the fuck!!!??" as we used to say back then.

221 book / journals

MY EDUCATION
William Burroughs

media: **HARDBACK**
released: **1995**
created: **1959-92**
commerce
critical
WSB quotient

 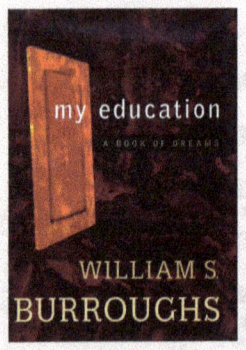

WSB's dream journal. Although dreams were a rich source of material for his writing, none of the entries here found their way into audio-visual performances, which is strange as most of the book is eminently filmic. WSB was an advocate of J.W. Dunne's theories of serialism that contend that dreams afford a higher-dimensional viewpoint that allows past and future impressions to co-occupy the focus of attention. I urge all WSB fans to read Dunne's *An Experiment With Time* at the earliest opportunity, or try *Nothing Dies* if that one looks a bit hard, or *The Serial Universe* if it looks easy.

222 multimedia / experimental

PANTOPON ROSE
Andrea di Castro

media: **CD-ROM**
released: **1995**
created
commerce
critical
WSB quotient

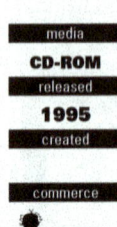 

Bilingual CD-Rom focussed on WSB in Mexico. Various sections present historic photos and press clippings, a biblio/filmo/discography, paintings (the Seven Deadly Sins series) via an attractive point-and-click interface. Given its Mexican origin, some of the material is unfamiliar but, like all popular multimedia, it's really aimed at the neophyte. The music, by Rosino Serrano, is very effective.

223 multimedia / animation

THE DARK EYE
Russell Lees.

media: **CD-ROM**
released: **1995**
created
commerce
critical
WSB quotient

WSB is the main voice actor in this point-and-click adventure that has gained cult status. The game unusually used stop-motion style animation and looks similar to *The Junky's Christmas* 197 short. The action is based around the stories of Edgar Allen Poe and, as well as in-game dialogue, WSB reads Poe's poem "Annabel Lee" (2:00) and story "The Masque of the Red Death" (15:55), the latter with music by Thomas Dolby.

224 recording / jazz

THE HEART/HERTZ FILES
Klange

media: **CD**
released: **1995**
created
commerce
critical
WSB quotient

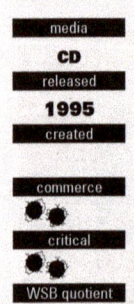 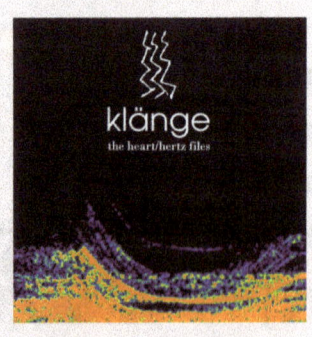

Italian ambient electronica on Minus Habens Records, the debut release from this outfit (actually I think it's just one guy) who are still around today. WSB samples from the *Commissioner of Sewers* 170 soundtrack appear on "Hypnosis Under Revelations" (3:49).

225	**recording**
	punk

THE MORTAL MICRONOTZ TRIBUTE!

Various

media: CD
released: 1995
created:
commerce: ●●●
critical: ●●
WSB quotient: ●

Compilation of mostly Lawrence, KS-based groups do versions of tunes by the local heroes 98. WSB joins up with The Eudoras for a version of "Old Lady Sloan" (3:02), which he'd originally penned the words for, and it's almost as if he's trying to sing. JWG provides a version of "Day after Day". Other groups here are: Mopar Funeral, Truck Stop Love, Shower Trick, Five-O, Beef Eaters, Means To An End, Sufferbus, Kill Creek, Stick, Slackjaw, Bubble Boys. None of that means shit to me. Sorry.

226	**recording**
	various

10%: FILE UNDER BURROUGHS

Various

media: 2CD
released: 1996
created:
commerce: ●●●
critical: ●●
WSB quotient: ●●●●

Comp put out by Joe Ambrose and Frank Rynne to complement the *Destroy All Rational Thought* video 238. WSB contributes "For Here to Go" (5:20), a recording of his reminiscences about Gysin (also used in the video), and the motley and mostly-star cast includes Bomb the Bass 217, Material 157, John Cale 118, Paul Bowles 239, Herbert Hunke and more. The first disc ("beats") is electro dance type stuff, mostly of an ambient bent with sporadic joujouka overtones. The second ("beat") is songs and recordings set to music. The set got savagely panned as self-indulgent on release but I reckon it's pretty cool in parts.

227	**recording**
	spoken word

NAKED LUNCH (AUDIOBOOK)

William Burroughs

media: 3CD/2CC
released: 1996
created:
commerce: ●●●●
critical: ●●●
WSB quotient: ●●●●●

The first full-length (approx. three hours) WSB audiobook, abridged by Nelson Lyon with WSB's approval. Recorded early 1995, and produced by Hal Willner and James Grauerholz with music by Bill Frisell, Eyvind Kang, Wayne Horvitz. An unabridged version 306, read by Mark Bramall, was issued in 2009.

228	**recording**
	rock

SONGS IN THE KEY OF X

Various

media: CD
released: 1996
created:
commerce: ●●●●
critical: ●●●
WSB quotient: ●●

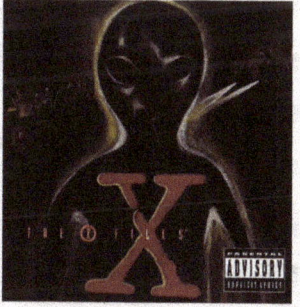

A CD spin-off of the then-popular sf tv show *The X-Files*. Inspired by Marlene Dietrich, WSB provides vocals for a version of REM's "Star Me Kitten" (3:30) earning the disc a Parental Advisory warning. Michael Stipe of REM was an self-confessed WSB fan and had visited him in Lawrence with Kim Gordon of Sonic Youth. He also appeared with Patti Smith at The Nova Convention Revisited event 246. Getting back to the disc, we also have the (ex-Nirvana 220) Foo Fighters doing a version of Gary Numan's 72 *Down in the Park* plus a bunch of other stuff.

1996

229 multimedia
documentary

THE BEAT EXPERIENCE
Red Hot Organization

media: CD-ROM
released: 1996

A CD-Rom produced by Voyager Interactive and The Red Hot Organization in conjunction with the Whitney Museum of American Art's comprehensive "Beat Culture and the New America: 1950-1965" exhibition. It's kinda fun for a little while, you get to explore a beatnik pad and can view short postage stamp size videos or readings. There's some WSB content including snippets of Antony Balch footage. Same folks who did the *Poetry in Motion* 210 CD-Rom.

230 film
documentary

THE MAN WHO INVENTED MODERN SEX
Clare Beavan dir.

media: 50M COL..
released: 1996

THIS SPACE
INTENTIONALLY
LEFT BLANK

This was an episode (s3e4) of the BBC series *Reputations* examining Alfred Kinsey, the noted sex researcher. I cannot find out anything about it, I'm afraid, but according to Herbert Huncke, quoted in Ted Morgan's *Literary Outlaw*, WSB was interviewed by Alfred Kinsey in 1946 for his study into male sexuality, and his sexual history and penis size (flaccid and erect) were entered on file at his institute.

1997

231 recording
jazz

COMMUNIQUÉ
Steve Lacy & Mal Waldron

media: CD
released: 1997

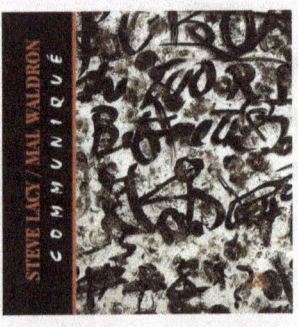

Steve Lacy (1934 – 2004) is remembered as one of greatest soprano saxophonists. He was a long-time friend of Brion Gysin and had worked with him on six songs for Antony Balch's unrealised film of *Naked Lunch* 2 and some other recordings. WSB provided the cover painting for this well-received release, and Lacy went on to do a sound portrait of WSB on his 1999 CD *Sands*, and a further track based on *Naked Lunch* on his 2003 *Beat Suite*.

232 recording
spoken word

JUNKY (AUDIOBOOK)
William Burroughs

media: 2CC
released: 1997

Unlike the scarce *Naked Lunch* audiobook 227, this Penguin version was very widely available until the switching over of in-car stereos from cassette to CD led to its being issued on in a three-disc set, with a different cover, in 1997.

233 recording — spoken word 🇺🇸
KEROUAC - KICKS JOY DARKNESS
Various

- media: CD/CC
- released: 1997
- created:
- commerce: ●●●
- critical: ●●
- WSB quotient: ●

Well, here's an oddity, a beatnik tribute album not overseen by Hal Willner. The all-star cast includes original beats (Ginsberg, Ferlinghetti and WSB), fellow travellers (Hunter S Thompson, Jim Carroll, Patti Smith, Lydia Lunch, John Cale, Sonic Youth), Rock Stars (Steven Tyler, Eddie Vedder) and movie stars (Matt Dillon, Johnny Depp). What could possibly go wrong? I'm not terribly sure. WSB reads Kerouac's "Old Western Movies" (2:32) with backing from Tom Hajdu & Andy Milburn who did the soundtrack for *The Mothman Prophecies*. I reckon the album is a crock of shit but I'm not that massively into Kerouac so others may like it.

234 book — critical 🇬🇧
NAKED LENS
Jack Sargeant

- media: PAPERBACK
- released: 1997
- created:
- commerce: ●●
- critical: ●●●
- WSB quotient: ●●

You have no business reading my nonsense here if you haven't already digested Jack Sargeant's fine book. There's a wealth of WSB info here. The coverage of Balch is especially excellent with Sargeant's notes complimented by an account by Genesis P-Orridge and a reprint of Arthur Cantrill's rare 1983 interview with Gysin. Also treated at length are *Chappaqua* 24, *Decoder* 110 (via a great interview with Klaus Maeck), and other beat-vehicles, with an emphasis on the more underground stuff. There are comprehensively annotated filmographies and appendices. I tried to avoid checking this too frequently or I would have hoovered up the whole shithouse!

235 recording — leide 🇨🇦
SEPTEMBER SONGS
Various

- media: CD
- released: 1997
- created:
- commerce: ●●●●
- critical: ●●
- WSB quotient: ●

An audio version of the 1994 Kurt Weill tribute film 232. WSB reprises "What Keeps Mankind Alive" (2.46) which sits alongside his version of "Falling in Love Again" on *Dead City Radio* 162 and *The Black Rider* 196 as his contribution to the German leide tradition. If anyone cares, Stan Ridgway was in the film but is missing from the line-up here. Hmmm...

236 film — drama 🇦🇺
XTRMN8MM
David Cox dir.

- media: 3M B/W
- released: 1997
- created:
- commerce: ●
- critical: ●
- WSB quotient: ●

Predating Primal Scream's 2000 album *XTRMNTR*, Dave shot this Jarmanesque romp of me in WSB drag drifting through Melbourne on his last reels of Super 8. Watch out for: Irving Gribbish's lab, The Monument to the Thing With No Name, Bernard's Magic Shop, the Domed Reading Room, a subterranean public convenience in Carlton, Harris's since-discharged gun shop etc. I got home to find that WSB had died from a heart attack during the filming. True. There a few versions of this circulating, most with "Demons of the Undergroove" by the WSB-citing Invisible Generation on the soundtrack.

1998

237 recording — spoken word 🇬🇧
CYBER-SADISM LIVE!
Stewart Home

- media: CD
- released: 1998
- created: —
- commerce: ●●
- critical: ●●●
- WSB quotient: ●

If WSB is the underground's Elvis of Letters that would make Stewart Home its Cliff Richard which is just stupid. Home's confronting and compelling oeuvre includes novels, cultural/political critique, experimental films, exhibitions, performance and shit there's not even words for yet. This spoken-word disc contains the track "William Burroughs in Hell" (0:55) recorded at the ICA, London 28 Oct. 1997. His mother, Julia Callan-Thompson, appears briefly in *Cain's Film* [28], and it may be fair to say that Home finds much more in Alex Trocchi than in WSB.

MORE: www.stewarthomesociety.org (25 Aug. 2013)

238 film — documentary 🇮🇪
DESTROY ALL RATIONAL THOUGHT
Joe Ambrose, Frank Rynne & Terry Wilson dirs.

- media: 60M COL..
- released: 1998
- created: 1992
- commerce: ●●
- critical: ●●
- WSB quotient: ●●●

Documenting The Here to Go Show, a festival organised by Wilson, Ambrose and Rynne in Dublin to celebrate the legacy of Brion Gysin and to mark WSB's 80th birthday. The film has one of the last filmed interviews with WSB and some great previously unavailable Anthony Balch footage. Also here are The Master Musicians of Joujouka, Bill Laswell, The Baby Snakes, Ira Cohen, Hakim Bey, Brian Downey (ex-Thin Lizzy) and many more. The show is pretty much stolen by Hamri The Painter of Morocco who charms and embarrasses the audience in equal measure. The disc had a mixed reception but, as a souvenir of the events, it's worth it.

239 film — documentary 🇨🇦
LET IT COME DOWN
Jennifer Baichwal dir.

- media: 75M COL..
- released: 1998
- created: —
- commerce: ●●
- critical: ●●
- WSB quotient: ●●●

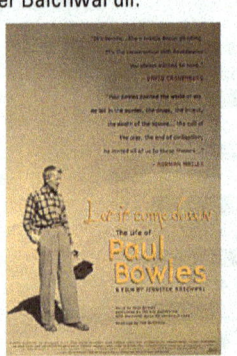

This well-received doco on the life of Paul Bowles (1910-1999) mixes archival footage with interviews from WSB, Allen Ginsberg and other beat-era writers who knew Bowles and his wife Jane during their fifty years in Morocco. Bowles advised WSB prior to the publication of *Junkie* and *Naked Lunch* and his recollections of WSB in Tangier are well worth seeking out, as are photos of the era, some of which include rare snaps of Ian Sommerville. Bowles was also a talented musician, a story told in the *Night Music* doco [259].

240 film — documentary 🇺🇸
MODULATIONS: CINEMA FOR THE EAR
Iara Lee dir.

- media: 75M COL..
- released: 1998
- created: —
- commerce: ●●
- critical: ●●●
- WSB quotient: ●●

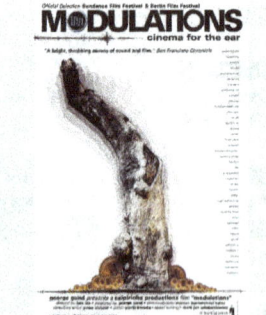

"Recalling All Active Agents" from BTIGR [124] opens this doco that "traces the evolution of electronic music as one of the most profound artistic developments of the 20th century". There's an interview with Genesis P-Orridge where he refers to the significance of cut/ups, although not specifically to Gysin or WSB. The stellar line-up of contributors includes Arthur Baker, Afrika Bambaataa, Carl Cox, Derrick May, Robert Moog, Giorgio Moroder, DJ Spooky and Karlheinz Stockhausen. The film was produced and directed by Korean-Brazilian activist Iara Lee, whose biography is well worth a look.

241 recording — hip hop

NEGRO NECRO NEKROS
Dälek

- media: LP/CD
- released: 1998
- created:
- commerce: ●●
- critical: ●●
- WSB quotient: ●

Not to be confused with the eighties synth group Dalek I Love You, this NJ experimental hip-hop dude is a mate of Techno Animal who worked with WSB on the *Hashisheen* 252 CD. Here, his track "Images of .44 Casings" (10:27) loops WSB's "Images, millions of images. That's what I eat..." from "Inflexible Authority" on *Call Me Burroughs* 11 to good effect. It's simultaneously creepy and groovy as all fuck. I really dig this but the disc is deleted now and getting pricey on the internet. Bah!

242 recording — spoken word

ONE NIGHT @ THE 1001
Brion Gysin

- media: 2CD
- released: 1998
- created:
- commerce: ●●
- critical: ●●●
- WSB quotient: ●

In 1953 Brion Gysin opened a restaurant, The 1001 Nights, in Tangiers, and engaged The Master Musicians of Jajouka 39 to play an extended residency. The first disc here includes remastered recordings of some of those performances. The second disc is a reading, by Gysin and WSB, of Gysin's "Dila-loo", an invocation based on the rites of Pan, with electronic backing by Ramuntcho Matta.

243 recording — spoken word

SELECTIONS FROM THE BEST OF WSB FROM GPS
William Burroughs

- media: CD
- released: 1998
- created:
- commerce: ●●●
- critical: ●●
- WSB quotient: ●●●●

A 23 (!) minute long recursive compilation promo for *The Best of WSB from GPS* box set 244 included with hardcover edition of *Word Virus* 250. Tracks included are "Twilight's Last Gleamings", "The Unworthy Vessel" and "The Name is Clem Snide" all from YTGIWTSMMW 88, "Dr. Benway is Operating in an Auditorium" and "My Protagonist Kim Carson" from *WSB/John Giorno* 54, "Roosevelt After Inauguration" from *The Nova Convention* 73, "The Mummy Piece" from *Life is a Killer* 91, and a short excerpt from "The Last Words of Hassan Sabbah" on NHNBTR 81.

244 recording — spoken word

THE BEST OF WSB FROM GPS
William Burroughs

- media: 4CD
- released: 1998
- created:
- commerce: ●●●
- critical: ●●●
- WSB quotient: ●●●●●

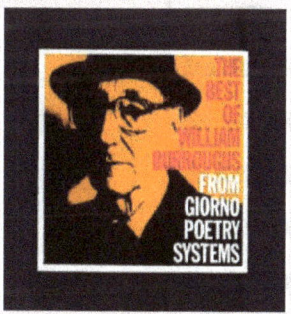

It does what it says on the packet, which was nominated for the 1999 Grammy for Best Boxed Recording Package but lost to Hank Williams. Includes cuts from *The Dial-A-Poem Poets* 44, YTGIWTSMMW 88, *WSB/John Giorno* 54, *The Nova Convention* 73, *Big Ego* 62, *Sugar, Alcohol & Meat* 76, *Totally Corrupt* 57, BOTTOAC 51, *You're a Hook* 116, *Life is a Killer* 91, ADHITMOAC 117, *Smack My Crack* 137, LAGIWYTKC 156, BAODTANG 109 together with some unreleased stuff and a long-awaited reissue of NHNBTR 81. The deluxe booklet has many unpublished photos and essays by John Giorno, JWG and David Gates plus WSB texts.

245 film — drama
THE BOOK OF LIFE
Hal Hartley dir.

media: 63M COL..
released: 1998
created:
commerce:
critical:
WSB quotient:

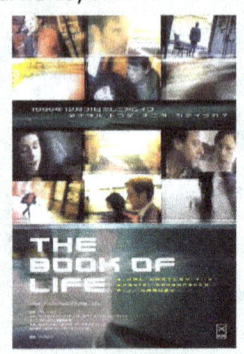

WSB's first posthumous film role was in this run-of-the-millennium tale about Christ returning for the rapture. It stars Martin Donovan as Jesus and chanteuse P.J. Harvey as Mary Magdalene as they wander round NYC opening the seven seals and angst about shit. WSB appears in voice only (for one minute) on the radio as a preacher giving a sermon about the imminent apocalypse. The film is obviously low-budget and has a student film vibe to it in parts. As might be expected given the subject matter it's overbearingly portentous, but all this is mitigated by the final frames which, like many NYC films of the time, lend it some retrospective gravity.

246 film — documentary
THE NOVA CONVENTION REVISITED
John Aes-Nihil dir.

media: UNKNOWN
released: 1998
created: 1996
commerce:
critical:
WSB quotient:

THIS SPACE INTENTIONALLY LEFT BLANK

On 26 Nov. 1996 The Lied Center at the University of Kansas hosted a reunion of participants from the Nova Convention 73. Guest performers included: Patti Smith (who played with Michael Stipe), Lenny Kaye, Deborah Harry and Chris Stein, John Giorno, Philip Glass, Laurie Anderson, and Ed Sanders. It was to be WSB's last public performance. Parts of the event were video-taped (by John Aes-Nihil who had made the cult-hit *Manson Family Movies*) and received limited release but reviews were critical of the quality of the recordings.

247 recording — electro
THE ROAD TO THE WESTERN LANDS
Material

media: 2LP/CD
released: 1998
created:
commerce:
critical:
WSB quotient:

Two new remixes of "Seven Souls" and five of "The Western Lands" from Material's *Seven Souls* 157. The mixes are by Bill Laswell himself and Talvin Singh, DJ Soul Slinger, Spring Heel Jack, The Audio Janitor (aka DJ Olive). Whereas the original was basically a spoken word release with musical backing, here the music takes prominence over the words, making the disc more accessible and likely to see rotation.

248 film — sf
VENUS BLUE
Gillian Ashurst dir.

media: 11M COL..
released: 1998
created:
commerce:
critical:
WSB quotient:

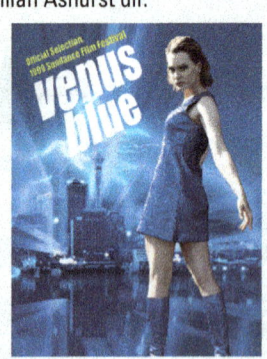

Okay. So I included this one just to get those groovy Kiwis on the map. SF short about an alien visitor to Auckland with mysterious powers. For eleven minutes it manages to pack in heaps of other popular poetic references including WSB, plus L. Frank Baum, Lord Byron, Albert Camus, Lewis Carroll, Leonard Cohen, Samuel Taylor Coleridge, René Descartes, Jean Genet, John Keats, Jack Kerouac, Arthur Rimbaud, Tom Robbins, William Shakespeare and Hunter S. Thompson,

249 book — critical

WISING UP THE MARKS
Timothy Murphy

media: **HARDBACK**
released: **1998**
created:

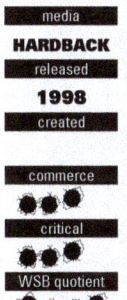
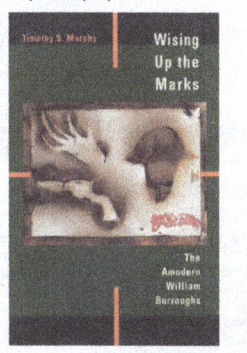

When it comes to critical theory, Adorno what Althfusser's about and it means Foucault to me. Once you get past all the pseudo bullshit (which academic publishers demand) this is my fave scholarly study of WSB – mainly because he sticks the welly into Cronenberg! With gusto! Murphy manages to articulate generalised reservations about WSB's admittance to the pantheon much better than what I ever could, even if I could be arsed. The conclusion, which examines WSB's dissemination through non-print media comprehensively, is particularly recommended.

250 book — critical

WORD VIRUS
James Grauerholz & Ira Silverberg (eds)

media: **HARDBACK**
released: **1998**
created:

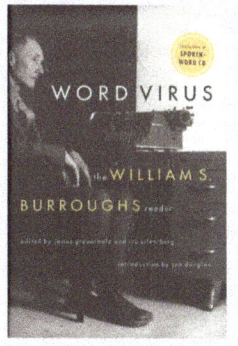

A comprehensive update of the concept of *A William Burroughs Reader* 89, with extracts from WSB's oeuvre from *Junkie* 1 to *My Education* 221 plus copious contextual notes by JWG and an essay ny Ann Charters. This also marks the first publication of parts of ATHWBITT 295 which wouldn't come out in full until ten years later. Initial hardback copies came with a sampler CD 243 for *The Best of WSB from GPS* 244.

251 recording — leide

ZUR HOLLE MAMA #3
Various

media: **CD**
released: **1998**
created:

Third in an acclaimed series compiled by Franz "The last gentleman of contemporary literature" Dobler, this comp of varied German styles includes WSB's take on "Ich Bin Von Kopf Bis Fuss Auf Liebe Eingestellt" (2:26) from *Dead City Radio* 162 along with varied germanophonic contributions from Tobias Gruben, Viva Maria!, Fink, Stella, Tom Combo, Knarf Rellöm, Richie Nell, Fred Is Dead, Quarks, Freundeskreis, Der Heitere Himmel, Katharina Franck, Kinderzimmer Productions, Bruno Ferrari Quintett, Isar 12, Fröhliche Menschen, Surrogat, A Million Mercies & Alles Wie Gross, Barbara Morgenstern, Monostars, Herbst In Peking and Halb.

252 recording — electro

HASHISHEEN: THE END OF LAW
Bill Laswell

media: **CD**
released: **1999**
created:

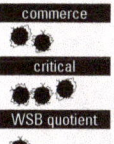

Compiled by Bill Laswell and Hakim Bey, a concept album based on Hassan I Sassah and his sect who should to be familiar to all WSB fans. WSB features here on "The Western Lands" (6:12) with music by Techno Animal and with Iggy Pop reading from a text by Bey. This is a new track based on WSB's readings from the *Seven Souls* sessions 157. Other readers include Patti Smith, Genesis P-Orridge, Ira Cohen, Anne Clark and Sussan Deyhim, and musical backing by Jah Wobble, Techno Animal (Kevin Martin), Nicky Skopelitis and Eyeless In Gaza. The album still has a very committed following. Not sure about the sect.

1999

253	film
	experimental

NOVA EXPRESS
Andre Perkowski dir.

media: 3HR+ COL..
released: 1999
created:
commerce: ●●
critical: ●●●
WSB quotient: ●●●●

For my money the most entertaining and faithful WSB adaptation yet! Started last century and probably never to be definitively completed, this is an exhausting and exhilarating mash-up of stock footage, collages, psychedelic fragments and other bits all stitched together seemingly haphazardly over recordings of WSB, other actors and synthesised voices reading out bits of my fave WSB novel 10. These type of videos are as easy to do as they are hard to do well, but this is like Craig Baldwin went back in time to take Antony Balch's place. More than an hour's worth of fragments have surfaced on the internet by now (2013). Sweet!

254	film
	documentary

THE SOURCE
Chuck Workman dir.

media: 88M COL..
released: 1999
created:
commerce: ●●
critical: ●●●
WSB quotient: ●●●

An all-star dramatised doco of the canonical story of the Beatic trinity with Johnny Depp as Kerouac, John Turturro as Ginsberg and, in the most inspired piece of casting since Stephen Fry played Oscar Wilde, Dennis Hopper as WSB. Also has new interviews with Ginsberg, WSB, Kesey, Ferlinghetti, Mailer, Jerry Garcia, Tom Hayden, Gary Snyder and Ed Sanders. The film was very well-reviewed and got nominated for the Grand Jury Prize for Documentary at the Sundance Film Festival. Bonus fact! Workman is often the dude responsible for the In Memoriam montage segments for the Oscar ceremonies.

2000

255	film
	drama

BEAT
Gary Walkow dir.

media: 93M COL..
released: 2000
created:
commerce: ●●
critical: ●●
WSB quotient: ●●●●

Marketed as "a true story", which is true only in the sense that it is indeed a story, this movie demonstrates the principle that US films can address no topic other than via its relation to violent death. Set in Mexico, 1951, with Kiefer Sutherland playing WSB and Kurt Cobain's 185 widow Courtney Love playing the role of Joan, it focuses on the killings of David Kammerer (see ATHWBITT 295) and of Joan Vollmer. It may be significant that the movie was produced soon (in filmic terms) after WSB's own death, preventing him from commenting or, potentially, litigating. Readers interested in these events are advised to seek other sources.

256	film
	documentary

CONDO PAINTING
John McNaughton dir.

media: 84M COL..
released: 2000
created:
commerce: ●
critical: ●●
WSB quotient: ●●●

The US artist George Condo was a close friend of WSB. They had collaborated on paintings from 1988–96 and exhibited together. They also worked together on a collection of writings and etchings titled *Ghost of Chance* which was published in a limited edition by the Whitney Museum in 1991. This doco explores Condo's striking work and his idiosyncratic outlook. It's quite easy to see why he and WSB got along. Allen Ginsberg also puts in an appearance. The soundtrack includes DJ Spooky, Sonic Youth, Tom Waits. Condo was a pall-bearer at WSB's funeral.

257 recording	
jazz	

INNERMEDIUM
Robert Musso

media: **CD**
released: **2000**
created:
commerce: ●●●
critical: ●
WSB quotient: ●

WSB provided the cover painting for this release by Robert Musso, NYC-based multi-instrumentalist and technician who has featured on over a thousand records. The law of averages entails that he has been engineer on many Bill Laswell projects including *Seven Souls* 157, *The Road to the Western Lands* 247, *Words of Advice for Young People* 201, *Jahbulon* 311, *Incunabula* 309 and Sly and Robbie's *Rhythm Killers* 135. He has also engineered for Tom Waits, but not on *The Black Rider* 196. Phew. That was close.

258 book	
journals	

LAST WORDS
William Burroughs / James Grauerholz (ed)

media: **HARDBACK**
released: **2000**
created: **1996-97**
commerce: ●●●
critical: ●●
WSB quotient: ●●●

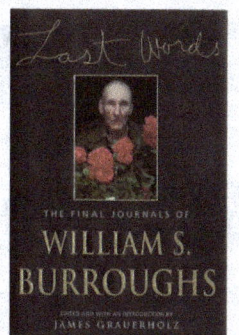

WSB's final journals (14 Nov. 1996 – 30 Jul. 1997) include a number of notes about past, future and then current film and music projects. WSB died on 2 Aug. 1997. Musical selections played at his memorial (6 Aug. 1997) included Schubert's "Opus 78 in G major", The Master Musicians of Joujouka's "Your Eyes are Like a Cup of Tea" 39, Ry Cooder's "Paris Texas", Duke Ellington's "East St Louis Toodle-Oo", "Black and Tan Fantasy", "The Moocher", Louis Armstrong's "Chinese Blues", "Texas Moaner Blues", "Wild Man Blues", "Ain't Misbehavin'", "Stardust" and Bessie Smith's "Down-Hearted Blues".

259 film	
documentary	

NIGHT WALTZ
Owsley Brown dir.

media: **89M COL..**
released: **2000**
created:
commerce: ●●
critical: ●●
WSB quotient: ●

Well-reviewed doco about author Paul Bowles' 239 first and lesser-known career as an avant-garde composer. His first-known work being a piano translation of some of Kurt Schwitters vocals. Here several of Bowles' compositions are played in their entirety over nice visuals of his adopted homeland of Morocco interspersed with one of his last interviews. There are also new interviews with Ginsberg and WSB who were long-time friends with Bowles in Tangiers. Interested punters can seek out the CD of Bowles' piano music which, it's probably redundant to say, is put out by Sub Rosa.

260 recording	
rock	

NYC GHOSTS AND FLOWERS
Sonic Youth

media: **CD**
released: **2000**
created:
commerce: ●●
critical: ●●
WSB quotient: ●

Formed in NYC in 1981 with a core of Thurston Moore, Kim Gordon, Lee Ranaldo, Steve Shelley, they became the highest-profile art/rock crossover band of all time and if you're reading a book about WSB then there's probably not much I can tell you about them that you don't already know. The cover of their 2000 release used WSB's screen-print "X-Ray Man", they contributed "Dr Benway's House" to *Dead City Radio* 162 and provided the soundtrack to *A Man Within* 308. There may be a brief glimpse of WSB in the video for "Teenage Riot" (1988). Some members visited WSB in Lawrence and elsewhere. They're nice people.

261 recording — electro
PLANET RAVE
Various

media: CD
released: 2000
created:
commerce: ●●
critical: ●●
WSB quotient: ●

A "Tribal House" comp from the influential "world music" label that had put out Material's *The Road to the Western Lands* 247, although the track here, "Ineffect" (7:27), is taken from its predecessor *Seven Souls* 157. Other tracks here are from Tulku, Emer Kenny, Dissidenten, Jai Uttal And The Pagan Love Orchestra, Material, Jai Uttal and the Pagan Love Orchestra and Badar Ali Khan. It's probably very nice if you like that sort of thing.

262 recording — rock
STONED IMMACULATE
Various

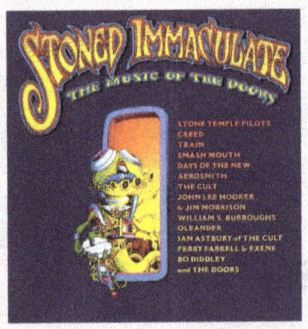

media: CD
released: 2000
created:
commerce: ●●
critical: ●
WSB quotient: ●

This uh "patchy" tribute album features WSB reading Jim Morrison's poem "Is Everybody In?" (2:48) with looped backing of Doors tunes and samples of Morrison. It could well be the least worst track here. Other contributors include Stone Temple Pilots, Creed, Train, Smash Mouth, Days Of The New, Aerosmith, The Cult, Oleander, Perry Farrell, John Lee Hooker and Bo Diddley. With the exception of the last two, could I really give a shit about these people?

263 recording — punk
STRANGLEHOLD
Various

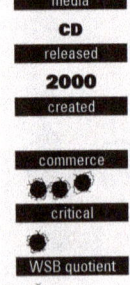

media: CD
released: 2000
created:
commerce: ●●
critical: ●
WSB quotient: ●

Budget-price comp of new young bands playing old dead music. WSB's contributes to the liner notes: "I always thought a punk was someone who took it up the ass." The names of the groups might tell you something: The Fucking Assholes, Limecell, The Bulemics, Nuclear Saturday, Turning Blue, Calamity Jones, Big Shrimp, Pushers, Talking to Lois, The Outside, Bullys, Advice to Addicts, Piss Ant, White Trash Debutantes, Kermit's Finger, New Society of Anarchists, Oppressed Logic, Shitloads of Fuckall, S.O.S., Lawndarts, and Resentments. Actually Shitloads of Fuckall is pretty funny. I take it back.

264 recording — various
THE NIGHT WATCH
Various

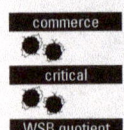

media: CD
released: 2000
created:
commerce: ●●
critical: ●●
WSB quotient: ●

Another comp on LTM records, recycling some tracks from the *Minutes* LP 133 including WSB's "On the Nova Lark" (3:05) from the *Talk Talk* flexi 82. Other names here include The Names, Josef K, Crispy Ambulance, Paul Haig, Bertholer, Ultramarine, Section 25, Paul Haig, Steven Brown & Blaine L. Reininger, Crispy Ambulance, Jazz, Minny Pops, Jean Cocteau, Jacques Derrida, Tuxedomoon. Came with a free Section 25 album. Woohoo!

265	**recording**
	spoken word

UP FROM THE ARCHIVES
Gerard Malanga

- media: **CD**
- released: **2000**
- created:
- commerce: ●
- critical: ●
- WSB quotient: ●

Gerard Malanga (b. 1943) is an American poet, photographer, filmmaker, curator and archivist. He got started in 1963 when he took a job as Andy Warhol's assistant, acting in many of his films, producing his "screen tests" and doing an embarrassing but influential whip dance with the Velvet Underground 22. Gerard also took some of the most iconic photos of WSB, including the one in front of Burroughs Corp. and on the Brooklyn Bridge shooting the WTC with a double-barrelled shotgun. This audio retrospective came out (where else?) on Sub Rosa and includes an untitled chat with WSB (5:02) recorded NY, 21 Jul. 1974.

266	**recording**
	spoken word

LAST WORDS: QUI VIVRE VERRA
William Burroughs / Ulrike Haage / Barbara Schäfer

- media: **CD**
- released: **2001**
- created: **1999**
- commerce: ●
- critical: ●●
- WSB quotient: ●●●

A very effective radio-play treatment of WSB's *Last Words* 258 produced for Bavarian radio in 1999. The show features readings, with some bilingual sections, backed by sparse but appropriate musical accompaniment. See *Tagebuch eines Ruckzuges* 275 for more groovy hörspiel action.

267	**film**
	documentary

SLEEP IN A NEST OF FLAMES
James Dowell & John Kolomvakis dirs.

- media: **118M COL..**
- released: **2001**
- created:
- commerce: ●●
- critical: ●●●
- WSB quotient: ●

THIS SPACE
INTENTIONALLY
LEFT BLANK

Documentary on Charles Henri Ford, from his bohemian days in Paris to his founding of *View* magazine in the forties, which would introduce the French surrealists, amongst others, to a US audience. Ford had featured WSB in his 1967 film *Poem Posters* 17 and here WSB provides a profile of Ford. Also appearing are Allen Ginsberg, Paul Bowles, Paul Morrissey, Edmund White, Dorothea Tanning and Ford himself.

268	**film**
	animation

THE LAST WORDS OF DUTCH SCHULTZ
Gerrit van Dijk dir.

- media: **24M COL..**
- released: **2001**
- created:
- commerce: ●
- critical: ●●
- WSB quotient: ●●

Shot with a mix of live action and rotoscoped animation, this is a film version of the (public domain) last words of "Dutch" Schultz as recorded by the police stenographer, rather than a production of WSB's 1970 text 35. It stars Rutger Hauer as the voice of Dutch but a different actor plays him on screen. I thought it was pretty cool.

269 film — music
LAST NIGHT ON EARTH
Richie Smyth dir.

media: 5M COL..
released: 2002
created:
commerce:
critical:
WSB quotient:

I assume that WSB got this in writing. Bono and his chums had already used the *A Thanksgiving Prayer* 174 video on their *Zoo TV* tour but now they invited WSB to be in their clip filmed, conveniently for him, in Kansas City and also featuring Sophie (Roald Dahl's daughter) Dahl. There has been some amusing discussion on Christian-oriented U2 forums re: who WSB is intended to symbolise. The clip warrants a brief mention in *Last Words* and was to be his final performance. Surely it's just a weird coincidence that Andy Warhol's last creative gesture had also been a cameo in a video for a shit band, in his case "Misfit" by Curiosity Killed the Cat.

270 recording — hip hop
MORE DUB INFUSIONS
Various

media: 2LP/CD
released: 2002
created:
commerce:
critical:
WSB quotient:

It's dub Jim but not as we know it. This German comp includes WSB & Gus Van Sant's "Millions of Images" (4:07) from *The Elvis of Letters* 123 alongside Rhythm & Sound, Swayzak/Benjamin Zephaniah, Williams Traffic, Juantrip, Recloose, Etienne De Crecy, Roots Manuva, Butch Cassidy Sound System, The Novak Project, Brooklyn Funk Essentials and Die Fantastischen Vier. Half those names don't mean owt to me but, for what it's worth, Benjamin Zephaniah (who is exceptionally good value if you don't know) had also appeared on Bomb The Bass's *Clear* LP 217.

271 recording — various
THE WIRE: 20 YEARS 1982-2002
Various

media: 3CD
released: 2002
created:
commerce:
critical:
WSB quotient:

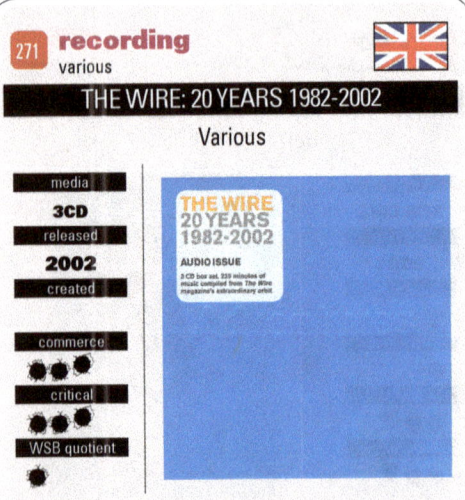

This three disc edition was put out to mark two decades of the celebrated British mag that specialises in experimental or neglected music. It's a worth comp with a massive track listing. WSB contributes "Silver Smoke of Dreams" (4:50) from BTIGR 124. The Wire had published some excellent coverage of WSB's sound work including Jack Sargeant's 234 definitive piece in Issue 300 (Feb. 2009). You have no business reading this book if you haven't checked it out. I must get round to it.

272 film — drama
ELEPHANT
Gus Van Sant dir.

media: 81M COL..
released: 2003
created:
commerce:
critical:
WSB quotient:

Gus Van Sant took his cues from neglected English master film-maker Alan Clarke's film of the same name, translating the "action" from sectarian killings in Ireland to school shootings in the US. He sneaks WSB's "Meeting of International Conference of Technological Psychiatry" (from *Call Me Burroughs* 11) onto the soundtrack, a thought-provoking gesture given WSB's pro-gun stance. Van Sant followed this film with *Last Days*, which was based on circumstances leading up to Kurt Cobain's 185 suicide.

273 recording
electro
NEW DEUTSCH
Various

- media: 2LP/CD
- released: 2003
- created: 1979-95
- commerce
- critical
- WSB quotient

WSB has an unknown contributor role on this compilation of German post-punk/new-wave ("Deutsche neue welle" if you like) curated by Thomas Bär and DJ Hell. Groups here include Blindgänger, Christof Glowalla, DAF, Der Plan, Die Gesunden, Die Hornissen, Echowest, Eiskalte Engel, Fehlfarben, Gleitzeit, Grauzone, Keine Ahnung, Neon, No More, Pyrolator, Stratis, Weltklang Za Za. If you're not familiar with this crazy driving electro slop I urge you to check out the genre. The closest thing in the anglosphere would be the Sheffield sound (Cabaret Voltaire etc.). Pyrolator and Der Plan in particular are worth a shufty. Cheers Zig!

274 film
documentary
PORTRAIT OF A BOOKSTORE AS AN OLD MAN
Gonzague Pichelin & Benjamin Sutherland dirs.

- media: 52M COL..
- released: 2003
- created
- commerce
- critical
- WSB quotient

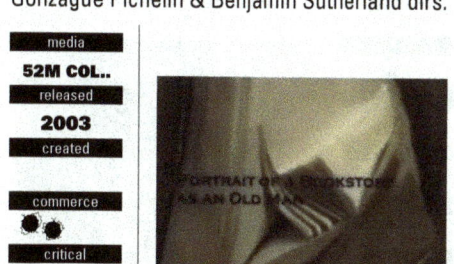

In 1951, US expatriate George Whitman opened Shakespeare and Co. at 37 Rue de la Bûcherie, Paris. He was celebrated for offering free food and lodging to hard-up visiting would-be writers. I had the great pleasure of visiting the shop and briefly meeting George in early 1992 so I can personally vouch that this fascinating and touching documentary is not hyperbolic. There is only a tenuous WSB connection and he appears elliptically in a couple of stills but highlights include pancake batter that doubles as carpet glue and the price of admission is worth it just for the final scene of George's "haircut" which is hilarious and terrifying in equal measure.

275 recording
spoken word
TAGEBUCH EINES RÜCKZUGES
William Burroughs

- media: CD
- released: 2003
- created
- commerce
- critical
- WSB quotient

Based on WSB's *The Retreat Diaries* 55, this is a bilingual German radio-play (49:00) directed by Kai Grehn, narrated by Hans-Peter Hallwachs, Harvey Friedmann and Tom Strauss with music by alva noto & Kai-Uwe Kohlschmidt. Whether it's down to the mastery of the hörspiel format and/or the bilingual approach, I found this a rare instance where a narrator other than WSB performs his texts effectively. The recording was put out in a tasty package by Galerie Vevaise in a hardback digipack with a 36 page booklet and also in a 100 limited edition with a numbered art-print.

276 recording
electro
POST INDUSTRIAL BOYS
Post Industrial Boys

- media: LP/CD
- released: 2004
- created
- commerce
- critical
- WSB quotient

From Georgia (the country), this collective type outfit play an ambient kind of avant-pop. The track "In the Kitchen" (3:05) on their debut release features a reading of a WSB text (maybe from *The Job* 34) by writer, performance artist and activist Irakli Kakabadze.

277 recording — spoken word
RADIO HYPER-YAHOO
Elliott Sharp

media: CD
released: 2004
created:
commerce:
critical:
WSB quotient:

Elliott Sharp (b. 1951) is an NYC-based multi-instrumentalist and composer who has released more than eighty albums of blues, jazz, orchestral music, noise, no wave rock, and techno. This is the third volume in Sharp's Swift-inspired Yahoos trilogy (the first volume came out during Reagan's reign, the second in Bush Snr's and this one in Bush Jr's). On this disc Steve Buscemi reads out a WSB text on "In the Film" (4:37). Buscemi was a friend of WSB and appears in *Lawrence Home Movies* 262 and, in 2011, it was announced that he was planning a film of WSB's *Queer* 121.

278 book — critical
RETAKING THE UNIVERSE
Davis Schneiderman & Jamie Russell (eds)

media: PAPERBACK
released: 2004
created:
commerce:
critical:
WSB quotient:

A bog-standard collection of peer-reviewed essays subtitled "William S. Burroughs in the Age of Globalization". Typical research-money generating academic work, except that one might have expected some analysis of WSB's engagement with the Control Machine here: Nike/Gap ads, work with corp-rockers U2 blah blah, publication by Murdoch-owned conglomerates and so on. Strangely this is all omitted. There's not much point pretending it didn't happen just coz it's too hard. At least WSB never pretended he was a lefty like some of these guys do, even if it is published by the venerable Pluto Press, who have done some cool shit through the ages.

279 recording — electro
RHYTHM SCIENCE
DJ Spooky

media: CD
released: 2004
created:
commerce:
critical:
WSB quotient:

Paul Miller (b. 1970) aka DJ Spooky is regarded as one of the leading theoreticians of sampling and dj culture. His influence from WSB is obvious in that his name is often suffixed "That Subliminal Kid", presumably in tribute to Ian Sommerville. Miller's 2004 book *Rhythm Science* was a runaway success and came with a mix CD of Spooky trawling through the archives of the Sub Rosa label, who also issued the disc separately here. The comp boasts a stellar cast and includes a medley (if the kids still called them that) of Scanner's "Fuse" with WSB & Martin Olsen's "The Five Steps" (2:35). Miller followed up the project with 2008 with *Sound Unbound* 299.

280 recording — spoken word
DIGGIN THE NEW BREED
Various

media: CD
released: 2005
created:
commerce:
critical:
WSB quotient:

Audio doco on "The Beat Generation & Post War America" put out by Chrome Dreams in their "Enlightenment" series. These CDs mix a commentary with documentary soundbites and cheesy incidental music. There are four chapters, a brief intro followed by sections focussing on Kerouac (16:24), WSB (24:04) and Ginsberg etc. (27.38). I've not been able to track these down in time and only heard snippets of this on all-music.com but they struck me as mindbogglingly inane and ill-informed. Apparently "jive talk" arrived in the US by slave ship at the beginning of the seventeenth century... wtf? srly... WTF!? Bonus! Kerouac was a racist... ooooookay.

281 recording
country/folk

LAND RUSH
Fletcher Harrington & Topeka

media: CD
released: 2005

Topeka (meaning "digging good potatoes" in the Kansa and the Ioway languages) is the captal city of Kansas, next along the turnpike after Lawrence 282. WSB spent some time in hospital there, and his pal Jack Kerouac 168 had once said "Anybody can make Paris holy, but I can make Topeka holy." In May 2004, the former Atchison Topeka and Santa Fe Tributary was officially named Burroughs Creek in honour of WSB. The record under discussion credits WSB with "spoken word" but unfortunately the MoR country pop stylings of this outfit prevented further research.

282 film
documentary

LAWRENCE HOME MOVIES
Wayne Propst dir.

media: 16M COL..
released: 2005

W.S.B.

Propst is a Lawrence-based [performance] artist who met WSB in 1981. His own artworks are informed by, though not derivative of, WSB's canon although they did in fact collaborate on a cannon, in order to shoot bowling balls at canvasses. Propst has also shot a couple of short films of WSB in his latter years (and also one called *Shotgun Paintings*, Col. 4:42). Propst himself appears in *The Junky's Christmas* 197, *A Man Within* 308 and *Words of Advice* 294.

283 recording
spoken word

NEWSPAPER TAXIS
Various

media: CD
released: 2005

Another Chrome Dreams production, but somewhat less inane than *Diggin The New Breed* 280 was. It's basically a survey of the most prominent drug advocates of the twentieth century, so we get Philip K. Dick, Aldous Huxley, Tim Leary, Ken Kesey and WSB, together with maybe less obvious candidates such as J.G. Ballard, H.R. Giger and Kenneth Anger. Like the previous one, I've only heard bits so maybe it's fantastic. What? It could happen.

284 recording
psyche

NOVA PSYCHEDELIA (1975-1985)
Todd Tamanend Clark

media: 2CD
released: 2005
created: 1984

Originally on Todd's 1984 debut LP "Into The Vision", the title track (8:37) features 30 second WSB sample (from BTIGR 124) with gnarly guitar antics from Cheetah Chrome, inept (?) theremin, things banging together... genius! This double disc comp collects most of his tunes made before going into extended hiatus. Four thumbs up! Expect him to be a household name, in strange houses everywhere, anytime now.

285 film
documentary
ABSOLUTE WILSON
Katharina Otto-Bernstein dir.

media: 105M COL...
released: 2006
created: 2006

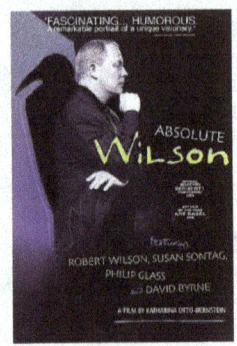

Robert Wilson (b. 1941) is a US avant-garde playwright and director, often regarded as the leading exponent of the field, his best known work being his 1976 opera *Einstein on the Beach* (with music by Philip Glass). In 1984 he developed his epic *the CIVIL warS*, which was the subject of a documentary by Howard Brookner 101. Whilst Wilson found international acclaim, US success eluded him until he collaborated with WSB and Tom Waits on *The Black Rider* 166 in 1990. This acclaimed biopic features interviews with WSB amongst others.

286 recording
electro
MAKROSOFT 'THEME'
Makrosoft

media: CD
released: 2006
created: 2006

Synthy lounge treatments of the music of Nirvana, Iggy Pop, Velvets, REM, John Lennon from this Dusseldorf outfit. Given that configuration of names, it's no surprise that the first track "MakroSoft 'Theme'" (1:45) samples WSB from Klaus Maeck's *Decoder* 110: "Looking for nothing special? Well... Here it is."

287 recording
electro
NOISE & ELECTRONIC MUSIC #4
Various

media: 2CD
released: 2006
created: 1937-2005

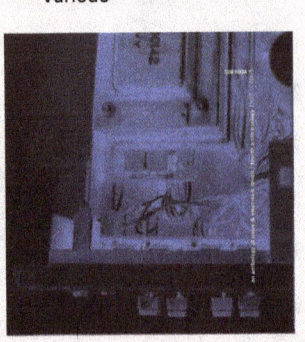

The fourth volume of this series of comps from Sub Rosa includes WSB doing "Present Time Exercises" (2:23) from BTIGR 124. Comes in an elaborate package with a fifty-page booklet bound in. Other contributors are: Halim El-Dabh, György Ligeti, Jean-Claude Risset, Beatriz Ferreyra, Maja Ratkje, Laurie Spiegel, Steve Reich, Stephen Vitiello, eRikm, Wang Changcun, Chlorgeschlecht, Gottfried Michael Koenig, Milan Knizak, Les Rallizes Denudes, Vibracathedral Orchestra, Andy Hawkins, Alvin Lucier, Loop Orchestra, The, John Waterman, François Bayle + Robert Wyatt + Kevin Ayers, James Whitehead, Jean-Marc Vivenza and Olivier Messiaen.

288 recording
electro
THE AUDIENCE'S LISTENING
Cut Chemist

media: 2LP/CD
released: 2006
created: 2006

Lucas MacFadden (b. 1970) is a US DJ and producer who has worked with popular groups like Jurassic 5, Less than Jake and Ozmatli, toured with Shakira and had his music used in ads for ipods. All these names will probably be entirely forgotten by the time this book comes out. Notwithstanding his mainstream credentials, Lucas' first solo album includes the track 'Storm' which has a sample of WSB ("Stay outta that time flak... Storm the studio") from "Towers Open Fire" on TDIOTM 128 and as used by Meat Beat Manifesto seventeen years previously 158.

289	film
	drama

THE SOPRANOS: MEMBERS ONLY
Timothy Van Patten dir.

- media: 52M COL..
- released: 2006
- created:
- commerce:
- critical:
- WSB quotient:

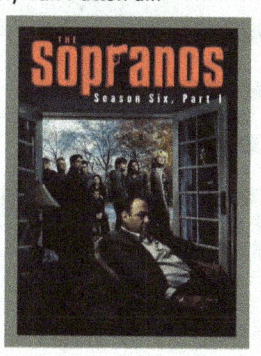

The first episode of the sixth season of this monumentally popular crime show (shown 31 Aug. 2006 in the US) opens and closes with "Seven Souls" by Material 157 on the soundtrack. This could be some kind of veiled or unconscious nod to WSB's *Last Words of Dutch Schultz* 35 ... or then again not. Apparently I'm a freak for having zero interest in post-WW2 gangster-chic but I have watched the clip on YouTube. Hope you appreciate it. The shit I gone through.

290	recording
	opera

THE THEATRE OF REPETITIONS
Johannes Kalitzke

- media: 2SACD
- released: 2006
- created:
- commerce:
- critical:
- WSB quotient:

Johannes Kalitzke (b. 1959) is a German composer of modern classical works. His 2003 opera is based on Deleuze's ideas of repetition, Deleuze's ideas of repetition and Deleuze's ideas of repetition. It's comprised of three parts – the first is based on texts by De Sade, the second on texts from WSB's TPODR 114, and the third on transcripts of the Nuremberg trials. This recording of a 2006 presentation, conducted by Bernhard Lang and recorded live in Graz, Austria, on 10 Oct. 2003.

291	recording
	jazz

TRANSFIXIONES
Hugo Westerdahl & Juan Belda

- media: CD
- released: 2006
- created:
- commerce:
- critical:
- WSB quotient:

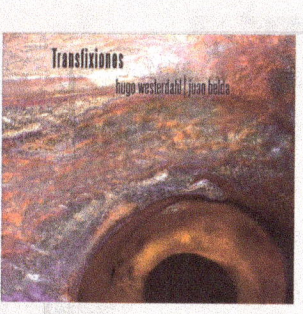

Westerdahl (b. 1957) is a Spanish musician and engineer. This is his only release so far. The material is kinda jazzy electro-ambient stuff. The track "Random" (5:47) has a sample from 'Origin and Theory of Cut-Ups' from BTIGR 124 and WSB is also reported to be on "TFX3" (2:57). Other tracks sample Brion Gysin and Don Van Vliet.

292	film
	documentary

OBSCENE
Daniel O'Connor & Neil Ortenberg dirs.

- media: 97M COL..
- released: 2007
- created:
- commerce:
- critical:
- WSB quotient:

Biopic of Barney Rosset (1922-2012), legendary US publisher of *Lady Chatterley's Lover*, *Tropic of Cancer*, *The Autobiography of Malcolm X* and many works by WSB. He also reprinted and popularised many of the classics of Victorian era erotica. A tireless defender of free expression in books and film, Rosset fought many court cases, effectively ending literary censorship in the US but not without putting with lawsuits, death-threats, grenade attacks, government surveillance, and the occupation of his premises by enraged feminists. Great and inspiring fun, WSB reads from *Naked Lunch* 2 amidst the coverage of its trial.

293 recording — experimental

REAL ENGLISH TEA MADE HERE
William Burroughs

- media: 3CD
- released: 2007
- created: 1964-65
- commerce: ●●○○○
- critical: ●●●○○
- WSB quotient: ●●●●○

Curated by Colin Fallows and Barry Miles, from Miles' archives, this is an amazing compilation of cut/up experiments from the mid-sixties, mostly recorded in NYC. The strength of these recordings is their duration, most being between 15 and 45 minutes long, which avoids the problem of NHNBTR [81] and BTIGR [124] where you're just starting to vibe into a track by the time it's over. The downside is that you may have to go out for a piss or a smoko halfway and miss a good bit. There's also a lovely illustrated booklet with customarily meticulous notes by Miles. The title comes from a passage in *Nova Express* [10] that crops up in a few other places too.

294 film — spoken word

WORDS OF ADVICE
Lars Movin & Steen Møller Rasmussen dir.

- media: 74M
- released: 2007
- created:
- commerce: ●●○○○
- critical: ●●●○○
- WSB quotient: ●●●●○

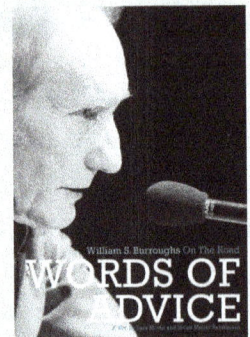

Subtitled "William S. Burroughs On The Road", this doco mixes previously unseen footage from the legendary reading in Copenhagen (29 Oct. 1983) and footage of WSB's latter years from Lawrence with new interviews by JWG, Hal Willner, John Giorno and others to explore WSB's relentless tour schedule promoting The Final Trilogy. very well-received and awarded by the Danish Film Institute for "outstanding efforts in documentary". Featuring a soundtrack by Material [157], Patti Smith and Islamic Diggers. The DVD version has the full unedited Copenhagen reading as an extra.

295 book — fiction

AND THE HIPPOS WERE BOILED IN THEIR TANKS
Jack Kerouac & William Burroughs

- media: HARDBACK
- released: 2008
- created: 1944
- commerce: ●●●○○
- critical: ●●●○○
- WSB quotient: ●●○○○

Kerouac had already written his self-admittedly shithouse *The Sea is My Brother* by the time he collaborated with WSB on this in 1944. Dismissed on-camera by WSB in *What Happened to Kerouac?* [130], he resisted attempts to publish it and it didn't come out until after the 2005 death of Lucien Carr, the real-life basis of one of the protagonists. An audiobook [302] soon followed, and in 2013 a film called *Kill Your Darlings*, based on the same events, came out starring Ben Foster as WSB and Daniel "Harry Potter" Radcliffe as Allen Ginsberg. You couldn't make this shit up but why would you want to?

296 film — documentary

CHELSEA ON THE ROCKS
Abel Ferrara dir.

- media: 89M COL..
- released: 2008
- created:
- commerce: ●●○○○
- critical: ●●○○○
- WSB quotient: ●○○○○

The eminent director's first documentary examines the history and changing climate at the Chelsea Hotel, NYC. Ferrara's informal and candid interviews are great value, especially the one with Milos Forman, but the re-enactments (Sid and Nancy, Janis Joplin etc.) are a bit wanky. He also includes footage from Nigel Finch's doco [78] from happier times, including a brief shot of WSB and Warhol, but no more than that. Bonus points for putting enthusiasm before coherence.

297 recording	
reggae	🇩🇪

CINEMASONICS
Doug Wimbish

- media: **CD**
- released: **2008**
- created:
- commerce: ●●●
- critical: ●●●
- WSB quotient: ●

Born in 1956, Wimbish got his start as bassist for Sugarhill Records and, with Skip McDonald and Keith LeBlanc 126, made up the rhythm section that played on countless tunes. In the mid-eighties the trio headed to London to join Adrian Sherwood in Tackhead 163 before nearly joining the Rolling Stones but ending up in Living Colour then going onto work with Mark Stewart 112 and others like Mick Jagger, Seal, Annie Lennox, Madonna, Little Annie (ex-Crass), Depeche Mode and Mos Def. This solo LP reunited him with the trio plus Sherwood and includes samples from WSB's "Last Words of HiS" from NHNBTR 81 on "Rockin Shoes" (4:17).

298 recording	
metal	🇫🇮

FLORA MEETS FAUNA
Violet Halo

- media: **CD**
- released: **2008**
- created:
- commerce: ●●●
- critical: ●●●
- WSB quotient: ●

This Finnish metal group has some WSB sampling on this LP but I haven't been able to find out any more than that. Sorry! If they'd played reggae I might have tried harder.

299 recording	
electro	🇧🇪

SOUND UNBOUND
DJ Spooky

- media: **CD**
- released: **2008**
- created:
- commerce: ●●●
- critical: ●●●
- WSB quotient: ●●●

Following 2004's *Rhythm Science* 270, That Subliminal Kid serves up a second helping of "excerpts and allegories from the Sub Rosa archives" to tie in with his follow-up volume. This time the CD finishes with an edit of WSB (with Iggy Pop and Techno Animal) doing "The Western Land" (4:10), originally from Bill Laswell's *Hashisheen* CD 252. Also, a cast of dozens including Allen Ginsberg, Jean Cocteau, Gertrude Stein, the Master Musicians of Joujouka, Marcel Duchamp, Aphex Twin, James Joyce, Erik Satie, Raoul Hausmann, John Cage, Antonin Artaud, Pauline Oliveros, Nam June Paik, Terry Riley, Steve Reich, Sonic Youth, Morton Subotnick etc.

300 recording	
spoken word	🇮🇪

THE INSTRUMENT OF CONTROL
William Burroughs

- media: **CD**
- released: **2008**
- created:
- commerce: ●●●
- critical: ●●●
- WSB quotient: ●●●●

An unofficial-looking Italian release subtitled "William S. Burroughs in conversation and readings", this disc has no track listing or recording info but the selection of tracks ("Introducing John Stanley Hart", "Twilight's Last Gleaming", "The Place of Dead Roads", "Progressive Education", "The Wild Fruits", "The Unworthy Vessel", "The Name is Clem Snide", "Cities of the Red Night" and a radio interview) indicates that it may be mostly condensed down from *The Best of WSB from GPS* 244.

301 **film**	
drama	

THE JAPANESE SANDMAN
Ed Buhr dir.

media: **12M COL..**
released: **2008**
created:
commerce:
critical:
WSB quotient:

Based on the first of *The Yage Letters* [3], this is a bittersweet love story cum travelogue. Told in flashback, it's the first film to use different actors for the old (1950s, b/w) and young (1930s, colour) portrayals of WSB. Shouldn't those film stocks be the other way round? The title comes from a 1920 song which is mentioned in the letter. I'm familiar with the tune but I haven't been able to see the film. It seems to have been well received on realitystudio.org. Apparently the director is interested in expanding it to feature length. It does sound promising.

302 **recording**	
spoken word	

AND THE HIPPOS WERE BOILED IN THEIR TANKS
Jack Kerouac & William Burroughs

media: **4CD/3CC**
released: **2009**
created:
commerce:
critical:
WSB quotient:

An unabridged (4h22m) recording of the 1944 novel [295] read by Ray Porter who got started voicing animated stories from the Book of Mormon and wound up in shows like *Lost* and *Sons of Anarchy*. I reckon he does a pretty good job switching not too jarringly from faux WSB to faux Kerouac with each alternating chapter. It's always tricky voicing something when the original speaker's voice is so familiar, so this would probably be more effective for readers unfamiliar with WSB's (or Kerouac's) work, were it not for the fact that this book is of limited interest to them. It was also released as a single mp3cd and a standalone PlayAway player thingummy.

303 **film**	
documentary	

CORSO: THE LAST BEAT
Gustave Reininger dir.

media: **89M COL..**
released: **2009**
created:
commerce:
critical:
WSB quotient:

Director Reininger has a penchant for organised crime topics so perhaps Corso's cameo in *The Godfather: Part III* made him the ideal candidate for this ten years in production biopic about The Fourth Beat. Following the death of Allen Ginsberg Corso embarked on a global road trip from Paris to Rome, Florence, Delphi, Athens and Venice, becoming preoccupied with finding out what happened to the mother he never knew. Somewhat miraculously, the director tracks her down, still alive, and they are reunited but Corso is diagnosed with cancer and died a year later. Warning. Contains spoilers. Hmmm. Should probably have put that first. Some WSB content.

304 **recording**	
rock	

EATS DARKNESS
Apostle of Hustle

media: **LP/CD**
released: **2009**
created:
commerce:
critical:
WSB quotient:

Canadian indie-rock group led by David Whiteman, who moonlights in the better-known Broken Social Scene. This, the Apostles' third album, has a number of inter-song short collage pieces with WSB samples on "Sign" (1:21) and "Nobody Bought It" (1:11). Actually, I prefer these bits to the tunes themselves. 8^(

305	recording
	electro

RIDING STRANGE HORSES
Dub Spencer & Trance Hill

media	CD
released	2009
created	
commerce	●●●
critical	●●●
WSB quotient	●

Before this Swiss outfit gained exposure through their dubby reworkings of the Clash's oeuvre, they put out this diverse collection which included versions of Metallica's "Enter Sandman", M's "Pop Muzik" and Martha and the Muffins' "Echo Beach". To some extent, it's irony-by-numbers but it's funky nevertheless. Their track here "The Saints Go Marching Through All the Popular Tunes" (6:32) samples the track from NHNBTR 81 and could be a liberal version of Dubblestandart's tune 312 of the same name if it didn't sound different to that and instead was similar to some stuff on *The Elvis of Letters* 123.

306	recording
	spoken word

NAKED LUNCH
William Burroughs

media	9CD/8CC
released	2009
created	
commerce	●●●
critical	●●●
WSB quotient	●●●●

Read by Mark Bramhall, this unabridged reading clocks in at 10h23m, although being based on The Restored Edition, it may be more true to call it anti-abridged. I have experimented briefly with processing the audio to more closely approximate WSB's voice on the previous abridged version 227 but then I wondered why I was doing it and stopped. This release also came out as an mp3cd and standalone PlayAway version.

307	recording
	spoken word

THREE ALLUSIVE TRACKS
William Burroughs

media	7"
released	2009
created	1960s
commerce	●●
critical	●●●
WSB quotient	●●●●

Limited edition (300 only) seven-inch vinyl release for three tracks from BTIGR 124 on Sub Rosa. Hand numbered in a die-cut sleeve with sticker.

308	film
	documentary

A MAN WITHIN
Yony Leyser dir.

media	87M COL..
released	2010
created	
commerce	●●●
critical	●●●●
WSB quotient	●●●●

A remarkable summation of WSB's life and oeuvre, all the more so when you discover it was the debut feature of a twenty-odd year old. Drawing on new interviews with WSB's associates and a host of other material, the most general criticism is that it could have been thirty minutes longer! Personally, I would have liked it better if it were a bit more incoherent and had some boring bits in. In fact, there's so little in the way of fucked up and tedious shit going on here that we can only assume that it's the director's intention. Still, you can't please everyone. The soundtrack is by Patti Smith and Sonic Youth but it's not intrusive.

309 recording — reggae 🇺🇸
INCUNABULA
Method of Defiance

media: CD
released: 2010
created:
commerce: ●●○
critical: ●●○
WSB quotient: ●○○

One of Bill Laswell's innumerable and ever-mutating projects, the first Method of Defiance-branded release was 2006's *The Only Way To Go Is Down*. In 2010 a new line-up, with contributions from Bernie Worrell, Toshinori Kondo, Guy Licata, DJ Krush, Dr. Israel and Herbie Hancock, started putting out more reggae-based material but still with a hard electronic edge. The paintings on each cover are taken from a work by WSB and can be tiled to form a larger work. The follow-up to this release was *Jahbulon* 311, released later that year.

310 recording — jazz 🇺🇸
INTERZONE
John Zorn

media: CD
released: 2010
created:
commerce: ●●○
critical: ●●○
WSB quotient: ●●○

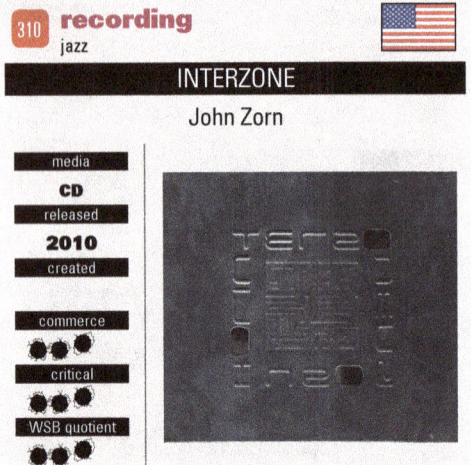

John Zorn (b. 1953) is a US composer, producer and multi-instrumentalist, probably best-known for his saxophonic work. Zorn had been a fan of WSB and Gysin since the sixties and has himself noted the influence of their cut/up experiments on his jump-cut compositional style. This is a 55 minute long piece in three movements for a septet of players, and got to #46 in the *Billboard* Jazz charts. The first of a trio of WSB/Gysin tributes, it was followed by *Nova Express* 315 and *Dreamachines* 232.

311 recording — reggae 🇺🇸
JAHBULON
Method of Defiance

media: CD
released: 2010
created:
commerce: ●●○
critical: ●●○
WSB quotient: ●○○

Another section of the painting by WSB graces the cover of the follow-up to *Incunabula* 309 by Bill Laswell's second (?) incarnation of this reggae/hard electro outfit. The following year a dub album, *Dub Arcanum Arcandrum*, would be issued with versions by such luminaries as Scientist and Mad Professor. Surely it cannot be very long before WSB samples crop up on an MoD track?

312 recording — reggae 🇦🇹
MARIJUANA DREAMS
Dubblestandart

media: CD
released: 2010
created:
commerce: ●●○
critical: ●●○
WSB quotient: ●●○

One of the surprising WSB-posthumous developments is his growing stature in the field of reggae. Given his endorsement by Bill Laswell (who has worked with many singers and players, including Lee Perry, probably THE most influential musician/producer evah!) and Adrian Sherwood (of the legendary On-U Sound and Pressure Sounds labels), both significant players in the US and UK scenes, this is not surprising. These Austrian guys do laid back mash-up style grooves and their tune "Saints Go Marchin Through All the Popular Tunes" (6:08) features copious WSB samples from NHNBTR 81. No relation to the Dub Spencer & Trance Hill tune 305.

313 recording — various 🇬🇧
STEP RIGHT UP!
Various

- media: CD
- released: 2010
- created:
- commerce: ●●
- critical: ●●
- WSB quotient: ●

Since 2001 the British music monthly Mojo has usually come with a thematic cover-mounted CD. Catering for an informed readership, these comps heavily feature obscure archive gems and idiosyncratic covers of classic tunes. The July 2010 edition was guest-curated by Tom Waits who included WSB's "Ich bin von Kopf bis Fuß auf Liebe Eingestellt" (2:23) from *Dead City Radio* 162 alongside tracks by Tennessee Ernie Ford, Son House, Hank Williams, Prisonaires, Ray Charles, Blind Mamie Forehand, Hank Ballard and the Midnighters, Paul Robeson, Howlin' Wolf, Harry Belafonte, Bob Dylan, Gavin Briars, Big Mama Thornton and Cliff Edwards.

314 recording — joujouka 🇬🇧
THE SOURCE
The Master Musicians of Jajouka

- media: LP/CD
- released: 2010
- created:
- commerce: ●●
- critical: ●●
- WSB quotient: ●

WSB provided a quote for the sleeve of this release by the Bachir Attar led version of the Sufi group. Space here permits mention of this faction's appearance with Debbie Harry and Chris Stein on the GPS comp *Cash Cow* 191, their soundtrack work for *Ornette: Made in America* 120, *Naked Lunch* 182 amongst others, and their appearance, on one of the most eclectic bills ever for a show, at Psychic TV's *Time's Up Live* at Royal Festival Hall, London 1 May 1999 which also featured Billy Childish and the Headcoats, Question Mark and the Mysterians and Scanner.

315 recording — jazz 🇺🇸
NOVA EXPRESS
John Zorn

- media: CD
- released: 2011
- created:
- commerce: ●●
- critical: ●●●
- WSB quotient: ●●●

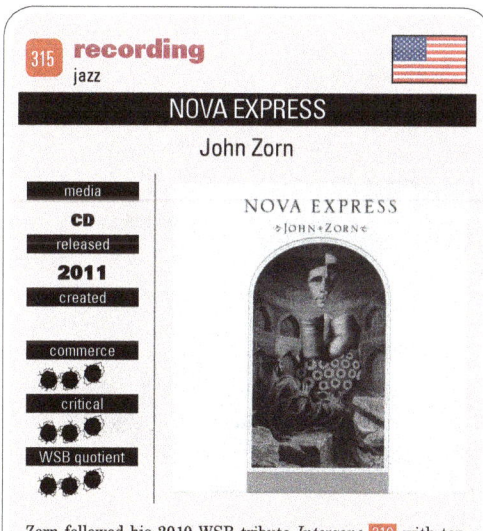

Zorn followed his 2010 WSB tribute *Interzone* 310 with ten tracks worth of "modern chamber music" performed by a quartet of piano (John Medeski), vibraphone (Kenny Wollesen), bass (Trevor Dunn) and drums (Joey Baron). Pleasant enough but it didn't blow my socks off. Next up came *Dreamachines* 323.

316 film — documentary 🇺🇸
THE BALLAD OF GENESIS AND LADY JAYE
Marie Losier dir.

- media: 75M COL..
- released: 2011
- created:
- commerce: ●●
- critical: ●●●
- WSB quotient: ●

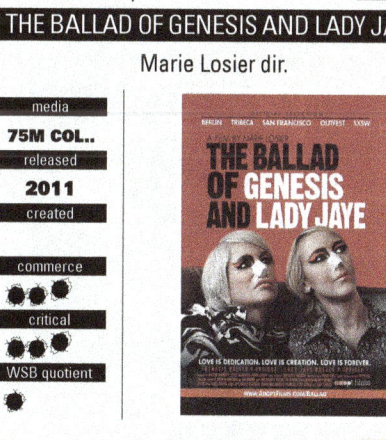

Widely acclaimed doco about Genesis P-Orridge's 136 relationship with Lady Jaye and their quest to create the first "pandrogynous" being. Starting in 2000 they undertook cosmetic surgery and adopted gender neutral and alternating pronouns to become as alike as possible. The project was extended to immaterial dimensions upon Lady Jaye's physical death, from a heart attack, in 2007. The doco has a lot of info about Gen's career including info on h/er work with WSB and appears only in (uncredited) archive footage.

317	**film**
	documentary

THE BEAT HOTEL
Alan Governar dir.

media	
88M COL..	
released	
2011	
created	
commerce	
critical	
WSB quotient	

A doco about the hotel at 9, Rue Git le Coeur which became the European hq of various Beats and friends from 1957–63. Ginsberg, Orlovsky, Corso were soon joined by WSB (who finished *Naked Lunch* there) and by Ian Sommerville and Brion Gysin (who invented the dreamachine there). The film is based around the evocative photos of Harold Chapman, who lived in the attic and didn't say a word for two years because he wanted to be invisible and document the scene as it happened. Other contributors include: Miles, Lars Movin 294, Oliver Harris, and... George Whitman! 274 YAY!

MORE: Miles, Barry. *The Beat Hotel* (Grove, 2000).

318	**recording**
	country/folk

HELL MONEY
Rome

media	
CD	
released	
2012	
created	
commerce	
critical	
WSB quotient	

Jérôme Reuter started this outfit out of Luxembourg in 2005. Apparently there's a WSB quote on the sleeve, and given titles like "Tangier Fix" and "Among the Wild Boys" that's no surprise. They're one of those new-fangled neo-folk, dark gothic groups. Not my thing. FYI "Hell Money" is joss paper printed to look like currency, for use in the afterlife.

319	**film**
	experimental

MENTALLUSIONS
Benjamin Meade dir.

media	
2DVD	
released	
2012	
created	
commerce	
critical	
WSB quotient	

Ben Meade has made several fictional and documentary features and co-produced 2004's well-received alternate history *Confederate States of America*. Meade had used WSB in his debut short *Image is Virus* in 1975 but I have been unable to view it and details are scant. He also used Gus Van Sant's *Millions of Images* 123 on the soundtrack of his 2007 short *Seratonin*.

320	**film**
	documentary

OUTTAKES FROM THE LIFE OF A HAPPY MAN
Jonas Mekas dir.

media	
68M COL..	
released	
2012	
created	
commerce	
critical	
WSB quotient	

Jonas Mekas (b. 1922) is an NY-based Lithuanian filmmaker, poet and artist who, like Stan Brakhage 64, has been called "the godfather of American avant-garde cinema." His 2012 auto-biographical study includes archive footage of WSB and others. According to Brion Gysin, Mekas and other members of the influential NY Film Co-op had been very unreceptive to Balch's WSB films due to his "heavy" reputation, and also disparaged Balch's version of *Witchcraft through the Ages* 26 in a *Village Voice* review (12 Feb. 70). This probably contributed to the wide critical disinterest in the films until their revival by Genesis P-Orridge in the eighties 129.

321 film — drama
THE BLACK MEAT
Matthew Roe dir.

media: 14M COL..
released: 2012

Short two-hander based on texts from *Naked Lunch* made by a young film-maker from Maryland. Unambitious but effective nonetheless. Stars Chris Barnhart (Sall) and David Short (Malleck). According to his website, Roe has produced over a dozen productions for film, video, television and Internet distribution, and become known for his naturalistic dialogue and fascination with counterculture themes and characters. He has also published a personal film theory titled *The Anarchic Filmmaker Manifesto*.

322 recording — spoken word
THE SPOKEN WORD
William Burroughs & Brion Gysin

media: 2CD
released: 2012

Issued by The British Library from their archives, the first disc includes WSB reading (from TPODR 114) at the Centre Hotel, Liverpool, 5 Oct. 1982. The second is mostly Gysin's permutated poems, recorded 1960–62, and WSB's "Invisible Art" 22 Mar. 1970. Comes with a 16-page booklet. WSB had also contributed an interview to the British Library's earlier *American Writers: The Spoken Word* comp.

323 recording — jazz
DREAMACHINES
John Zorn

media: CD
released: 2013

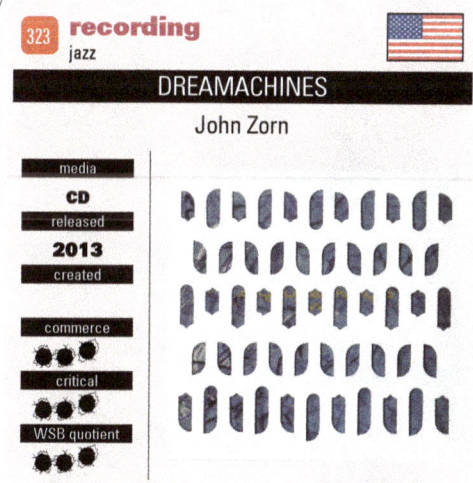

Zorn's third WSB/Gysin tribute in as many years is the most plush of the lot. The cover is from Gysin artwork from his collection and has a WSB quote about the citadels of enlightenment. You know the one. The die-cut sleeve could easily be adapted into a miniature dreamachine if you could just make yourself tiny enough to use it. There are nine tracks here by the same quartet as on his *Nova Express* 315.

324 recording — jazz
WANDERLUST
Cliff Hines

media: CD
released: 2013

Cliff Hines is a US jazz guitarist/composer. This, his second LP features New Orleans jazz legends such as James Singleton, Bill Summers, Kent Jordan, includes a WSB-inspired track "Interzone", and its successor, "Interzone Reprise" (2:54) has a section of that WSB piece read by one Lloyd Dillon.

ANY NUMBER CAN PLAY

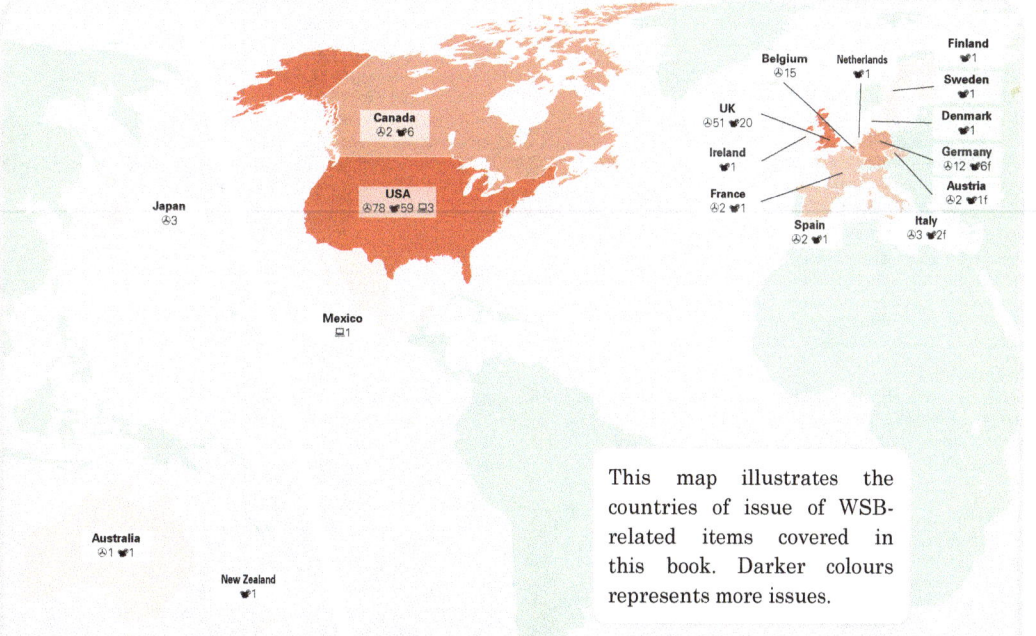

This map illustrates the countries of issue of WSB-related items covered in this book. Darker colours represents more issues.

Index by type

BOOKS

RECORDINGS

BOOKS BY WSB

fiction
Junkie – William Lee (US, 1953) 1
The Naked Lunch – William Burroughs (FR, 1959) 2
Valentine's Day Reading – William Burroughs (US, 1965) ... 12
Ali's Smile – William Burroughs (UK, 1969) 27
The Wild Boys: A Book of the Dead – William Burroughs (US, 1971) ... 40
Exterminator! – William Burroughs (US, 1973) 45
Port of Saints – William Burroughs (UK, 1975) 52
Doctor Benway – William Burroughs (US, 1979) 67
Cities of the Red Night – William Burroughs (US, 1981) ... 79
The Burroughs File – William Burroughs (US, 1984) 113
The Place of Dead Roads – William Burroughs (US, 1984) ... 114
Queer – William Burroughs (US, 1985) 121
The Western Lands – William Burroughs (US, 1987) 141
Interzone – William Burroughs (US, 1989) 155
And the Hippos… – Jack Kerouac & William Burroughs (US, 2008) ... 295

cut/ups
Minutes to Go – Burroughs / Gysin / Beiles / Corso (FR, 1960) ... 3
The Exterminator – William Burroughs & Brion Gysin (US, 1960) .. 4
The Soft Machine – William Burroughs (FR, 1961) 5
The Ticket That Exploded – William Burroughs (FR, 1962) .. 6
Dead Fingers Talk – William Burroughs (UK, 1963) 7
Nova Express – William Burroughs (US, 1964) 10
The Braille Film – Carl Weissner & William Burroughs (US, 1970) ... 33

interviews, journals, letters
The Yage Letters – William Burroughs & Allen Ginsberg (US, 1963) ... 8
The Job – William Burroughs & Daniel Odier (UK, 1970) 34
Snack: Two Tape Transcripts – William Burroughs & Eric Mottram (UK, 1975) ... 53
With William Burroughs – Victor Bockris (US, 1981) 87
The Retreat Diaries – William Burroughs (US, 1976) 55
My Education – William Burroughs (US, 1995) 221
Last Words – William Burroughs / James Grauerholz (ed) (US, 2000) ... 258

non-fiction
Electronic Revolution – William Burroughs (UK, 1971) 37
The Third Mind – William Burroughs & Brion Gysin (FR, 1976) ... 56
Ah Pook is Here and Other Texts – William Burroughs (UK, 1979) ... 65
The Adding Machine – William Burroughs (UK, 1985) 122
The Cat Inside – William Burroughs (US, 1986) 127

screenplays
The Last Words of Dutch Schultz – William Burroughs (UK, 1970) ... 35
Blade Runner: A Movie – William Burroughs (US, 1979) 66
The Naked Lunch (Screenplay) – David Cronenberg (UK, 1989) ... 159

CRITICAL WORKS
A William Burroughs Reader – John Calder (ed) (UK, 1982) .. 89
Re/Search 4/5 – Burroughs / Gysin / TG (US, 1982) 94
The Final Academy – Roger Ely (ed) (UK, 1982) 97
Everything is Permitted – Ira Silverberg (ed) (UK, 1992) . 180
Wireless Imagination – Douglas Kahn & Gregory Whitehead (eds) (US, 1992) ... 188
Naked Lens – Jack Sargeant (UK, 1997) 234
Wising up the Marks – Timothy Murphy (US, 1998) 249
Word Virus – James Grauerholz & Ira Silverberg (eds) (US, 1998) ... 250
Retaking the Universe – Davis Schneiderman & Jamie Russell (eds) (UK, 2004) ... 278

WSB RECORDS

readings
Call Me Burroughs – William Burroughs (FR, 1965) 11
Live at the Kabuki – William Burroughs (US, 1983) 102
The Doctor is on the Market – William Burroughs (UK, 1986) ... 128
Uncommon Quotes – William Burroughs (US, 1988) 148
Vaudeville Voices – William Burroughs (US, 1993) 200
Naked Lunch (Audiobook) – William Burroughs (US, 1996) ... 227
Junky (Audiobook) – William Burroughs (UK, 1997) 232
Selections from The Best of WSB from GPS – William Burroughs (US, 1998) ... 243
The Best of WSB from GPS – William Burroughs (US, 1998) . 244
The Instrument of Control – William Burroughs (IT, 2008) . 300
The Spoken Word – William S Burroughs & Brion Gysin (UK, 2012) ... 322

readings with music
The Elvis of Letters – William Burroughs & Gus Van Sant (US, 1985) ... 123
Seven Souls – Material (US, 1989) 157
Dead City Radio – William Burroughs (US, 1990) 162
Millions of Images – William Burroughs & Gus Van Sant (US, 1990) ... 164
Just One Fix – Ministry (US, 1992) 181
The "Priest" They Called Him – William Burroughs & Kurt Cobain (US, 1992) ... 185
Spare Ass Annie and Other Tales – William Burroughs (US, 1993) ... 194
The Black Rider – Tom Waits (US, 1993) 196
The Operator's Manual – William Burroughs (US, 1993) 198
Words of Advice For Young People – William Burroughs (US, 1993) ... 201
The Road to the Western Lands – Material (US, 1998) 247

cut/ups & experimental
Nothing Here Now but the Recordings – William Burroughs (UK, 1981) ... 81
On the Nova Lark – William Burroughs (US, 1981) 82
Break Through in Grey Room – William Burroughs (BE, 1986) . 124
The Coldspring Tape – Gysin / Burroughs / P-Orridge (UK, 1989) ... 154
Real English Tea Made Here – William Burroughs (UK, 2007) . 293
Three Allusive Tracks – William Burroughs (BE, 2009) 307

WSB ON COMPS

spoken word on GPS albums
The Dial-A-Poem Poets – Various (US, 1972) 44
Disconnected – Various (US, 1974) 49
Biting Off the Tongue of a Corpse – Various (US, 1975) ... 51
William Burroughs / John Giorno – William Burroughs & John Giorno (US, 1975) ... 54
Totally Corrupt – Various (US, 1976) 57
Big Ego – Various (US, 1978) 62
The Nova Convention – Various (US, 1979) 73
Sugar, Alcohol & Meat – Various (US, 1980) 76
You're the Guy I Want to Share My… – Giorno / Burroughs / Anderson (US, 1981) ... 88
Life is a Killer – Various (US, 1982) 91
One World Poetry – Various (US, 1982) 92
Better an Old Demon Than a New God – Various (US, 1984) .. 109
You're a Hook – Various (US, 1984) 116
A Diamond Hidden in the Mouth of a Corpse – Various (US, 1985) ... 117
Smack My Crack – Various (US, 1987) 137
Like a Girl, I Want You to Keep Coming – Various (US, 1989) ... 156
Cash Cow – Various (US, 1993) 191

cut/ups & experimental
Aspen 5+6 – Various (US, 1967) 15
Klacto/23 – Various (DE, 1967) 16
OU Revuedisque 40-41 – Various (UK, 1972) 43
OU Revuedisque 42-43-44 – Various (UK, 1973) 47

Index by type

Revolutions Per Minute – Various (US, 1982) 95
Myths: Instructions 1 – Various (BE, 1984) 112

songs
Mister Heartbreak – Laurie Anderson (UK, 1983) 103
World Turning – Tony Trischka (US, 1993) 202
Hallucination Engine – Material (US, 1994) 207
Cough it Up! – Various (US, 1995) 219
The Mortal Micronotz Tribute! – Various (US, 1995) 225
Songs in the Key of X – Various (US, 1996) 228
September Songs – Various (CA, 1997) 235
Stoned Immaculate – Various (US, 2000) 262

spoken word
10%: File under Burroughs – Various (BE, 1996) 226
Kerouac - Kicks Joy Darkness – Various (US, 1997) 233
Hashisheen: The End of Law – Bill Laswell (BE, 1999) 252
Up from the Archives – Gerard Malanga (BE, 2000) 265

reissues
The Fruit of the Original Sin – Various (BE, 1981) 84
Minutes – Various (UK, 1987) 133
Minutes to Go – Various (BE, 1988) 144
The Beat Generation – Various (US, 1992) 186
Big Hard Disk Vol. 2 – Various (US, 1994) 204
The Myths Collection Part Two – Various (BE, 1994) 215
Zur Holle Mama #3 – Various (DE, 1998) 251
Planet Rave – Various (US, 2000) 261
The Night Watch – Various (UK, 2000) 264
More Dub Infusions – Various (DE, 2002) 270
The Wire: 20 Years 1982-2002 – Various (UK, 2002) 271
Noise & Electronic Music #4 – Various (BE, 2006) 287
Step Right Up! – Various (UK, 2010) 313

WSB READ BY OTHERS
Last Words: Qui Vivre Verra – Burroughs / Haage / Schäfer (DE, 2001) 266
Tagebuch eines Rückzuges – William Burroughs (DE, 2003) 275
The Theatre of Repetitions – Johannes Kalitzke (AT, 2006) 290
And the Hippos.. (Audiobook) – Jack Kerouac & William Burroughs (US, 2009) 302
The Naked Lunch (Audiobook) – William Burroughs (US, 2009) 306

WSB ARTWORK
Communiqué – Steve Lacy & Mal Waldron (IT, 1997) 231
Innermedium – Robert Musso (JP, 2000) 257
NYC Ghosts and Flowers – Sonic Youth (US, 2000) 260
Incunabula – Method of Defiance (US, 2010) 309
Jahbulon – Method of Defiance (US, 2010) 311

SAMPLES & INSPIRATION

ambient
The White Arcades – Harold Budd (UK, 1987) 142
Bajo El Sol Jaguar – Jorge Reyes (ES, 1991) 169
Ambient - 152 minutes 33 seconds – Various (UK, 1993) 189

country/folk
The Mugwumps – The Mugwumps (US, 1967) 20
William Burrito Brothers – William Burrito Brothers (US, 1976) 59
Land Rush – Fletcher Harrington & Topeka (US, 2005) 281
Hell Money – Rome (DE, 2012) 318

electro
Rabies – Naked Lunch (US, 1979) 71
Replicas – Tubeway Army (UK, 1979) 72
The Wild Boys – Duran Duran (UK, 1984) 115
Artificial Intelligence – John Cale (UK, 1985) 118
Code – Cabaret Voltaire (UK, 1987) 134
Queer – Manapsara (BE, 1988) 145
Routine (extended mix) – Manapsara (BE, 1988) 146
Friendly as a Hand Grenade – Tackhead (UK, 1990) 163
Technodon – Yellow Magic Orchestra (JP, 1993) 195
The Greatest Show of Truth – The Sacred Sawdust Ring (UK, 1994) 213
In Extremis (The Remixes) – Nirvana (UK, 1995) 220
New Deutsch – Various (DE, 2003) 273
Post Industrial Boys – Post Industrial Boys (DE, 2004) 276
Rhythm Science – DJ Spooky (BE, 2004) 279

MakroSoft 'Theme' – Makrosoft (DE, 2006) 286
The Audience's Listening – Cut Chemist (US, 2006) 288
Sound Unbound – DJ Spooky (BE, 2008) 299
Riding Strange Horses – Dub Spencer & Trance Hill (DE, 2009) 305

experimental
Audiopoems – Henri Chopin (UK, 1971) 36
Megaton for Wm. Burroughs – Gordon Mumma (US, 1979) 70
ReR Quarterly, Vol. 1 Selections – Various (UK, 1991) 172

hip hop
Action! – The Alliance (DE, 1988) 143
Clear – Bomb the Bass (UK, 1995) 217
Negro Necro Nekros – Dälek (US, 1998) 241

industrial
The Gospel Comes to New Guinea – 23 Skidoo (UK, 1981) 85
Major Malfunction – Keith LeBlanc (UK, 1986) 126
Anarchy in the UK – P.J. Proby (UK, 1987) 131
Jane's Addiction – Jane's Addiction (US, 1987) 132
The Mugwump Dance – P.J. Proby (UK, 1987) 140
End of the Century Party – Gary Clail (UK, 1989) 151
Storm the Studio – Meat Beat Manifesto (UK, 1989) 158

joujouka
The Pipes of Pan at Joujouka – The Master Musicians of Joujouka (UK, 1971) 39
Apocalypse Across the Sky – The Master Musicians of Jajouka (UK, 1992) 177
The Source – The Master Musicians of Jajouka (UK, 2010) 314

jazz
Chappaqua – Ravi Shankar (US, 1968) 24
Take Another Little Piece of My Heart – Nova Express (AU, 1969) 29
Obsolete – Dashiell Hedayat (FR, 1971) 38
Can't Buy a Thrill – Steely Dan (US, 1972) 42
Naked Lunch (Soundtrack) – Howard Shore / Ornette Coleman / LPO (US, 1992) 182
The Heart/Hertz Files – Klange (IT, 1995) 224
Transfixiones – Hugo Westerdahl & Juan Belda (ES, 2006) 291
Interzone – John Zorn (US, 2010) 310
Nova Express – John Zorn (US, 2011) 315
Dreamachines – John Zorn (US, 2013) 323
Wanderlust – Cliff Hines (US, 2013) 324

metal
Burning in Water Drowning in Flame – Skrew (US, 1992) 178
Nowhere – Therapy? (UK, 1994) 209
Flora Meets Fauna – Violet Halo (FI, 2008) 298

psychedelic
Sgt. Pepper's Lonely Hearts Club Band – The Beatles (UK, 1967) 18
The Velvet Underground and Nico – The Velvet Underground (US, 1967) 22
The Soft Machine – The Soft Machine (UK, 1968) 25
The Master – Nick Haeffner (UK, 1987) 139
Twelve Selves – Daevid Allen (UK, 1993) 199
Dreamspeed – Anton Fier (JP, 1994) 205
Nova Psychedelia (1975-1985) – Todd Tamanend Clark (US, 2005) 284

punk
Orgasm Addict – Buzzcocks (UK, 1977) 61
Storm the Reality Studio – Dead Fingers Talk (UK, 1978) 63
Unknown Pleasures – Joy Division (UK, 1979) 69
The Mortal Micronotz – The Mortal Micronotz (US, 1982) 98
Suicide Alley – Manic Street Preachers (UK, 1991) 173
The Longest Line – NOFX (US, 1992) 187
Stranglehold – Various (US, 2000) 263

reggae
Rhythm Killers – Sly and Robbie (UK, 1987) 135
CinemaSonics – Doug Wimbish (DE, 2008) 297
Marijuana Dreams – Dubblestandart (AT, 2010) 312

rock
The Insect Trust – The Insect Trust (US, 1966) 14
Born to be Wild – Steppenwolf (US, 1968) 23
Diamond Dogs – David Bowie (UK, 1974) 48
Rollercoaster – The Jesus and Mary Chain (UK, 1990) 165
The Nova Mob – The Nova Mob (US, 1991) 175
Eats Darkness – Apostle of Hustle (CA, 2009) 304

Index by type

spoken word

The Jack Kerouac Collection – Jack Kerouac (US, 1990) 168
Prison – Steven Jesse Bernstein (US, 1992) 184
Holy Soul Jelly Roll – Allen Ginsberg (US, 1994) 208
Cyber-Sadism Live! – Stewart Home (US, 1998) 237
One Night @ the 1001 – Brion Gysin (BE, 1998) 242
Radio Hyper-Yahoo – Elliott Sharp (US, 2004) 277
Diggin the New Breed – Various (UK, 2005) 280
Newspaper Taxis – Various (UK, 2005) 283

FILMS & MULTIMEDIA

FILMS BASED ON WSB TEXTS

The Discipline of DE – Gus Van Sant dir. (US, 1982) 96
Taking Tiger Mountain – Tom Huckabee dir. (UK, 1983) 105
The Black Rider – Robert Wilson dir. (AT, 1990) 166
Naked Lunch – David Cronenberg dir. (CA, 1991) 171
A Thanksgiving Prayer – Gus Van Sant dir. (US, 1991) 174
The Junky's Christmas – Nick Donkin & Melodie McDaniel dir. (US, 1993) 197
Ah Pook Is Here – Philip Hunt dir. (DE, 1994) 203
Nova Express – Andre Perkowski dir. (US, 1999) 253
The Last Words of Dutch Schultz – Gerrit van Dijk dir. (NL, 2001) 268
The Japanese Sandman – Ed Buhr dir. (US, 2008) 301
The Black Meat – Matthew Roe dir. (US, 2012) 321

WSB DOCOS

William Burroughs with Kathy Acker – Fenella Greenfield dir. (US, 1982) 99
Burroughs – Howard Brookner dir. (US, 1983) 101
Commissioner of Sewers – Klaus Maeck dir. (DE, 1991) 170
Burroughs! – Graham Duff dir. (UK, 1992) 179
Lawrence Home Movies – Wayne Propst dir. (US, 2005) 282
Words of Advice – Lars Movin & Steen Møller Rasmussen dir. (DK, 2007) 294
A Man Within – Yony Leyser dir. (US, 2010) 308

WSB FILM APPEARANCES

advert
Nike Ads – Wieden & Kennedy Agency (1994) 216

comedy
Twister – Michael Almereyda dir. (US, 1988) 147
Bloodhounds of Broadway – Howard Brookner dir. (US, 1989) 149
Beavis and Butthead: Tornado – Mike Judge dir. (US, 1993) 190
Even Cowgirls Get the Blues – Gus Van Sant dir. (US, 1993) 192

documentary
Witchcraft Through the Ages – Benjamin Christensen dir. (SE, 1968) 26
Cain's Film – Jamie Wadhawan dir. (UK, 1969) 28
Underground and Emigrants – Rosa von Praunheim dir. (DE, 1976) 58
90 Minutes Live – William Burroughs & Peter Gzowski dir. (CA, 1977) 60
Fried Shoes Cooked Diamonds – Costanzo Allione dir. (US, 1979) 68
Chelsea Hotel – Nigel Finch dir. (UK, 1981) 78
Shamans of the Blind Country – Michael Oppitz dir. (DE, 1981) 83
Poetry in Motion – Ron Mann dir. (CA, 1982) 93
William Buys a Parrot – Antony Balch dir. (UK, 1982) 100
Kerouac, the Movie – John Antonelli dir. (US, 1985) 119
Ornette: Made in America – Shirley Clarke dir. (US, 1985) 120
What Happened to Kerouac? – Lerner & MacAdams dir. (US, 1986) 130
The Beat Generation: An American Dream – Janet Forman dir. (US, 1987) 138
Gang of Souls – Maria Beatty dir. (US, 1989) 152
Heavy Petting – Obie Benz dir. (US, 1989) 153
The Black Rider (Documentary) – Theo Janssen & Ralph Quinke dir. (DE, 1990) 167
Naked Making Lunch – Chris Rodley dir. (US, 1992) 183
Einstein's Brain – Kevin Hull dir. (UK, 1994) 211
The Life & Times of Allen Ginsberg – Jerry Aronson dir. (US, 1994) 214
The Man Who Invented Modern Sex – Clare Beavan dir. (UK, 1996) 230
Destroy All Rational Thought – Ambrose, Rynne & Wilson dirs. (IE, 1998) 238
Let It Come Down – Jennifer Baichwal dir. (CA, 1998) 239
The Nova Convention Revisited – John Aes-Nihil dir. (US, 1998) 246
The Source – Chuck Workman dir. (US, 1999) 254
Condo Painting – John McNaughton dir. (US, 2000) 256
Night Waltz – Owsley Brown dir. (US, 2000) 259
Sleep in a Nest of Flames – James Dowell & John Kolomvakis dirs. (US, 2001) 267
Absolute Wilson – Katharina Otto-Bernstein dir. (US, 2006) 285
Obscene – Daniel O'Connor & Neil Ortenberg dirs. (US, 2007) 292
Corso: The Last Beat – Gustave Reininger dir. (IT, 2009) 303
The Beat Hotel – Alan Governar dir. (US, 2011) 317
Outtakes from the Life of a Happy Man – Jonas Mekas dir. (US, 2012) 320

drama
Chappaqua – Conrad Rooks dir. (US, 1966) 13
Prologue – Robin Spry dir. (CA, 1970) 32
Energy and How to Get It – Robert Frank dir. (US, 1981) 80
Decoder – Klaus Maeck dir. (DE, 1984) 110
It Don't Pay to Be an Honest Citizen – Jacob Burckhardt dir. (US, 1984) 111
Drugstore Cowboy – Gus Van Sant dir. (US, 1989) 150
The Book of Life – Hal Hartley dir. (US, 1998) 245

experimental
Towers Open Fire – Antony Balch dir. (UK, 1963) 9
Poem Posters – Charles Henri Ford dir. (US, 1967) 17
The Cut-Ups – Antony Balch dir. (UK, 1967) 19
Bill and Tony – Antony Balch dir. (UK, 1972) 41
Thot-Fal'N – Stan Brakhage dir. (US, 1978) 64
Ghosts at no. 9 – Antony Balch dir. (UK, 1982) 90
Pirate Tape – Derek Jarman dir. (UK, 1983) 104
The Dream Machine – Derek Jarman dir. (UK, 1983) 106
This Song for Jack – Robert Frank dir. (US, 1983) 108
Thee Films – Antony Balch dir. (UK, 1986) 129
Towers Open Fire & other films – Anthony Balch dir. (US, 1989) 160
Wax – David Blair dir. (US, 1991) 176
Glitterbug – Derek Jarman dir. (UK, 1994) 206
Mentallusions – Benjamin Meade dir. (US, 2012) 319

multimedia
Poetry in Motion – Ron Mann (US, 1994) 210
Pantopon Rose – Andrea di Castro (MX, 1995) 222
The Dark Eye – Russell Lees / Inscape (US, 1995) 223
The Beat Experience – Red Hot Organization (US, 1996) 229

music
Home of the Brave – Laurie Anderson dir. (US, 1986) 125
Scared to Live – Psychic TV (UK, 1987) 136
September Songs – Larry Weinstein dir. (CA, 1994) 212
Last Night on Earth – Richie Smyth dir. (US, 2002) 269

readings
Gay Sunshine Reading – William Burroughs (US, 1974) 50
Saturday Night Live – William Burroughs (US, 1981) 86
The Final Academy Documents – Balch / Whitehead dirs. (UK, 1983) 107

INFLUENCES & REFERERENCES

The Nude Restaurant – Andy Warhol dir. (US, 1967) 21
Secrets of Sex – Antony Balch dir. (UK, 1969) 30
Performance – Donald Cammell & Nicholas Roeg dirs. (UK, 1970) 31
Horror Hospital – Antony Balch dir. (UK, 1973) 46
Heart Beat – John Byrum dir. (US, 1980) 74
Lunatics, Lovers and Poets – Andrea Andermann dir. (IT, 1980) 75
The Exterminator – James Glickenhaus dir. (US, 1980) 77
A Short Conversation from the Grave – Patti Podesta dir. (US, 1990) 161
Kika – Pedro Almodóvar dir. (ES, 1993) 193
Clueless – Amy Heckerling dir. (US, 1995) 218
Xtrmn8mm – David Cox dir. (AU, 1997) 236
Modulations: Cinema for the Ear – Iara Lee dir. (US, 1998) 240
Venus Blue – Gillian Ashurst dir. (NZ, 1998) 248
Beat – Gary Walkow dir. (US, 2000) 255
Elephant – Gus Van Sant dir. (US, 2003) 272
Portrait of a Bookstore as an Old Man – Pichelin & Sutherland dirs. (FR, 2003) 274
The Sopranos: Members Only – Timothy Van Patten dir. (US, 2006) 289
Chelsea on the Rocks – Abel Ferrara dir. (US, 2008) 296
The Ballad of Genesis and Lady Jaye – Marie Losier dir. (US, 2011) 316

Index of creators

Names of groups are listed without articles here. This listing excludes mentions of WSB as they occur in all items. It does not account for mentions in blurbs.

#

23 Skidoo . . . . *The Gospel Comes to New Guinea* (1981) 85

A

Aes-Nihil, John . . . . *The Nova Convention Revisited* (1998) 246
Allen, Daevid . . . . *Twelve Selves* (1993) 199
Alliance, The . . . . *Action!* (1988) 143
Allione, Costanzo . . . . *Fried Shoes Cooked Diamonds* (1979) 68
Almereyda, Michael . . . . *Twister* (1988) 147
Almodóvar, Pedro . . . . *Kika* (1993) 193
Ambrose, Joe . . . . *Destroy All Rational Thought* (1998) 238
Andermann, Andrea . . . . *Lunatics, Lovers and Poets* (1980) 75
Anderson, Laurie . . . . *You're the Guy I Want to Share My..* (1981) . . 88
Anderson, Laurie . . . . *Mister Heartbreak* (1983) 103
Anderson, Laurie . . . . *Home of the Brave* (1986) 125
Antonelli, John . . . . *Kerouac, the Movie* (1985) 119
Apostle of Hustle . . . . *Eats Darkness* (2009) 304
Aronson, Jerry . . . . *The Life & Times of Allen Ginsberg* (1994) . . . 214
Ashurst, Gillian . . . . *Venus Blue* (1998) 248

B

Baichwal, Jennifer . . . . *Let It Come Down* (1998) 239
Balch, Antony . . . . *The Final Academy Documents* (1982) 106
Balch, Antony . . . . *Towers Open Fire* (1963) 9
Balch, Antony . . . . *The Cut-Ups* (1967) 19
Balch, Antony . . . . *Secrets of Sex* (1969) 30
Balch, Antony . . . . *Bill and Tony* (1972) 41
Balch, Antony . . . . *Horror Hospital* (1973) 46
Balch, Antony . . . . *Ghosts at no. 9* (1982) 90
Balch, Antony . . . . *William Buys a Parrot* (1982) 100
Balch, Antony . . . . *Thee Films* (1986) 129
Balch, Antony . . . . *Towers Open Fire & other films* (1989) 160
Beatles, The . . . . *Sgt. Pepper's Lonely Hearts Club Band* (1967) . . 18
Beatty, Maria . . . . *Gang of Souls* (1989) 152
Beavan, Clare . . . . *The Man Who Invented Modern Sex* (1996) . . 230
Beiles, Sinclair . . . . *Minutes to Go* (1960) 3
Belda, Juan . . . . *Transfixiones* (2007) 292
Benz, Obie . . . . *Heavy Petting* (1989) 153
Bernstein, Steven Jesse . . . . *Prison* (1992) 184
Blair, David . . . . *Wax* (1991) 176
Bockris, Victor . . . . *With William Burroughs* (1981) 87
Bomb the Bass . . . . *Clear* (1995) 217
Bowie, David . . . . *Diamond Dogs* (1974) 48
Brakhage, Stan . . . . *Thot-Fal'N* (1978) 64
Brookner, Howard . . . . *Burroughs* (1983) 101
Brookner, Howard . . . . *Bloodhounds of Broadway* (1989) 149
Brown, Owsley . . . . *Night Waltz* (2000) 259
Budd, Harold . . . . *The White Arcades* (1987) 142
Buhr, Ed . . . . *The Japanese Sandman* (2008) 301
Burckhardt, Jacob . . . . *It Don't Pay to Be an Honest Citizen* (1984) . . 111
Buzzcocks . . . . *Orgasm Addict* (1977) 61
Byrum, John . . . . *Heart Beat* (1980) 74

C

Cabaret Voltaire . . . . *Code* (1987) 134
Calder, John . . . . *A William Burroughs Reader* (1982) 89
Cale, John . . . . *Artificial Intelligence* (1985) 118
Cammell, Donald . . . . *Performance* (1970) 31
Chopin, Henri . . . . *Audiopoems* (1971) 36
Christensen, Benjamin . . . . . *Witchcraft Through the Ages* (1968) 26
Clail, Gary . . . . *End of the Century Party* (1989) 151

Clarke, Shirley . . . . *Ornette: Made in America* (1985) 120
Cobain, Kurt . . . . *The "Priest" They Called Him* (1992) 185
Coleman, Ornette . . . . *Naked Lunch (Soundtrack)* (1993) 183
Corso, Gregory . . . . *Minutes to Go* (1960) 3
Cox, David *Xtrmn8mm* (1997) 236
Cronenberg, David . . . . *The Naked Lunch (Screenplay)* (1989) 159
Cronenberg, David . . . . *Naked Lunch* (1991) 171
Cut Chemist . . . . *The Audience's Listening* (2006) 288

D

Dälek . . . . *Negro Necro Nekros* (1998) 241
Dead Fingers Talk . . . . *Storm the Reality Studio* (1978) 63
di Castro, Andrea . . . . *Pantopon Rose* (1995) 222
DJ Spooky . . . . *Rhythm Science* (2004) 279
DJ Spooky . . . . *Sound Unbound* (2008) 299
Donkin, Nick . . . . *The Junky's Christmas* (1993) 197
Dowell, James . . . . *Sleep in a Nest of Flames* (2001) 267
Dub Spencer & Trance Hill . . *Riding Strange Horses* (2009) 305
Dubblestandart . . . . *Marijuana Dreams* (2010) 312
Duff, Graham . . . . *Burroughs!* (1992) 179
Duran Duran . . . . *The Wild Boys* (1984) 115

E

Ely, Roger . . . . *The Final Academy* (1982) 97

F

Ferrara, Abel . . . . *Chelsea on the Rocks* (2008) 296
Fier, Anton . . . . *Dreamspeed* (1994) 205
Finch, Nigel . . . . *Chelsea Hotel* (1981) 78
Ford, Charles Henri . . . . *Poem Posters* (1967) 17
Forman, Janet . . . . *The Beat Generation: An American Dream* (1987) . . 138
Frank, Robert . . . . *Energy and How to Get It* (1981) 80
Frank, Robert . . . . *This Song for Jack* (1983) 108

G

Ginsberg, Allen . . . . *The Yage Letters* (1963) 8
Ginsberg, Allen . . . . *Holy Soul Jelly Roll* (1994) 208
Giorno, John . . . . *You're the Guy I Want to Share My ...* (1981) . . 88
Giorno, John . . . . *William Burroughs / John Giorno* (1975) 54
Glickenhaus, James . . . . *The Exterminator* (1980) 77
Governar, Alan . . . . *The Beat Hotel* (2011) 317
Grauerholz, James . . . . *Last Words* (2000) 258
Grauerholz, James . . . . *Word Virus* (1998) 250
Greenfield, Fenella . . . . *William Burroughs with Kathy Acker* (1982) . . 99
Gysin, Brion . . . . *Minutes to Go* (1960) 3
Gysin, Brion . . . . *Re/Search 4/5* (1982) 94
Gysin, Brion . . . . *The Coldspring Tape* (1989) 154
Gysin, Brion . . . . *The Exterminator* (1960) 4
Gysin, Brion . . . . *The Third Mind* (1976) 56
Gysin, Brion . . . . *One Night @ the 1001* (1998) 242
Gysin, Brion . . . . *The Spoken Word* (2012) 322
Gzowski, Peter . . . . *90 Minutes Live* (1977) 60

H

Haage, Ulrike . . . . *Last Words: Qui Vivre Verra* (2001) 266
Haeffner, Nick . . . . *The Master* (1987) 139
Harrington, Fletcher . . . . *Land Rush* (2004) 280
Hartley, Hal . . . . *The Book of Life* (1998) 245
Heckerling, Amy . . . . *Clueless* (1995) 218
Hedayat, Dashiell . . . . *Obsolete* (1971) 38
Hines, Cliff . . . . *Wanderlust* (2013) 324
Home, Stewart . . . . *Cyber-Sadism Live!* (1998) 237
Huckabee, Tom . . . . *Taking Tiger Mountain* (1983) 105
Hull, Kevin . . . . *Einstein's Brain* (1994) 211
Hunt, Philip . . . . *Ah Pook Is Here* (1994) 203

111

Index of creators

I
Insect Trust, The............*The Insect Trust* (1966).................... 14

J
Jane's Addiction.............*Jane's Addiction* (1987)................... 132
Janssen, Theo................*The Black Rider* (Documentary) (1990)...... 167
Jarman, Derek................*Pirate Tape* (1983)........................ 104
Jarman, Derek................*The Dream Machine* (1983).................. 106
Jarman, Derek................*Glitterbug* (1994)......................... 206
Jesus and Mary Chain, The....*Rollercoaster* (1990)...................... 165
Joy Division.................*Unknown Pleasures* (1979).................. 69
Judge, Mike..................*Beavis and Butthead: Tornado* (1993)....... 190

K
Kahn, Douglas................*Wireless Imagination* (1991)............... 187
Kalitzke, Johannes...........*The Theatre of Repetitions* (2006)......... 290
Kerouac, Jack................*And the Hippos...* (2008).................. 295
Kerouac, Jack................*The Jack Kerouac Collection* (1990)........ 168
Kerouac, Jack................*And the Hippos...* (Audiobook) (2009)...... 302
Klange.......................*The Heart/Hertz Files* (1995).............. 224
Kolomvakis, John.............*Sleep in a Nest of Flames* (2002).......... 268

L
Lacy, Steve..................*Communiqué* (1997)......................... 231
Laswell, Bill................*Hashisheen: The End of Law* (1999)......... 252
LeBlanc, Keith...............*Major Malfunction* (1986).................. 126
Lee, Iara....................*Modulations: Cinema for the Ear* (1998)... 240
Lee, William.................*Junkie* (1953)............................. 1
Lees, Russell................*The Dark Eye* (1995)....................... 223
Lerner, Richard..............*What Happened to Kerouac?* (1986).......... 130
Leyser, Yony.................*A Man Within* (2010)....................... 308
London Philharmonic Orch.....*Naked Lunch* (Soundtrack) (1994)........... 184
Losier, Marie................*The Ballad of Genesis and Lady Jaye* (2011). 316

M
MacAdams, Lewis..............*What Happened to Kerouac?* (1987).......... 131
Maeck, Klaus.................*Decoder* (1984)............................ 110
Maeck, Klaus.................*Commissioner of Sewers* (1991)............. 170
Makrosoft....................*MakroSoft 'Theme'* (2006).................. 286
Malanga, Gerard..............*Up from the Archives* (2000).............. 265
Manapsara....................*Queer* (1988).............................. 145
Manapsara....................*Routine* (extended mix) (1988)............. 146
Manic Street Preachers.......*Suicide Alley* (1991)...................... 173
Mann, Ron....................*Poetry in Motion* (1982)................... 93
Mann, Ron....................*Poetry in Motion* (1994)................... 210
Master Musicians of Jajouka, The *Apocalypse Across the Sky* (1992).... 177
Master Musicians of Jajouka, The *The Source* (2010).................. 314
Master Musicians of Joujouka, The *The Pipes of Pan at Joujouka* (1971). 39
Material.....................*Seven Souls* (1989)........................ 157
Material.....................*Hallucination Engine* (1994)............... 207
Material.....................*The Road to the Western Lands* (1998)..... 247
McDaniel, Melodie............*The Junky's Christmas* (1994).............. 198
McNaughton, John.............*Condo Painting* (2000)..................... 256
Meade, Benjamin..............*Mentallusions* (2012)...................... 319
Meat Beat Manifesto..........*Storm the Studio* (1989)................... 158
Mekas, Jonas.................*Outtakes from the Life of a Happy Man* (2012). 320
Method of Defiance...........*Incunabula* (2010)......................... 309
Method of Defiance...........*Jahbulon* (2010)........................... 311
Ministry.....................*Just One Fix* (1992)....................... 181
Mortal Micronotz, The........*The Mortal Micronotz* (1982)............... 98
Mottram, Eric................*Snack: Two Tape Transcripts* (1975)....... 53
Movin, Lars..................*Words of Advice* (2007).................... 294
Mugwumps, The................*The Mugwumps* (1967)....................... 20
Mumma, Gordon................*Megaton for Wm. Burroughs* (1979).......... 70
Murphy, Timothy..............*Wising up the Marks* (1998)................ 249
Musso, Robert................*Innermedium* (2000)........................ 257

N
Naked Lunch..................*Rabies* (1979)............................. 71
Nirvana......................*In Extremis* (The Remixes) (1995).......... 220
NOFX.........................*The Longest Line* (1992)................... 187

Nova Express.................*Take Another Little Piece of My Heart* (1969). 29
Nova Mob, The................*The Nova Mob* (1991)....................... 175

O
O'Connor, Daniel.............*Obscene* (2007)............................ 292
Odier, Daniel................*The Job* (1970)............................ 34
Oppitz, Michael..............*Shamans of the Blind Country* (1981)...... 83
Ortenberg, Neil..............*Obscene* (2008)............................ 293
Otto-Bernstein, Katharina....*Absolute Wilson* (2006).................... 285

P
Perkowski, Andre.............*Nova Express* (1999)....................... 253
Pichelin, Gonzague...........*Portrait of a Bookstore as an Old Man* (2003). 274
Podesta, Patti...............*A Short Conversation from the Grave* (1990). 161
P-Orridge, Genesis...........*The Coldspring Tape* (1989)................ 154
Post Industrial Boys.........*Post Industrial Boys* (2004)............... 276
Proby, P.J...................*Anarchy in the UK* (1987).................. 131
Proby, P.J...................*The Mugwump Dance* (1987).................. 140
Propst, Wayne................*Lawrence Home Movies* (2005)............... 282
Psychic TV...................*Scared to Live* (1987)..................... 136

Q
Quinke, Ralph................*The Black Rider* (Documentary) (1991)..... 168

R
Rasmussen, Steen Møller......*Words of Advice* (2008).................... 295
Red Hot Organization.........*The Beat Experience* (1996)................ 229
Reininger, Gustave...........*Corso: The Last Beat* (2009)............... 303
Reyes, Jorge.................*Bajo El Sol Jaguar* (1991)................. 169
Rodley, Chris................*Naked Making Lunch* (1992)................. 183
Roe, Matthew.................*The Black Meat* (2012)..................... 321
Roeg, Nicolas................*Performance* (1970)........................ 31
Rome.........................*Hell Money* (2012)......................... 318
Rooks, Conrad................*Chappaqua* (1966).......................... 13
Russell, Jamie...............*Retaking the Universe* (2005).............. 279
Rynne, Frank.................*Destroy All Rational Thought* (1999)....... 239

S
Sacred Sawdust Ring, The.....*The Greatest Show of Truth* (1994)......... 213
Sargeant, Jack...............*Naked Lens* (1997)......................... 234
Schäfer, Barbara.............*Last Words: Qui Vivre Verra* (2002)........ 267
Schneiderman, Davis..........*Retaking the Universe* (2004).............. 278
Shankar, Ravi................*Chappaqua OST* (1968)...................... 24
Sharp, Elliott...............*Radio Hyper-Yahoo* (2004).................. 277
Shore, Howard................*Naked Lunch* (Soundtrack) (1992)........... 182
Silverberg, Ira..............*Word Virus* (1999)......................... 251
Silverberg, Ira..............*Everything is Permitted* (1992)............ 180
Skrew........................*Burning in Water Drowning in Flame* (1992). 178
Sly and Robbie...............*Rhythm Killers* (1987)..................... 135
Smyth, Richie................*Last Night on Earth* (2002)................ 269
Soft Machine, The............*The Soft Machine* (1968)................... 25
Sonic Youth..................*NYC Ghosts and Flowers* (2000)............. 260
Spry, Robin..................*Prologue* (1970)........................... 32
Steely Dan...................*Can't Buy a Thrill* (1972)................. 42
Steppenwolf..................*Born to be Wild* (1968).................... 23
Sutherland, Benjamin.........*Portrait of a Bookstore as an Old Man* (2004). 275

T
Tackhead.....................*Friendly as a Hand Grenade* (1990)......... 163
Tamanend Clark, Todd.........*Nova Psychedelia (1975-1985)* (2005)....... 284
Therapy?.....................*Nowhere* (1994)............................ 209
Trischka, Tony...............*World Turning* (1993)...................... 202
Tubeway Army.................*Replicas* (1979)........................... 72

V
van Dijk, Gerrit.............*The Last Words of Dutch Schultz* (2001).... 268
Van Patten, Timothy..........*The Sopranos: Members Only* (2006)......... 289
Van Sant, Gus................*The Discipline of DE* (1982)............... 96
Van Sant, Gus................*The Elvis of Letters* (1985)............... 123
Van Sant, Gus................*Drugstore Cowboy* (1989)................... 150
Van Sant, Gus................*Millions of Images* (1990)................. 164

Van Sant, Gus	*A Thanksgiving Prayer* (1991)	174	
Van Sant, Gus	*Even Cowgirls Get the Blues* (1993)	192	
Van Sant, Gus	*Elephant* (2003)	272	
Velvet Underground, The	*The Velvet Underground and Nico* (1967)	22	
Violet Halo	*Flora Meets Fauna* (2008)	298	
von Praunheim, Rosa	*Underground and Emigrants* (1976)	58	
Whitehead, Malcolm	*The Final Academy Documents* (1983)	107	
Wieden & Kennedy Agency	*Nike Ads* (1994)	216	
William Burrito Brothers	*William Burrito Brothers* (1976)	59	
Wilson, Terry	*Destroy All Rational Thought* (2000)	240	
Wilson, Robert	*The Black Rider* (1990)	166	
Wimbish, Doug	*CinemaSonics* (2008)	297	
Wladron, Mal	*Communiqué* (1998)	232	
Workman, Chuck	*The Source* (1999)	254	

W

Wadhawan, Jamie	*Cain's Film* (1969)	28	
Waits, Tom	*The Black Rider* (1993)	196	
Walkow, Gary	*Beat* (2000)	255	
Warhol, Andy	*The Nude Restaurant* (1967)	21	
Weinstein, Larry	*September Songs* (1994)	212	
Weissner, Carl	*The Braille Film* (1970)	33	
Westerdahl, Hugo	*Transfixiones* (2006)	291	
Whitehead, Gregory	*Wireless Imagination* (1992)	188	

Y

Yellow Magic Orchestra	*Technodon* (1993)	195	

Z

Zorn, John	*Interzone* (2010)	310	
Zorn, John	*Nova Express* (2011)	315	
Zorn, John	*Dreamachines* (2013)	323	

Index of titles

#

10%: File under Burroughs – Various (BE, 1996)	226	
90 Minutes Live – William Burroughs & Peter Gzowski (CA, 1977)	60	

A

Absolute Wilson – Katharina Otto-Bernstein dir. (US, 2006)	285	
Action! – The Alliance (DE, 1988)	143	
(The) Adding Machine – William Burroughs (UK, 1985)	122	
Ah Pook Is Here – Philip Hunt dir. (DE, 1994)	203	
Ah Pook is Here and Other Texts – William Burroughs (UK, 1979)	65	
Ali's Smile – William Burroughs (UK, 1969)	27	
Ambient - 152 minutes 33 seconds – Various (UK, 1993)	189	
Anarchy in the UK – P.J. Proby (UK, 1987)	131	
And the Hippos… – Jack Kerouac & William Burroughs (US, 2008)	295	
And the Hippos… (Audiobook) – Jack Kerouac & William Burroughs (US, 2009)	302	
Apocalypse Across the Sky – The Master Musicians of Jajouka (UK, 1992)	177	
Artificial Intelligence – John Cale (UK, 1985)	118	
Aspen 5+6 – Various (US, 1967)	15	
(The) Audience's Listening – Cut Chemist (US, 2006)	288	
Audiopoems – Henri Chopin (UK, 1971)	36	

B

Bajo El Sol Jaguar – Jorge Reyes (ES, 1991)	169	
(The) Ballad of Genesis and Lady Jaye – Marie Losier dir. (US, 2011)	316	
Beat – Gary Walkow dir. (US, 2000)	255	
(The) Beat Experience – Red Hot Organization (US, 1996)	229	
(The) Beat Generation – Various (US, 1992)	186	
(The) Beat Generation: An American Dream – Janet Forman dir. (US, 1987)	138	
(The) Beat Hotel – Alan Govenar dir. (US, 2011)	317	
Beavis and Butthead: Tornado – Mike Judge dir. (US, 1993)	190	
(The) Best of WSB from GPS – William Burroughs (US, 1998)	244	
Better an Old Demon Than a New God – Various (US, 1984)	109	
Big Ego – Various (US, 1978)	62	
Big Hard Disk Vol. 2 – Various (US, 1994)	204	
Bill and Tony – Antony Balch dir. (UK, 1972)	41	
Biting Off the Tongue of a Corpse – Various (US, 1975)	51	
(The) Black Meat – Matthew Roe dir. (US, 2012)	321	
(The) Black Rider – Robert Wilson dir. (AT, 1990)	166	
(The) Black Rider – Tom Waits (US, 1993)	196	
(The) Black Rider (Documentary) – Janssen & Quinke dir. (DE, 1990)	167	
Blade Runner: A Movie – William Burroughs (US, 1979)	66	
Bloodhounds of Broadway – Howard Brookner dir. (US, 1989)	149	
(The) Book of Life – Hal Hartley dir. (US, 1998)	245	
Born to be Wild – Steppenwolf (US, 1968)	23	
(The) Braille Film – Carl Weissner & William Burroughs (US, 1970)	33	
Break Through in Grey Room – William Burroughs (BE, 1986)	124	
Burning in Water Drowning in Flame – Skrew (US, 1992)	178	
Burroughs – Howard Brookner dir. (US, 1983)	101	
Burroughs! – Graham Duff (UK, 1992)	179	
(The) Burroughs File – William Burroughs (US, 1984)	113	

C

Cain's Film – Jamie Wadhawan dir. (UK, 1969)	28	
Call Me Burroughs – William Burroughs (FR, 1965)	11	
Can't Buy a Thrill – Steely Dan (US, 1972)	42	
Cash Cow – Various (US, 1993)	191	
(The) Cat Inside – William Burroughs (US, 1986)	127	
Chappaqua – Conrad Rooks dir. (US, 1966)	13	
Chappaqua – Ravi Shankar (US, 1968)	24	
Chelsea Hotel – Nigel Finch dir. (UK, 1981)	78	
Chelsea on the Rocks – Abel Ferrara dir. (US, 2008)	296	
CinemaSonics – Doug Wimbish (DE, 2008)	297	
Cities of the Red Night – William Burroughs (US, 1981)	79	
Clear – Bomb the Bass (UK, 1995)	217	
Clueless – Amy Heckerling dir. (US, 1995)	218	
Code – Cabaret Voltaire (UK, 1987)	134	
(The) Coldspring Tape – Gysin / Burroughs / P-Orridge (UK, 1989)	154	
Commissioner of Sewers – Klaus Maeck dir. (DE, 1991)	170	
Communiqué – Steve Lacy & Mal Waldron (IT, 1997)	231	
Condo Painting – John McNaughton dir. (US, 2000)	256	
Corso: The Last Beat – Gustave Reininger dir. (IT, 2009)	303	
Cough it Up! – Various (US, 1995)	219	
(The) Cut-Ups – Antony Balch dir. (UK, 1967)	19	
Cyber-Sadism Live! – Stewart Home (UK, 1998)	237	

D

(The) Dark Eye – Russell Lees / Inscape (US, 1995)	223	
Dead City Radio – William Burroughs (US, 1990)	162	
Dead Fingers Talk – William Burroughs (UK, 1963)	7	
Decoder – Klaus Maeck dir. (DE, 1984)	110	
Destroy All Rational Thought – Ambrose, Rynne & Wilson dirs. (IE, 1998)	238	
(The) Dial-A-Poem Poets – Various (US, 1972)	44	
Diamond Dogs – David Bowie (UK, 1974)	48	
(A) Diamond Hidden in the Mouth… – Various (US, 1985)	117	
Diggin the New Breed – Various (UK, 2005)	280	
(The) Discipline of DE – Gus Van Sant dir. (US, 1982)	96	
Disconnected – Various (US, 1974)	49	
Doctor Benway – William Burroughs (US, 1979)	67	
(The) Doctor is on the Market – William Burroughs (UK, 1986)	128	
(The) Dream Machine – Derek Jarman dir. (UK, 1983)	106	
Dreamachines – John Zorn (US, 2013)	323	
Dreamspeed – Anton Fier (JP, 1994)	205	
Drugstore Cowboy – Gus Van Sant dir. (US, 1989)	150	

113

Index of titles

E

Eats Darkness – Apostle of Hustle (CA, 2009)....304
Einstein's Brain – Kevin Hull dir. (UK, 1994)....211
Electronic Revolution – William Burroughs (UK, 1971)....37
Elephant – Gus Van Sant dir. (US, 2003)....272
(The) Elvis of Letters – William Burroughs & Gus Van Sant (US, 1985)....123
End of the Century Party – Gary Clail (UK, 1989)....151
Energy and How to Get It – Robert Frank dir. (US, 1981)....80
Even Cowgirls Get the Blues – Gus Van Sant dir. (US, 1993)....192
Everything is Permitted – Ira Silverberg (ed) (UK, 1992)....180
(The) Exterminator – James Glickenhaus dir. (US, 1980)....77
(The) Exterminator – William Burroughs & Brion Gysin (US, 1960)....4
Exterminator! – William Burroughs (US, 1973)....45

F

(The) Final Academy – Roger Ely (ed) (UK, 1982)....97
(The) Final Academy Documents – Balch / Whitehead dirs. (UK, 1983)....107
Flora Meets Fauna – Violet Halo (FI, 2008)....298
Fried Shoes Cooked Diamonds – Costanzo Allione dir. (US, 1979)....68
Friendly as a Hand Grenade – Tackhead (UK, 1990)....163
(The) Fruit of the Original Sin – Various (BE, 1981)....84

G

Gang of Souls – Maria Beatty dir. (US, 1989)....152
Gay Sunshine Reading – William Burroughs (US, 1974)....50
Ghosts at no. 9 – Antony Balch dir. (UK, 1982)....90
Glitterbug – Derek Jarman dir. (UK, 1994)....206
(The) Gospel Comes to New Guinea – 23 Skidoo (UK, 1981)....85
(The) Greatest Show of Truth – The Sacred Sawdust Ring (UK, 1994)....213

H

Hallucination Engine – Material (US, 1994)....207
Hashisheen: The End of Law – Bill Laswell (BE, 1999)....252
Heart Beat – John Byrum dir. (US, 1980)....74
(The) Heart/Hertz Files – Klange (IT, 1995)....224
Heavy Petting – Obie Benz dir. (US, 1989)....153
Hell Money – Rome (DE, 2012)....318
Holy Soul Jelly Roll – Allen Ginsberg (US, 1994)....208
Home of the Brave – Laurie Anderson dir. (US, 1986)....125
Horror Hospital – Antony Balch dir. (UK, 1973)....46

I

In Extremis (The Remixes) – Nirvana (UK, 1995)....220
Incunabula – Method of Defiance (US, 2010)....309
Innermedium – Robert Musso (JP, 2000)....257
(The) Insect Trust – The Insect Trust (US, 1966)....14
(The) Instrument of Control – William Burroughs (IT, 2008)....300
Interzone – John Zorn (US, 2010)....310
Interzone – William Burroughs (US, 1989)....155
It Don't Pay to Be an Honest Citizen – Jacob Burckhardt dir. (US, 1984)....111

J

(The) Jack Kerouac Collection – Jack Kerouac (US, 1990)....168
Jahbulon – Method of Defiance (US, 2010)....311
Jane's Addiction – Jane's Addiction (US, 1987)....132
(The) Japanese Sandman – Ed Buhr dir. (US, 2008)....301
(The) Job – William Burroughs & Daniel Odier (UK, 1970)....34
Junkie – William Lee (US, 1953)....1
Junky (Audiobook) – William Burroughs (US, 1997)....232
(The) Junky's Christmas – Nick Donkin & Melodie McDaniel dir. (US, 1993)....197
Just One Fix – Ministry (US, 1992)....181

K

Kerouac - Kicks Joy Darkness – Various (US, 1997)....233
Kerouac, the Movie – John Antonelli dir. (US, 1985)....119
Kika – Pedro Almodóvar dir. (ES, 1993)....193
Klacto/23 – Various (DE, 1967)....16

L

Land Rush – Fletcher Harrington & Topeka (US, 2005)....281
Last Night on Earth – Richie Smyth dir. (US, 2002)....269
Last Words – William Burroughs / James Grauerholz (ed) (US, 2000)....258
(The) Last Words of Dutch Schultz – Gerrit van Dijk dir. (NL, 2001)....268
(The) Last Words of Dutch Schultz – William Burroughs (UK, 1970)....35
Last Words: Qui Vivre Verra – Burroughs / Haage / Schäfer (DE, 2001)....266
Lawrence Home Movies – Wayne Propst dir. (US, 2005)....282
Let It Come Down – Jennifer Baichwal dir. (CA, 1998)....239
(The) Life & Times of Allen Ginsberg – Jerry Aronson dir. (US, 1994)....214
Life is a Killer – Various (US, 1982)....91
Like a Girl, I Want You to Keep Coming – Various (US, 1989)....156
Live at the Kabuki – William Burroughs (US, 1983)....102
(The) Longest Line – NOFX (US, 1992)....187
Lunatics, Lovers and Poets – Andrea Andermann dir. (IT, 1980)....75

M

Major Malfunction – Keith LeBlanc (UK, 1986)....126
MakroSoft 'Theme' – Makrosoft (DE, 2006)....286
(The) Man Who Invented Modern Sex – Clare Beavan dir. (UK, 1996)....230
(A) Man Within – Yony Leyser dir. (US, 2010)....308
Marijuana Dreams – Dubblestandart (AT, 2010)....312
(The) Master – Nick Haeffner (UK, 1987)....139
Megaton for Wm. Burroughs – Gordon Mumma (US, 1979)....70
Mentallusions – Benjamin Meade dir. (US, 2012)....319
Millions of Images – William Burroughs & Gus Van Sant (US, 1990)....164
Minutes – Various (UK, 1987)....133
Minutes to Go – Burroughs / Gysin / Beiles / Corso (FR, 1960)....3
Minutes to Go – Various (BE, 1988)....144
Mister Heartbreak – Laurie Anderson (US, 1983)....103
Modulations: Cinema for the Ear – Iara Lee dir. (US, 1998)....240
More Dub Infusions – Various (DE, 2002)....270
(The) Mortal Micronotz – The Mortal Micronotz (US, 1982)....98
(The) Mortal Micronotz Tribute! – Various (US, 1995)....225
(The) Mugwump Dance – P.J. Proby (UK, 1987)....140
(The) Mugwumps – The Mugwumps (US, 1967)....20
My Education – William Burroughs (US, 1995)....221
(The) Myths Collection Part Two – Various (BE, 1994)....215
Myths: Instructions 1 – Various (BE, 1984)....112

N

Naked Lens – Jack Sargeant (UK, 1997)....234
Naked Lunch – David Cronenberg dir. (CA, 1991)....171
(The) Naked Lunch – William Burroughs (FR, 1959)....2
Naked Lunch (Audiobook) – William Burroughs (US, 1996)....227
Naked Lunch (Audiobook) – William Burroughs (US, 2009)....306
(The) Naked Lunch (Screenplay) – David Cronenberg (UK, 1989)....159
Naked Lunch (Soundtrack) – Howard Shore / Ornette Coleman / LPO (US, 1992)....182
Naked Making Lunch – Chris Rodley dir. (US, 1992)....183
Negro Necro Nekros – Dälek (US, 1998)....241
New Deutsch – Various (DE, 2003)....273
Newspaper Taxis – Various (UK, 2005)....283
Night Waltz – Owsley Brown dir. (US, 2000)....259
(The) Night Watch – Various (UK, 2000)....264
Nike Ads – Wieden & Kennedy Agency (US, 1994)....216
Noise & Electronic Music #4 – Various (BE, 2006)....287
Nothing Here Now but the Recordings – William Burroughs (UK, 1981)....81
(The) Nova Convention – Various (US, 1979)....73
(The) Nova Convention Revisited – John Aes-Nihil dir. (US, 1998)....246
Nova Express – Andre Perkowski dir. (US, 1999)....253
Nova Express – John Zorn (US, 2011)....315
Nova Express – Various (UK, 1964)....10
(The) Nova Mob – The Nova Mob (US, 1991)....175
Nova Psychedelia (1975-1985) – Todd Tamanend Clark (US, 2005)....284
Nowhere – Therapy? (UK, 1994)....209
(The) Nude Restaurant – Andy Warhol dir. (US, 1967)....21
NYC Ghosts and Flowers – Sonic Youth (US, 2000)....260

O

Obscene – Daniel O'Connor & Neil Ortenberg dirs. (US, 2007)....292
Obsolete – Dashiell Hedayat (FR, 1971)....38
On the Nova Lark – William Burroughs (US, 1981)....82

114

Index of titles

One Night @ the 1001 – Brion Gysin (BE, 1998)	242
One World Poetry – Various (US, 1982)	92
(The) Operator's Manual – William Burroughs (US, 1993)	198
Orgasm Addict – Buzzcocks (UK, 1977)	61
Ornette: Made in America – Shirley Clarke dir. (US, 1985)	120
OU Revuedisque 40-41 – Various (UK, 1972)	43
OU Revuedisque 42-43-44 – Various (UK, 1973)	47
Outtakes from the Life of a Happy Man – Jonas Mekas dir. (US, 2012)	320

P

Pantopon Rose – Andrea di Castro (MX, 1995)	222
Performance – Donald Cammell & Nicholas Roeg dirs. (UK, 1970)	31
(The) Pipes of Pan at Joujouka – The Master Musicians of Joujouka (UK, 1971)	39
Pirate Tape – Derek Jarman dir. (UK, 1983)	104
(The) Place of Dead Roads – William Burroughs (US, 1984)	114
Planet Rave – Various (US, 2000)	261
Poem Posters – Charles Henri Ford dir. (US, 1967)	17
Poetry in Motion – Ron Mann dir. (US, 1994)	210
Poetry in Motion – Ron Mann dir. (CA, 1982)	93
Port of Saints – William Burroughs (UK, 1975)	52
Portrait of a Bookstore as an Old Man – Pichelin & Sutherland dirs. (FR, 2003)	274
Post Industrial Boys – Post Industrial Boys (DE, 2004)	276
(The) "Priest" They Called Him – William Burroughs & Kurt Cobain (US, 1992)	185
Prison – Steven Jesse Bernstein (US, 1992)	184
Prologue – Robin Spry dir. (CA, 1970)	32

Q

Queer – Manapsara (BE, 1988)	145
Queer – William Burroughs (US, 1985)	121

R

Rabies – Naked Lunch (UK, 1979)	71
Radio Hyper-Yahoo – Elliott Sharp (US, 2004)	277
Re/Search 4/5 – Burroughs / Gysin / TG (US, 1982)	94
Real English Tea Made Here – William Burroughs (UK, 2007)	293
Replicas – Tubeway Army (UK, 1979)	72
ReR Quarterly, Vol. 1 Selections – Various (UK, 1991)	172
Retaking the Universe – Davis Schneiderman & Jamie Russell (eds) (UK, 2004)	278
(The) Retreat Diaries – William Burroughs (US, 1976)	55
Revolutions Per Minute – Various (US, 1982)	95
Rhythm Killers – Sly and Robbie (UK, 1987)	135
Rhythm Science – DJ Spooky (BE, 2004)	279
Riding Strange Horses – Dub Spencer & Trance Hill (DE, 2009)	305
(The) Road to the Western Lands – Material (US, 1998)	247
Rollercoaster – The Jesus and Mary Chain (UK, 1990)	165
Routine (extended mix) – Manapsara (BE, 1988)	146

S

Saturday Night Live – William Burroughs (US, 1981)	86
Scared to Live – Psychic TV (UK, 1987)	136
Secrets of Sex – Antony Balch dir. (UK, 1969)	30
Selections from The Best of WSB from GPS – William Burroughs (US, 1998)	243
September Songs – Larry Weinstein dir. (CA, 1994)	212
September Songs – Various (US, 1997)	235
Seven Souls – Material (US, 1989)	157
Sgt. Pepper's Lonely Hearts Club Band – The Beatles (UK, 1967)	18
Shamans of the Blind Country – Michael Oppitz dir. (DE, 1981)	83
(A) Short Conversation from the Grave – Patti Podesta dir. (US, 1990)	161
Sleep in a Nest of Flames – James Dowell & John Kolomvakis dirs. (US, 2001)	267
Smack My Crack – Various (US, 1987)	137
Snack: Two Tape Transcripts – William Burroughs & Eric Mottram (UK, 1975)	53
(The) Soft Machine – The Soft Machine (UK, 1968)	25
(The) Soft Machine – William Burroughs (FR, 1961)	5
Songs in the Key of X – Various (US, 1996)	228
(The) Sopranos: Members Only – Timothy Van Patten dir. (US, 2006)	289
Sound Unbound – DJ Spooky (BE, 2008)	299
(The) Source – Chuck Workman dir. (US, 1999)	254
(The) Source – The Master Musicians of Jajouka (UK, 2010)	314
Spare Ass Annie and Other Tales – William Burroughs (US, 1993)	194
(The) Spoken Word – William S Burroughs & Brion Gysin (UK, 2012)	322
Step Right Up! – Various (UK, 2010)	313
Stoned Immaculate – Various (US, 2000)	262
Storm the Reality Studio – Dead Fingers Talk (UK, 1978)	63
Storm the Studio – Meat Beat Manifesto (UK, 1989)	158
Stranglehold – Various (US, 2000)	263
Sugar, Alcohol & Meat – Various (US, 1980)	76
Suicide Alley – Manic Street Preachers (UK, 1991)	173

T

Tagebuch eines Rückzuges – William Burroughs (DE, 2003)	275
Take Another Little Piece of My Heart – Nova Express (AU, 1969)	29
Taking Tiger Mountain – Tom Huckabee dir. (UK, 1983)	105
Technodon – Yellow Magic Orchestra (JP, 1993)	195
(A) Thanksgiving Prayer – Gus Van Sant dir. (US, 1991)	174
(The) Theatre of Repetitions – Johannes Kalitzke (AT, 2006)	290
(The) Third Mind – William Burroughs & Brion Gysin (FR, 1976)	56
Thee Films – Antony Balch dir. (UK, 1986)	129
This Song for Jack – Robert Frank dir. (US, 1983)	108
Thot-Fal'N – Stan Brakhage dir. (US, 1978)	64
Three Allusive Tracks – William Burroughs (BE, 2009)	307
(The) Ticket That Exploded – William Burroughs (FR, 1962)	6
Totally Corrupt – Various (US, 1976)	57
Towers Open Fire – Antony Balch dir. (UK, 1963)	9
Towers Open Fire & other films – Anthony Balch (US, 1989)	160
Transfixiones – Hugo Westerdahl & Juan Belda (ES, 2006)	291
Twelve Selves – Daevid Allen (UK, 1993)	199
Twister – Michael Almereyda dir. (US, 1988)	147

U

Uncommon Quotes – William Burroughs (US, 1988)	148
Underground and Emigrants – Rosa von Praunheim (DE, 1976)	58
Unknown Pleasures – Joy Division (UK, 1979)	69
Up from the Archives – Gerard Malanga (BE, 2000)	265

V

Valentine's Day Reading – William Burroughs (US, 1965)	12
Vaudeville Voices – William Burroughs (UK, 1993)	200
(The) Velvet Underground and Nico – The Velvet Underground (US, 1967)	22
Venus Blue – Gillian Ashurst dir. (NZ, 1998)	248

W

Wanderlust – Cliff Hines (US, 2013)	324
Wax – David Blair dir. (US, 1991)	176
(The) Western Lands – William Burroughs (US, 1987)	141
What Happened to Kerouac? – Lerner & MacAdams dirs. (US, 1986)	130
(The) White Arcades – Harold Budd (UK, 1987)	142
(The) Wild Boys – Duran Duran (UK, 1984)	115
(The) Wild Boys: A Book of the Dead – William Burroughs (US, 1971)	40
William Burrito Brothers – William Burrito Brothers (US, 1976)	59
William Burroughs / John Giorno – William Burroughs & John Giorno (US, 1975)	54
(A) William Burroughs Reader – John Calder (ed) (UK, 1982)	89
William Burroughs with Kathy Acker – Fenella Greenfield dir. (US, 1982)	99
William Buys a Parrot – Antony Balch dir. (UK, 1982)	100
(The) Wire: 20 Years 1982-2002 – Various (UK, 2002)	271
Wireless Imagination – Douglas Kahn & Gregory Whitehead (eds) (US, 1992)	188
Wising up the Marks – Timothy Murphy (US, 1998)	249
Witchcraft Through the Ages – Benjamin Christensen dir. (SE, 1968)	26
With William Burroughs – Victor Bockris (US, 1981)	87
Word Virus – James Grauerholz & Ira Silverberg (eds) (US, 1998)	250
Words of Advice – Lars Movin & Steen Møller Rasmussen dir. (DK, 2007)	294
Words of Advice For Young People – William Burroughs (US, 1993)	201
World Turning – Tony Trischka (US, 1993)	202

X

Xtrmn8mm – David Cox dir. (AU, 1997)	236

Y

(The) Yage Letters – William Burroughs & Allen Ginsberg (US, 1963)	8
You're a Hook – Various (US, 1984)	116
You're the Guy I Want to Share My.. – Giorno / Burroughs / Anderson (US, 1981)	88

Z

Zur Holle Mama #3 – Various (DE, 1998)	251

About the author

Simon Strong was born in Sheffield, South Yorkshire, in the mid-sixties and attended local comprehensive schools. He extrapolated an early interest in science fiction to become proficient in the then-new science of computer programming, writing programs and columns for hobbyist magazines. Upon leaving school Simon moved to the south coast to work in artifical intelligence research, but dropped out as he became increasingly politicised. Several years of extreme poverty and sporadic homelessness followed and he decided to become a writer so as to derive some utility from these experiences. Simon survived via occasional freelance programming, specialising in interface design, and so-called menial jobs such as bouncer or toilet cleaner. He eventually landed a job as a temporary bookseller and by the end of the eighties was living above an Indian takeaway in the red light district with other unpublished writers and unsigned musicians. Encouraged and advised by experimental novelist Stewart Home, Simon had completed his third novel *A259 Multiplex Bomb "Outrage"* and had it accepted for publication.

By the early nineties, Simon was working as factotum for local independent record labels and dealers, specialising in graphic design. He was now compiling a book about William Burroughs' recording career, and was appointed co-conven-

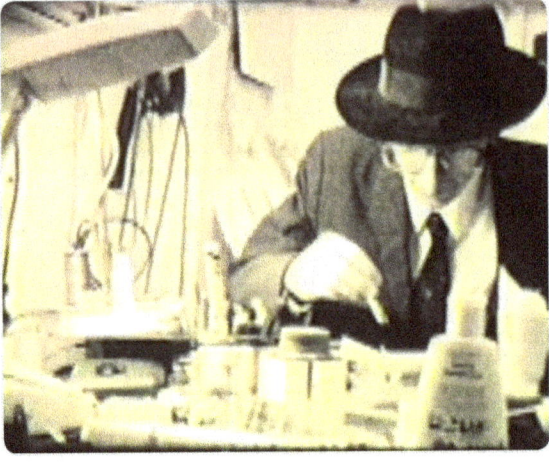

or of the 1994 Happy Burroughsday! event. Soon afterwards he founded CodeX Books and Records and issued works by authors including Stewart Home, Kathy Acker, Richard Hell and Billy Childish, as well as publishing the first book about Gysin's dreamachine, edited by Paul Cecil of the Temple of Psychic Youth. Frustrated by delays with his own book, Simon retrieved the rights and issued the book himself. Due to its sensational content, it quickly became a cult item, being reprinted within three months and exported around the world.

By the mid-nineties, personal circumstances forced Simon to quit the UK and he emigrated to Melbourne, Australia, where he landed a job at PolyEster Books, the "World's Freakiest Bookshop", and then at the University of Melbourne, where he remained for fifteen years in academic publishing.

After some years of creative inactivity, Simon resurfaced in 2001 as front-man for psychedelic group Pink Stainless Tail, which also featured Nick Boddington, Harry Howard and Sönke Rickertsen. They established a solid local reputation and issued three records in their ten year career.

During this period, Simon also worked on Jason Crest's Olympia Press project, which resulted in two books, *66mindfuck99* and *Rape vs. Murder*. Despite their samizdat distribution, these books attracted the attention of Ken Goldsmith of ubu.com who asked Simon to provide material for his archive.

Having produced several clips for his own group, Simon was now more interested in film projects and in 2008 completed *Totally Weird Shit!* about his experiences at PolyEster Books. It was followed by a feature length critique of David Cronenberg's Burroughs adaptation, and two years later by Simon's take on the Australian gold-rush insurgency *Bring Me the Head of Rafaello Carboni!*

Simon continues to write, make films, and currently presents a community radio show about the limits of protest music.

THE LEDATAPE ORGANISATION

our shit beats their gold

www.ledatape.net

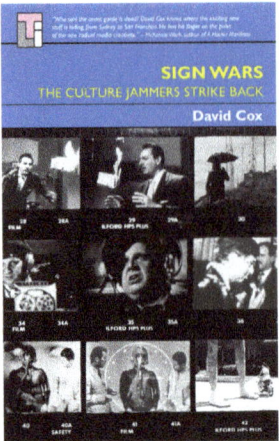
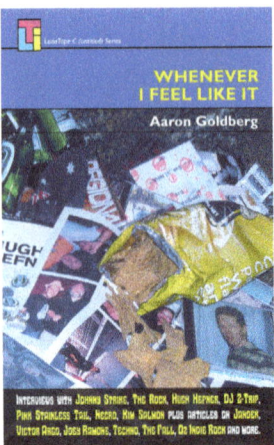

Tadhg Taylor
TOP FELLAS
THE STORY OF MELBOURNE'S SHARPIE CULT

2013, 5½ x 8½ in., 124pp

Gang Wars! Rock n' Roll! Fine Knits! Sharpie was born in mid-sixties Melbourne, progeny of mod, rocker and Mediterranean tailoring. For nigh on twenty years sharpies bossed the teenage world of coffee bars, pool halls, suburban dances and roller rinks. They loved dancing, spiffy threads and belting ten shades of sugar out of each other.

Top Fellas is the full story of the great sharp epic, told in a lively, borderline amoral, style. Packed with first hand accounts from ex-sharps and rock n' rollers like Lobby Loyde, Angry Anderson and Skyhooks Greg Macainsh, illustrated with over fifty photos of teenagers in cardigans,

"...a fast-paced, slang-laced, laddish style - plenty of first hand recollections... loaded with photos... highly enjoyable" (Mike Stax, *Ugly Things*).

David Cox
SIGN WARS
THE CULTURE JAMMERS STRIKE BACK

2005, 5½ x 8½ in., 266pp

A whole new generation of media activists and culture jammers have taken on the government and corporate advertising worlds. New technologies have greatly assisted artists, writers, film makers and activists to challenge and reverse the one-way flow of mind-numbing mainstream media. Camcorders, amateur and ham radio, mobile phones, the Internet and various other inexpensive means of exchanging signals have empowered this new generation.

David Cox takes us on a fascinating journey as he traverses the west coast of the United States and the east coast of Australia with descriptions of successful jamming and innovative campaigns.

"Who said the avant garde is dead? David Cox knows where the exciting new stuff is hiding, from Sydney to San Francisco. He has his finger on the pulse of the new radical media creativity." (McKenzie Wark, author of *A Hacker Manifesto*)

Aaron Goldberg
WHENEVER I FEEL LIKE IT
INTERVIEWS & ARTICLES

2010, 5½ x 8½ in., 114pp

Inspired by New York's legendary 'noise boys', 80s and 90s fanzines like Forced Exposure, B-side and Motorbooty and a lack of sex, Melbourne writer, musician, filmmaker and suburban struggler, Aaron Goldberg presents in 'real' print for the first time, a collection of non-fiction written works exploring his love for the not-quite popular pulp culture.

Includes interviews with: Johnny Strike (Crime) / Kim Salmon / Hugh Hefner / The Rock / Z-trip / DJ Necro / Pink Stainless Tail and articles on: AFL / Jandek / Joey Ramone / Techno / Victor Argo / Chopper / The Fall / Oz indie rock plus 'bonus' snapshot segment featuring HUGE celebrities!

Neil Palmer
EXECUTIVE SUFFICIENCY

2010, 5½ x 8½ in., 120pp

In the uptight world of the London media elite, even the opening of a new exhibition of Prison Art is regarded as an exciting adventure. Senses dulled and out of his depth in the face of an unfolding story of the real elite - the one that wields the real power - Bryn Nolan rouses himself from his cocoon of self-confidence and rises to a challenge that only he, London's premier public relations operator, can overcome.

The wild valleys and mountains of the Caucasus and the even wilder alleys and concrete rifts of the London landscape collide in this meticulously researched novel of high adventure happening elsewhere to other people, while the urban-exiled narrator finds himself embroiled in his own grave drama, picking up the loose threads of distant hazard that lead inexorably to his home town.

Nolan quickly discovers that in time of danger the tale becomes the truth, spurious anecdote becomes fact, and plausibility itself becomes a vehicle for transmutation.

Neil Palmer
PLACE EXPLOSION

2010, 5½ x 8½ in., 136pp

From Magic Localism to post-regionalist eco-apocalypse realism, from materialist anti-irrationality to the livin' end of punk rock mythology, from collective identities to utter individualism, from alienation to belonging, from Cambridge Royal Mail sorting office to Hove public library, the stories collected together in *Place Explosion* describe the fistula between knowledge and consciousness that has emerged in this totally precedented era of total control.

Place Explosion delves deep into the unlucky dip of popular culture in the long late-20th century, drags out its most enduring archetypes and ciphers – politics, identity, culture and the weird – and makes them sing and dance for their very existence.

Aaron Goldberg
FOUTRE LA MERDE, DANS

2011, 5 x 7 in., 120pp

Multi award-winning novelist Aaron Goldberg returns with his debut award-winning novel *Foutre la merde, dans*. A recipient of a $400,000 Arts Grant from Merde-och University, *Foutre la merde, dans* is a by-the-dots piece of contemporary literature, exploring notions of identity, sexuality, multi-multiculturalism, oppression from the dominant paradigm, persecution, depression, repression, acceptance and the ultimate triumph of getting your own retrospective at the Wheeler Dealer Centre, as well as increasing your Facebook friend count and your industry currency by 100,000 points/friends.

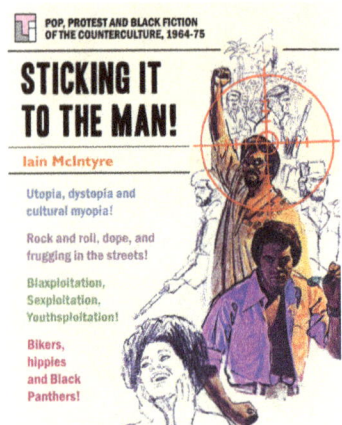

Michael Helms
FATAL VISIONS
THE WONDER YEARS

2012, 7½ x 9¼ in., 248pp

Melbourne's own infamous trash film zine, has congealed into perfect bound format!

This compilation covers the earliest and rarest entries in FVs decade-long publication history. Devoted to sleaze, violence and sexploitation, bottom of the package video titles, late late night TV movies, films that played as drive-in supports and in hard tops where they were lucky to play for one week only.

Thee Rockhunter
SONIC ANTIQUARIAN

2011, 7½ x 9¼ in., 128pp

From the back alleys of pub rock to the heady myths of classical Hauntiquarianism, The Rockhunter accompanies you on a journey without a destination in a land with so many names the map's worn through by over-printing. Rock history's never made more (or less) sense.

Profusely illustrated and featuring a comprehensive bibliography and index (conditions apply).

Iain McIntyre
STICKING IT TO THE MAN!
POP PROTEST & BLACK FICTION OF THE COUNTERCULTURE

2012, 7½ x 9¼ in., 80pp

Rock n roll, dope and frugging in the streets! Utopia, dystopia and cultural myopia! Blaxsploitation, Sexsploitation, Youthsploitation! Bikers, hippies and Black Panthers!

Featuring works by everyone from hipsters to hack authors and genres ranging across crime, sci-fi, teen novels and more. *Sticking It To The Man* features over 120 covers and reviews of fictional novels drawing upon the political and social upheaval of the counterculture era. Dig in to discover a lost world of of mind-bending militants, thinly veiled manifestoes and trashy exploitation.

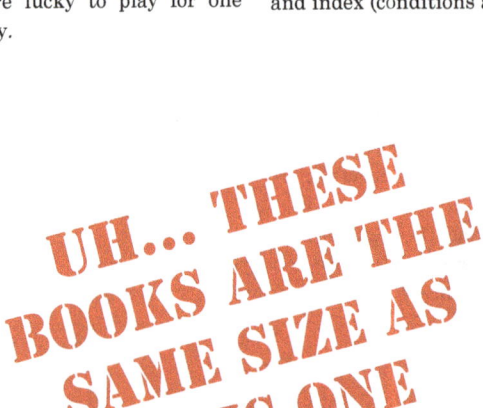

UH... THESE BOOKS ARE THE SAME SIZE AS THIS ONE

www.ingramcontent.com/pod-product-compliance
Lightning Source LLC
Chambersburg PA
CBHW080405170426
43193CB00016B/2818